KU-455-458

The Ham
The Wessex Hillforts
Proj

DRAWN.
LIBRARY

C014750654

The Wessex Hillforts Project

*Extensive survey of hillfort interiors
in central southern England*

Andrew Payne, Mark Corney and Barry Cunliffe

with contributions by N Burton, T Cromwell, S Cross, S Crutchley, N Linford, F Small and J Vallender

ENGLISH HERITAGE

HAMPSHIRE COUNTY LIBRARY	
C014750654	
HJ	25-Aug-2009
R936.2	£25.00
187359285X	

Published by English Heritage, 23 Savile Row, London W1S 2ET
www.english-heritage.org.uk
English Heritage is the Government's statutory adviser on all aspects of the
historic environment.

© English Heritage 2006

All images, unless otherwise specified, are either © English Heritage or
© Crown copyright. NMR. The negative numbers for English Heritage and
NMR images are noted in square brackets in the captions where possible.
Every effort has been made to trace copyright holders and we apologise in
advance for any unintentional omissions, which we would be pleased to
correct in any subsequent edition of the book.

First published 2006

ISBN 1 873592 85 X
     978 1 8735292 85 4

Product Code 51072

British Library Cataloguing in Publication Data
A CIP catalogue record for this book is available from the British Library.

All rights reserved
No part of this publication may be reproduced or transmitted in any form or
by any means, electronic or mechanical, including photocopying, recording,
or any information storage or retrieval system, without permission in writing
from the publisher.

Application for the reproduction of images should be made to the National
Monuments Record. Every effort has been made to trace the copyright
holders and we apologise in advance for any unintentional omissions, which
we would be pleased to correct in any subsequent edition of this book.

The National Monuments Record is the public archive of English Heritage.
For more information, contact NMR Enquiry and Research Services,
National Monuments Record Centre, Kemble Drive, Swindon SN2 2GZ;
telephone (01793) 414600.

Edited and brought to publication by David M Jones, Publishing,
English Heritage, Kemble Drive, Swindon SN2 2GZ.

Cover design and page layout by Mark Simmons
Indexed by Alan Rutter

Printed and bound in Great Britain by 4edge Ltd, Hockley. www.4edge.co.uk

Contents

Illustrations

Summary

The numerous earthwork forts that crown many of the hills of Southern England are among the largest and most dramatic of the prehistoric features that still survive in our modern rural landscape. These enclosures, occupied from the end of the Bronze Age to the last few centuries before the Roman conquest, have long attracted archaeological interest and debate on their function and significance remains central to the academic study of the Iron Age. The sheer scale of the enclosing earthworks at many sites indicates great expenditure of communal effort and a high degree of social organisation. Despite the attention given to these sites it remains unclear whether they were strongholds of Celtic chiefs and their retinues, communal centres of population akin to large villages or temporary refuges occupied seasonally or in times of unrest. Reliable interpretation of their role continues to be hampered by the small number that have been extensively examined archaeologically. The Wessex Hillforts Survey was designed in response to the need for more wide-ranging data on hillfort interiors, which realistically was unlikely to be obtainable by traditional more costly, time consuming and damaging intrusive excavation.

The research published in this book is the result of a three year partnership project between the former Ancient Monuments Laboratory of English Heritage and Oxford University. The project was designed to shed new light on the internal character of a wide range of hillfort sites in Central Southern England with a view to improving the future management and furthering greater public understanding of the monuments.

The Wessex Hillforts Survey was based entirely on non-invasive methodology primarily involving the use of fluxgate magnetometry or gradiometry. This technique locates archaeological features by means of the slight magnetic variations caused by past human activity and unlike excavation does not cause any damage to in-situ archaeological remains. At a selected number of sites, the magnetometer surveys were supplemented by magnetic susceptibility survey and digital terrain modelling. The surveys of each hillfort interior were further augmented by analysis of the aerial photographic record from a two km radius around each site firmly anchoring the individual hillforts in the context of the archaeological landscapes of which they were a part.

The results of the project significantly advance our comprehension of hillfort interiors in the eastern part of the region of Wessex, which in the absence of excavation, would otherwise have remained poorly understood and characterised. The eighteen hillforts surveyed across Hampshire, Wiltshire, Oxfordshire and Berkshire produced very varied results. These range from sites largely devoid of internal features to sites containing complex patterns of round structures, pits, roadways and in some cases internal enclosures and ditched boundaries. Overall assessment of the results has enabled more elaborate distinctions to be made between different classes of hillforts than has hitherto been possible. The wealth of new data revealed illustrates the great complexity of the archaeological record preserved inside these sites and it is apparent that this complexity can vary considerably locally from one site to the next opening up many new archaeological questions to explore further. The survey has also highlighted the fact that hillforts are far from isolated features in their contemporary landscape settings.

Résumé

Les nombreuses forteresses avec terrassement qui couronnent bien des collines du sud de l'Angleterre se classent parmi les plus étendus et les plus dramatiques des vestiges préhistoriques qui survivent encore dans notre paysage rural moderne. Ces enclos occupés de la fin de l'âge du bronze jusqu'aux tous derniers siècles avant la conquête romaine, ont depuis longtemps suscité l'intérêt des archéologues et le débat sur leur fonction et leur signification demeure au centre des recherches universitaires sur l'âge du fer. Sur beaucoup de ces sites, l'énormité de l'échelle des levées de terre qui les ceinturent témoigne des gigantesques efforts fournis par l'ensemble de cette société et atteste qu'elle jouissait d'un niveau élevé d'organisation. Malgré l'attention qui a été apportée à ces sites, il n'est toujours pas clair s'ils étaient des forteresses des princes celtes et de leur entourage, des centres communautaires de population apparentés à un village ou des refuges temporaires occupés en fonction des saisons ou en période d'instabilité. Le fait qu'un petit nombre seulement a fait l'objet d'une étude archéologique extensive continue à entraver toute interprétation fiable de leur rôle. L'étude des forteresses du Wessex a été conçue en réponse à ce besoin de données plus étendues sur l'intérieur des forteresses, ce qu'avec réalisme, il aurait été peu probable d'arriver à obtenir par des fouilles traditionnelles plus coûteuses, plus longues et susceptibles de causer plus de dégâts en pénétrant le site.

Les recherches publiées dans cet ouvrage sont le résultat d'un projet sur trois ans en partenariat entre l'ancien Laboratoire des Monuments Anciens d'English Heritage et l'Université d'Oxford. Le projet fut conçu pour jeter un nouveau jour sur les caractéristiques internes d'une importante gamme de sites de forteresses dans le centre de l'Angleterre du sud afin d'en améliorer la gestion dans l'avenir et de favoriser une meilleure compréhension des monuments parmi les membres du public.

L'Etude des Forteresses du Wessex reposait entièrement sur une méthodologie non-envahissante impliquant essentiellement l'usage de magnétométrie par induction ou de gradiométrie. Cette technique localise les vestiges archéologiques grâce aux légères variations magnétiques causées par des activités humaines dans le passé et contrairement aux fouilles, elle ne cause aucun dommage aux restes archéologiques in-situ. Sur un nombre de sites sélectionnés, les prospections au magnétomètre furent accompagnées d'une étude de susceptibilité magnétique et d'un modelage numérique du terrain. De plus, aux examens de l'intérieur de chaque forteresse vinrent s'ajouter une analyse des photographies aériennes répertoriées, à partir d'un rayon de deux kilomètres autour de chaque site, ancrant ainsi les forteresses individuelles dans le contexte des paysages archéologiques dont elles faisaient partie.

Les résultats de ce projet ont fait avancer de manière significative notre compréhension de l'intérieur des forteresses dans la partie est de la région du Wessex, qui autrement, en l'absence de fouilles, serait resté insuffisamment compris et caractérisé. Les dix-huit forteresses étudiées dans les comtés de Hampshire, Wiltshire, Oxforshire et Berkshire ont produit des résultats très divers. Ceux-ci vont de sites en grande partie dépourvus de traces internes jusqu'à des sites contenant des traces complexes de structures rondes, de puits, de voies et dans certains cas d'eneintes internes et de limites avec fossés. L'évaluation d'ensemble des résultats nous a permis d'établir des distinctions plus élaborées entre les différentes classes de forteresses qu'il n'avait été possible de le faire jusqu'alors. L'abondance de nouvelles données révélées illustre la grande complexité des traces archéologiques préservées à l'intérieur de ces sites et il est apparent que cette complexité peut varier considérablement dans un même lieu, d'un site à un autre, ce qui pose beaucoup de nouvelles questions archéologiques à explorer plus en profondeur. L'étude a également souligné le fait que les forteresses sont loin d'être des traits isolés dans le cadre de leur environnement contemporain.

Traduction: Annie Pritchard

Zusammenfassung

Die zahlreichen Erdforte, welche viele Hügel in Südengland krönen, zählen zu den größten und dramatischsten prähistorischen Merkmalen, die bis in die heutige Zeit in unserer modernen ländlichen Umgebung überleben. Diese Befestigungen wurden seit dem Bronzezeitalter bis ind die letzten Jahrhundert vor der römischen Eroberung besiedelt und haben seit langem archäologisches Interresse auf sich gezogen. Die Debatte über ihre Funktion und Bedeutung ist ein zentrales Thema der akademischen Studie des Eisenzeitalters. Der schiere Umfang der Erdanlagen an vielen der Standorte deutet auf einen grossen Aufwand an kommunalen Anstrengungen und auf ein hohes Maß sozialer Organisation hin. Trotz der großen Aufmerksamkeit, welche diesen Standorten gewidmet wird, ist es bisher unklar, ob sie Befestigungsanlagen keltischer Häuptlinge und ihres Gefolges, kommunale Zentren ähnlich großer Dörfer oder temporäre Zuflucht für verschiedene Jahreszeiten und in Zeiten von Gefahr waren. Zuverlässige Deutungen ihrer Rolle wird durch die relativ kleine Zahl an umfangreichen archäologischen Ausgrabungen behindert. Die Wessex Hügelfort Untersuchung wurde als Antwort auf den Bedarf für mehr weitragende Daten über Hügelfortinnenanlagen entwickelt, welche normalerweise nicht ohne traditionell teure, zeitaufwendige und beschädigende intrusive Ausgrabungen möglich sind.

Die in diesem Buch publizierten Nachforschungen sind das Resultat eines dreijährigen Partnerschaftsprojekts zwischen dem ehemaligen Altertümlichkeitslabor von English Heritage und der Universität von Oxford. Das Projekt wurde konstruiert um neues Licht auf den internen Charakter vieler Hügelforts in Südengland zu werfen und um das zukünftige Management und öffentliche Verständnis der Monumente zu verbessern.

Die Wessex Hügelfort Untersuchung basiert ausschließlich auf nicht-invasiven Methodologien, welche die primäre Nutzung von Fluxgate Magnetometern und Gradiometern beinhaltete. Diese Technik macht archäologische Merkmale durch die unterschiedlichen magnetischen Variationen ausfindig, welche durch vergangene menschliche Aktivitäten hervorgerufen wurden. Ungleich zu Ausgrabungen beschädigt diese Methodik keine der in-situ liegenden Überreste. An ausgesuchten Standorten wurden die Magnetometer-Untersuchungen durch magnetischen Empfindlichkeitstests und digitale Terrainmodellierung ergänzt. Die Untersuchungen der Hügelfortinnenanlagen wurden durch die Analyse von Luftaufnahmen mit einem 2km Radius um jedem Standort erweitert. Damit wird jedes Hügelfort fest in seinem Zusammenhang mit dem archeologischen Umfeld verankert, von welchem es ein Teil war.

Die Resultate dieses Projektes tragen wesentlich zur Förderung unseres Wissens von Hügelfortinnenanlagen in der östlichen Hälfte von Wessex bei, welche in der Abwesenheit von Ausgrabungen schlecht verstanden und charaktesiert geblieben wären. Die achtzehn untersuchten Hügelforts in Hampshire, Wiltshire, Oxfordshire und Berkshire produzierten verschiedene Resultate. Diese umfangen Standorte ohne irgentwelche wesentlichen Innenanlagen und andere mit komplexen Mustern von rundlichen Strukturen, Gruben, Straßenwegen sowie in einigen Fällen interne Einfriedungen und Grabenanlagen. Die allgemeine Beurteilung der Resultate erlaubt eine wesentlich detailiertere Unterscheidung zwischen den verschiedenen Klassen von Hügelforts, was bisher nicht möglich war. Der zum Vorschein gebrachte Reichtum an neuen Daten, illustriert die große Komplexität der archäologischen Überreste, welche in diesen Standorten erhalten sind, und verdeutlicht, daß diese Komplexität sehr unterschiedlich ist von einem Standort zum nächsten. Dieses öffnet die Möglichkeit vieler neuer archäologischer Fragen, welche weiter untersucht werden können. Die Untersuchung hebt den Fakt hervor, daß Hügelforts keine isolierten Merkmale in ihrer zeitgenössigen Landschaft waren.

Überzetzung: Norman Behrend

Acknowledgements

Numerous individuals and several organisations contributed to the work of the Wessex Hillforts Survey. The project was carried out with the financial backing of English Heritage and with the assistance and support of the Oxford University, Institute of Archaeology.

Project initiation:
Steve Trow for valuable support and advice, in particular for drafting the original project proposal and for his considerable contribution to the project in the early stages of initiation, planning and development.

Geoff Wainwright, Kate Foley, Andrew David, Barry Cunliffe, Chris Dunn, and Mark Corney all encouraged and supported the initial development of the project and also provided the resources and personal time for it to all happen.

Fieldwork:
First and foremost I would like to acknowledge the indispensable role of the two geophysical surveyors employed by the project – Emma Bray and Peter Cottrell whose contribution was vital to the successful outcome. Largely working on their own initiative Emma and Peter worked unstintingly over the course of two long summers with great energy and dedication to produce the unparalleled magnetometer data-set that underpins this publication. Without their willingness to get involved in such a major undertaking the project would never have reached fruition and they are warmly thanked for their marathon contribution. Occasional support was given to the core survey team in the field by Mark Cole and Tim Horsley who are both thanked for their assistance. Paul Linford supported the project throughout by ensuring that data processing and storage facilities were available for manipulating the large geophysical data-sets involved.

The project would not have been possible without the support of all the members of the Archaeometry Branch of the former Ancient Monuments Laboratory of English Heritage (now part of the Centre For Archaeology). Under the leadership of Andrew David the Archaeometry Branch was responsible for providing overall supervision of the project during the fieldwork stages and beyond, data processing facilities, additional field survey equipment, and additional staff for fieldwork.

Tom Cromwell, Nick Burton, Miles Hitchen and Pip Stevenson collected the GPS data in the field used to model the terrain of the hillforts at Alfred's Castle, Barbury Castle, Beacon Hill, Ladle Hill and Oldbury. Tom Cromwell subsequently processed the GPS data and produced the raw digital terrain models of the hillforts that were used to drape the magnetometer data-sets over.

Neil Linford generously gave of his time in the production of the relief-draped magnetometer survey images of Alfred's Castle, Barbury Castle, Ladle Hill and Oldbury. Sarah May and Nick Burton produced the detailed shaded relief model of the interior of Beacon Hill and Sarah May subsequently produced the relief-draped images of the magnetometer data from Beacon Hill.

Alister Bartlett carried out a series of detailed magnetic susceptibility surveys for the project at Castle Ditches, Wiltshire and Norsebury Ring, Hampshire generously dedicating considerably more time to the project than his fees should have covered.

The authors would like to express their thanks to all the landowners and tenant farmers who generously allowed access to the sites.

Support, encouragement, information and advice:
Gary Lock for commenting on sections of the text and for kindly providing information on his excavations at Alfred's Castle and Segsbury Camp. Also for helpful discussion on the project in general.

Mark Bowden for information on the earthwork surveys of Barbury and Liddington Castles and helpful discussion and comment. Dave McOmish for providing a copy of the analytical earthwork survey of Old Winchester Hill.

The English Heritage regional teams for the South of England (particularly Amanda Chadburn and Steve Trow), the County Archaeologists of Hampshire and Wiltshire (Dave Hopkins and Roy Canham) for SMR information, Anne Upson of Berkshire County Council for SMR information.

Tim Cromack and Gareth Watkins for co-ordinating the EH grant aid and Lidia Lozano at the Institute of Archaeology for providing staunch administrative support and financial management.

Material:
The National Monuments Record for providing the aerial photographic illustrative material published in the book, notably Damian Grady and Bob Bewley for giving generously of their time by helping to retrieve and make available appropriate aerial photographs of the hillforts. Simon Crutchley and Fiona Small kindly helped with the preparation of the sections on Alfred's Castle and St Catherine's Hill in Chapter 2 by providing additional material based upon aerial photography. I would also like to thank Rose Desmond at the University of Cambridge, Unit of Landscape Modelling – Air Photograph Library for permission to reproduce selected aerial images in their collection.

Publication:
John Vallender dedicated a considerable amount of time and expertise towards the production of publication quality graphics presenting the results of the 19 geophysical surveys in Chapter 3 (based on an original set of plans prepared by A Payne).

Mark Bowden kindly read and commented on the text in advance of publication.

Andy Payne would like to thank all the other long suffering people who have had to live with the Wessex Hillforts and its impact for as long as I have, particularly my close work colleagues in the Archaeometry Branch: Andrew, Louise, Neil and Paul, and my wife and children Jane, James and Jennifer.

1

Hillfort studies and the Wessex Project

by Andrew Payne

The *Wessex Hillforts Project* was initiated in 1996 to answer a need for more wide-ranging data on hillfort interiors for the purposes of placing their future management on a sounder footing and enhancing knowledge of the internal character of the various hillfort types represented in Wessex. It was hoped that the combined results of the project would considerably extend academic understanding of the socio-economic role of hillforts in southern England during the 1st millennium BC, thereby allowing a greater level of interpretation to be offered to visitors at those sites with public access.

The primary methodology employed by the project was geophysical survey supplemented by examination of aerial photographic evidence, documentary research and selective digital modelling of site microtopography. The examination of each hillfort was to be as comprehensive as possible without resorting to more costly and unnecessarily destructive intrusive techniques.

The context of the study

Hillforts have attracted archaeological interest for much of the last century and debate on their function and significance continues to be central to the academic study of the later Bronze Age and Iron Age (broadly the 1st millennium BC). Although some hillforts have been damaged by development or levelled through ploughing, those that remain are some of the most impressive ancient monuments still visible in the countryside today. Such prominent landmarks naturally attracted the interest of antiquaries and pioneers in archaeology from earliest times, an interest that has continued with the development of scientific field techniques and modern methods of excavation. Writing on social organisation in Iron Age Wessex, Haselgrove (1994, 1) concluded, 'there can be little doubting the significance of Iron Age hillforts, given the labour invested in their construction, so understanding their role is clearly vital'. While it is clear from the scale of these sites that great

effort and organisation must have been involved in their construction, the reasons why they were constructed are more difficult to comprehend. The term hillfort has been applied to many different types of site and their varying sizes, morphologies and situations strongly suggest a range of different motives for their construction, spanning a considerable date range (Fig 1.1).

We usually associate hillforts with the Iron Age, the period when many new hillforts were built, but the origins of hillfort building lie at least as far back as the Bronze Age. During the 800 years before the Roman invasion of Britain (the period that we conventionally term the Iron Age) the role of hillforts seems to have changed. New evidence is only gradually being uncovered that helps to extend our understanding and we still have very little information about hillfort interiors in general and the range of functions they might have fulfilled.

Generally, but not exclusively, set on elevated or other locations conferring natural defensive advantages, sites classed as hillforts in southern Britain can range in size from less than one hectare to many tens of hectares. Their structural complexity varies from simple univallate earthworks to vast multivallate fortresses with labyrinthine entrance passages. Although hillforts are among the most numerous of all our surviving prehistoric monuments – nearly 1500 were listed in the Ordnance Survey's 1962 *Map of Southern Britain in the Iron Age* alone (Fig 1.2) – our knowledge of the majority of sites is still quite limited because often their sheer scale is such that there have seldom been sufficient resources for extensive examination of their interiors.

Conventionally, hillforts have always been seen as primarily constructed for defence, but their disparate sizes, topographical settings and architectural forms, suggest that this need falls far short of providing a wholly adequate explanation for all of them (Harding 1979; Ralston 1996). The vast majority of the sites examined in this project are classic hillforts occupying highly

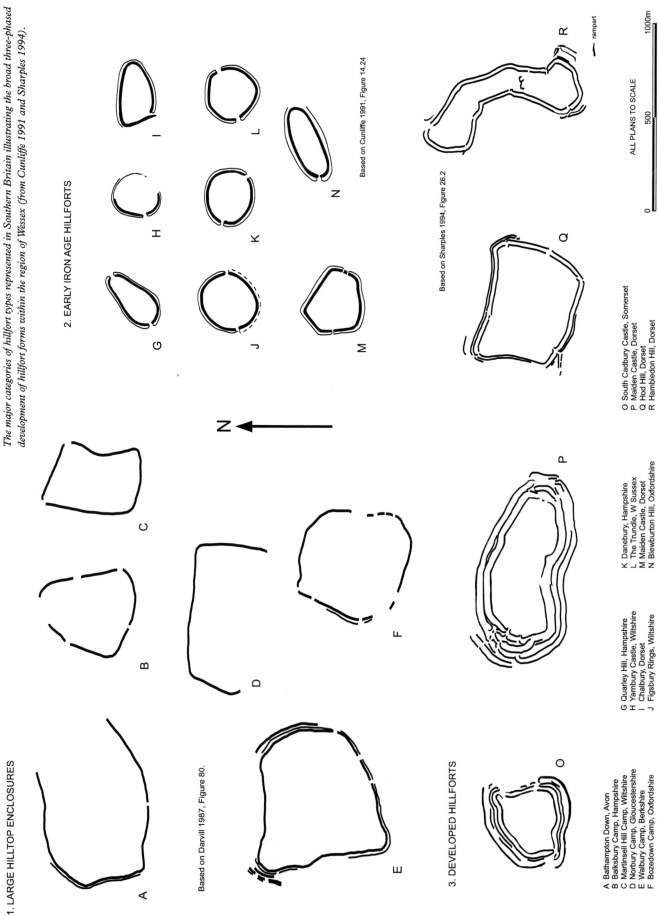

Fig 1.1

The major categories of hillfort types represented in Southern Britain illustrating the broad three-phased development of hillfort forms within the region of Wessex (from Cunliffe 1991 and Sharples 1994).

1. LARGE HILLTOP ENCLOSURES

Based on Darvill 1987, Figure 80.

2. EARLY IRON AGE HILLFORTS

Based on Cunliffe 1991, Figure 14.24

Based on Sharples 1994, Figure 26.2

3. DEVELOPED HILLFORTS

N

~ rampart

ALL PLANS TO SCALE

0   500   1000m

A Bathampton Down, Avon
B Balksbury Camp, Hampshire
C Martinsell Hill Camp, Wiltshire
D Norbury Camp, Gloucestershire
E Walbury Camp, Berkshire
F Bozedown Camp, Oxfordshire

G Quarley Hill, Hampshire
H Yarnbury Castle, Wiltshire
I   Chalbury, Dorset
J Figsbury Rings, Wiltshire

K Danebury, Hampshire
L The Trundle, W Sussex
M Maiden Castle, Dorset
N Blewburton Hill, Oxfordshire

O South Cadbury Castle, Somerset
P Maiden Castle, Dorset
Q Hod Hill, Dorset
R Hambledon Hill, Dorset

visible elevated positions dominating their surroundings (such as ridge ends or escarpment edges), where the hillfort ramparts enhance an already naturally defensible position. A minority of the sites examined possess defences that are of hillfort proportions but are situated in locations that confer little or no altitudinal advantage. Clearly defence was not always the primary consideration and it is likely that the wide spectrum of sites to which we apply the term hillfort performed a range of functions of which defence was but one.

Until the 1960s hillfort studies were dominated by problems of cultural affinity and chronology and, with a few exceptions, fieldwork was concentrated on the comparatively small-scale excavation of hillfort defences and gate structures. The question of the function of the hillfort in its social and economic environment was hardly voiced (Collis 1981, 66).

Although some hillforts had been dug into before 1900 by pioneers of field archaeology such as Augustus Lane Fox (better known as Pitt Rivers), it was not until the early years of the 20th century that archaeological interest was sufficiently awakened for major campaigns of excavation to be organised on regional groupings of sites. Between

Fig 1.2

Hillfort distribution in southern Britain (based on Cunliffe 1991 without revision) – not intended to be definitive. Non-verified, less visible hillfort-type sites probably exist in the survey area; evidence for some is discussed in Chap 2. Classification as hillforts of newly or recently identified ploughed-out sites depends on how strict our definition is. 'Hillfort' is often applied loosely to some low-lying sites and sites of less obvious defensive character.

1907 and the 1940s the combined work of Maud Cunnington in Wiltshire, E Cecil Curwen in Sussex and Christopher Hawkes in Hampshire was instrumental in transforming knowledge of the many examples of hillforts in these areas. The lack of a professional infrastructure and resources for funding and employing archaeological staff at this point in time did not allow for long term or extensive programmes of archaeological investigation. They nevertheless provided a useful sample of evidence from a large number of sites.

The first serious attempt to bring together the evidence amassed through these excavations in a nationwide synthesis was a paper entitled simply 'Hill-Forts' published by C F C Hawkes in the journal *Antiquity* in 1931. The paper reflected the historical paradigm then current among prehistorians, which sought to explain changes in the archaeological record and defensive architecture at hillfort sites during the Iron Age as a product of successive waves of population movements (or invasions) from continental Europe (Hawkes 1931; Wheeler 1943).

Invasionist theories of this nature are no longer widely accepted as the explanation for cultural change in the British Iron Age, but at the time they seemed to provide a plausible model against which to interpret the archaeological evidence. The view that there had been large-scale invasions in the prehistoric period had analogies with the historical period with its invasions of Normans, Vikings, Saxons and Romans; and Caesar, writing of Britain in the 1st century BC, talked of incursions of Belgae from northern France and the Low Countries into the south-east of the country. It was against this background that Christopher Hawkes in 1931 proposed a three-phase chronological system – the ABC of the British Iron Age – to explain the various stages of hillfort development in southern England. This system was to form the basic chronological framework for hillfort studies for the next 30 years or more.

The view propounded by the ABC system envisaged a movement of Celtic peoples from central and northern Europe spreading into the south-east of Britain in the 6th century BC and fusing with the native populace to form the Iron Age A culture. This period was associated with an initial phase of widespread hillfort building activity in central-southern and south-east England. The next stage of the scheme involved the arrival of a second wave of invaders arriving early in the 4th century BC. Originating from Spain and Brittany (Armorica) these invaders initially thrust into the western parts of Britain spreading into Dorset and the Cotswolds where they built hillforts characterised by massive multivallate defences. This second wave was assigned to the Iron Age B period. Finally, some time around 75 BC, Belgic invaders entered the Thames Valley and Kent, spreading into Essex, while a little later, as a result of Caesar's military conquests in Gaul, refugees from northern France landed on the shores of the Solent and moved into central southern Britain. These invaders were defined as the Iron Age C peoples. During this period in the south-east of England, hillforts declined and disappeared to be replaced by large fortified towns, usually in more low-lying situations commanding river crossings, as for example at *Orams Arbour* in Winchester (Whinney 1994). In territory that fringed the areas of Iron Age C penetration, such as Dorset, the continuation of old style hillforts marked native resistance to the Belgic influence.

Under the historical paradigm the most important question was 'when?' and involved the dating of hillfort horizons as indicators of political change. The excavation methods of the pre-Second World War era were almost entirely orientated to this problem with great emphasis on the trenching of ramparts and the clearance of entrances, but little work on the interiors (Collis 1981, 66). Excavations of this nature provide information concerning the chronology and structural history of individual sites and are a necessary prelude towards understanding a site, but were rarely taken forward to include investigation of the interior on a scale sufficient to enable the reconstruction of buildings, structures and features in the hillfort, let alone the spatial organisation of the interior. The first serious attempt to open up large areas of a hillfort interior was Sir Mortimer Wheeler's excavation at Maiden Castle in the late 1930s (Wheeler 1943).

Hawkes's ABC scheme, further elaborated by Gordon Childe and others (Childe 1935, 1946; Piggott C M 1950; Piggott S 1966) to embrace Iron Age defensive structures in the whole of Britain, found general acceptance and influenced most hillfort research published before the mid-1970s. However, with the increased use of radiometric dating and a changing theoretical stance from the late 1960s onwards this paradigm of invasion and response fell out of favour. Regional developments are now generally agreed to have been more influential on the growth of hillforts, including the demonstration of prestige or status on the part of the hillfort builders – or more particularly the decision makers who controlled their activities – as well as the wish to give physical definition to the limits of jurisdictions (social, ritual, economic or political) (Ralston 1996).

Since the collapse of the historical paradigm, a new chronological framework has only slowly begun to be developed. Unlike Hawkes's system and those tied to it, there is now no single chronological scheme that can be applied to hillfort development over the whole of Britain and currently we only have a detailed comprehension of the chronology of hillfort development in certain regions of Britain where sufficient research has been carried out. Prior to the use of radiometric dating, earlier pre-war dating saw hillforts as a relatively late development after 600 BC; most were not built until after 300–250 BC and multivallate forts not until after 50 BC. These dates are now known to be wrong, with radiocarbon evidence linked to changes in pottery form and decoration. It is evident that some hillforts were occupied as early as the Late Bronze Age and many more date from as early as the 7th or 6th centuries BC. At the same time it has become clear that many, if not most, hillforts in southern England were abandoned round about 100 BC (Atrebatic area) or shortly thereafter (Durotrigian area). This dramatic shift in possible time-span has superseded the chronologies in many older excavation reports, adding considerable confusion to an already complex picture.

From the 1960s onwards, following the abandonment of the Hawkes ABC system of culture change, an increasing concern with the definition of hillforts led to the appearance of a number of proposals for their classification. These rested mainly on the structure and placement of the ramparts, siting (for example cliff-edge forts) and the size of area enclosed (see, for example, Avery 1976). Closer consideration of such evidence suggests, however, that any typology based on shape and situation will be an oblique record of the local topography and may carry little archaeological significance. Much of the discussion on hillforts still focuses on the form of construction of the hillfort ramparts and less on internal character, which is generally more elusive without resort to excavation.

The post-war period saw the emergence of open area excavation and a growing interest in both the form of occupation within hillforts and in the economic and social stimuli that led to their development. In the 1960s and 70s, the realisation that the social and economic functions of hillforts could only be addressed through an understanding of their internal layout led to the large scale excavation of a number of hillfort interiors including South Cadbury in Somerset (Alcock 1968a, 1968b, 1969, 1970, 1980; Barrett *et al* 2000); Crickley Hill in Gloucestershire (Dixon 1976, 1994); Croft Ambrey, Credenhill and Midsummer Hill in the Welsh Marches (Stanford 1967, 1974; Stanford 1971; Stanford 1981); and Balksbury, Winklebury and Danebury in Hampshire (Wainwright and Davies 1995; Smith 1977, 1979; Cunliffe 1984a, 1995, Cunliffe and Poole 1991). Despite the increased attention given to hillfort interiors since the 1960s, only a very small proportion nationally have yet been investigated on anything approaching a reasonable scale. The problem has been accentuated by the general lack of success of aerial photography at revealing features inside hillforts, even when they are regularly ploughed and cultivated, often in contrast to their surrounding landscapes. This continuing lack of extensive data is reflected in the most recent comprehensive survey of hillfort studies (Cunliffe 1991) where much of the discussion of the available evidence continues to revolve around the morphology of hillfort defences. Within the small sample of hillforts that have been examined on a sufficient scale for the nature and density of their internal features to be adequately characterised, there is considerable variation in the complexity of internal characteristics and intensity of occupation. Some sites reveal evidence of free-standing buildings within their enclosed areas while others contain few traces of occupation. The latter group are believed to have served a variety of purposes including a range of agricultural uses (such as coralling of livestock), settings for ritual or display and as temporary refuges (Ralston 1996). Some of the earliest known Wessex hillfort sites such as Balksbury in Hampshire (Wainwright and Davies 1995; Cunliffe 2000) contained very few internal features (Fig 1.3). This suggests that they performed a very different function from the later hillforts, such as Danebury (Fig 1.4) and Maiden Castle, that developed in the early Iron Age but continued in use into the

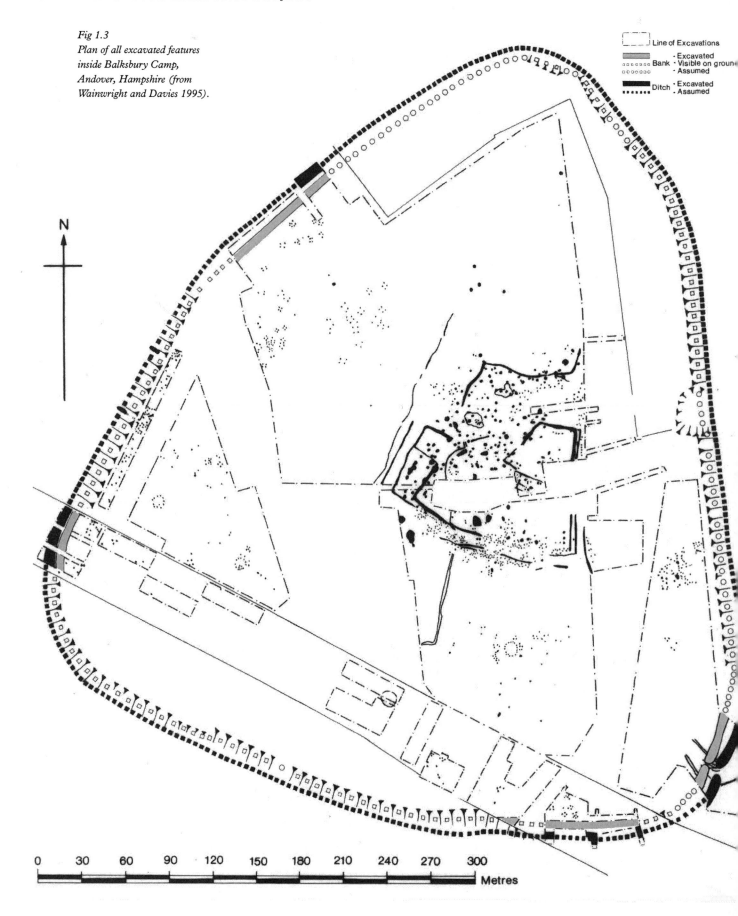

Fig 1.3
Plan of all excavated features
inside Balksbury Camp,
Andover, Hampshire (from
Wainwright and Davies 1995).

Line of Excavations

Bank
- Excavated
- Visible on ground
- Assumed

Ditch
- Excavated
- Assumed

N

0 30 60 90 120 150 180 210 240 270 300

Metres

Middle Iron Age by which time they were intensively occupied and strongly defended fortress town-like settlements with structures laid out on a rudimentary street-plan (Sharples 1991; Cunliffe 1984a, 1995, Cunliffe and Poole 1991).

Often over-shadowed by excavation, non-invasive archaeological techniques, led by analytical earthwork survey continue to make an important contribution to broadening understanding of hillforts through detailed mapping and investigation of their surface remains. Deserving of mention in this respect are the numerous hachured surveys of hillforts undertaken by the Royal Commission on the Historical Monuments of England in the counties of Dorset, Wiltshire and Hampshire and the work of the former Archaeological Division of the Ordnance Survey (working between the 1920s and 1970s) on whose surveys the majority of the plans in this volume are based. The RCHME surveys were initially undertaken for county inventories in the case of Dorset (RCHM, 1952, 1970a, 1970b, 1970c). Following the abandonment of this county-by-county approach, more recent analytical

earthwork surveys (Corney 1994) have tended to form part of more geographically restricted archaeological surveys of particular landscapes rich in cultural remains (*see* for example McOmish *et al* 2002; Riley and Wilson-North 2001), thematic studies of regional or national distributions of specific monument types (*see* for example Oswald *et al* 2001), or casework and project led surveys of individual sites such as Maiden Castle, South Cadbury Castle and Cissbury (Balaam *et al* 1991; Riley and Dunn 2000, Donachie and Field 1994). The historical contribution of earthwork survey to the study of hillforts is discussed in greater depth in Chapter 3. More recently, geophysical survey has played an increasingly significant role in revealing patterns of occupation inside hillforts that complements the evidence obtainable from the study of the surviving earthwork evidence. Traditionally used as an aid to the planning and targeting of excavations, as at South Cadbury in the 1960s, geophysical survey is increasingly employed in its own right or alongside earthwork survey as a powerful non-invasive tool in hillfort archaeology.

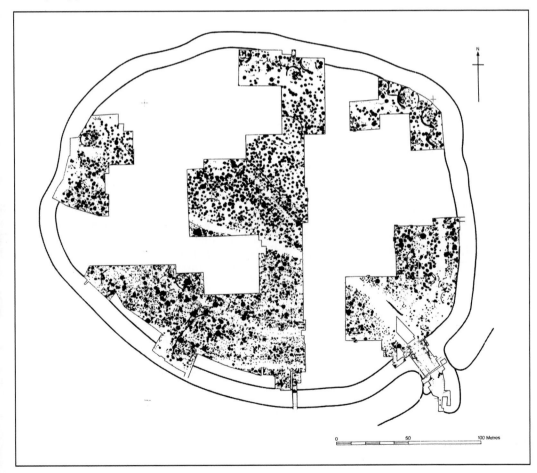

Fig 1.4
Plan of all excavated features inside Danebury hillfort, Hampshire (from Cunliffe 1995).

A number of criticisms of traditional approaches to Iron Age archaeology began to emerge from the late 1980s. The generalised, pan-European view of the 'Celts' was replaced by an emphasis on the distinctive nature of relatively small regions. This view relied directly on archaeological evidence and took a more critical approach to the literary sources that had formed the main plank of the traditional view. At the same time, the idea of hillforts as 'central places' and elite residences came under increased scrutiny and was found wanting, since even extensively excavated settlements yielded remarkably little evidence of social differentiation. The very existence of elites in the Middle Iron Age was questioned (Hill 1995) although the reduction in the number of occupied hillforts after 300 BC does nonetheless suggest some concentration of power at this time (Haselgrove 1999). The view of the period as one dominated by endemic warfare is also being overturned. The construction of fortified enclosures appears to have been connected as much with status as defence (Haselgrove 1999, Ralston 1996) and increasing emphasis is being placed on the non-defensive aspects of the role of hillforts, concentrating on issues such as the symbolic use of enclosed space (eg Bowden and McOmish 1987; Hingley 1990) and the cosmological significance of east and west-facing entrances (Hill 1996). There are numerous examples in southern England of the placement of hillfort defences well down-slope, thus rendering the interiors visible from the adjacent lowland. This may indicate a largely non-military purpose and suggests that display of power was more important.

> That power was based on more than simply the control of armed force seems clear for many Celtic-speaking societies. The wish to demonstrate status, the need to monitor access to markets, to industries, to food, or to luxuries, or the desire to control participation in ritual activities, are amongst many factors which may equally have contributed to the decision to erect hill-fort type earthworks, as well as influencing the form they took (Ralston 1996).

It is increasingly appreciated that much of the Iron Age material recovered during excavation provides only a selective and distorted picture of everyday life owing to the ritual nature of many deposits placed in settlement contexts. These new theoretical and synthetic studies have resulted in the publication of a number of volumes (eg Champion and Collis 1996; Gwilt and Haselgrove 1997; Hill and Cumberpatch 1995) though no thoroughly worked-though new Iron Age 'story' has yet emerged.

In 2001, *Understanding the British Iron Age – An Agenda for Action* (Haselgrove et al 2001) was published. This detailed research agenda based on five themes: chronological issues, settlements, landscapes and people, material culture, regionality and processes of change proved relevant to hillfort studies in several ways. Despite completion before the publication of the agenda, the Wessex hillforts survey and geophysical survey of Iron Age settlements in general had already begun to address in part some of the recommended avenues for future research, including:

- revealing spatial organisation of settlements and divisions of settlement space
- exploring the landscape for evidence of activity outside visible settlement boundaries
- carrying out surveys of poorly understood sites of the earlier Iron Age
- analysing landscapes around important loci of activity such as the environs of hillforts

In areas with established frameworks, such as Wessex, new fieldwork should focus on clearly defined research themes, as well as exploiting any significant new opportunities that may arise. Although the Wessex Hillforts Survey was opportunistic in nature it is hoped that it might stimulate other similar projects elsewhere in Britain where the methodology is effectively applicable and information is lacking. A major survey of Northumberland hillforts on the flanks of the Cheviot Hills was started in 2000. The three-year project, involving detailed analytical earthwork survey of twelve hillforts, is being carried out by the Archaeological Investigation team from the York Office of English Heritage in partnership with the Northumberland National Park Authority (Ainsworth et al 2001; Frodsham 2004). Detailed mapping of the surface evidence is more appropriate at these sites than geophysical survey because much of the archaeological evidence is spectacularly well preserved and observable above ground. Geophysical techniques are also less effective here due to underlying igneous geology, thin soil cover and bare rock exposures.

One of the few parts of the country that can confidently claim to possess a well understood hillfort chronology is the Danebury area, following four decades of intensive research by Cunliffe (Cunliffe 2000). The excavation campaign at Danebury was the most sustained investigation of any hillfort in Western Europe, taking place over some 20 years and resulting in the excavation of some 57 per cent of the interior of the site (Fig 1.4). The research on Danebury has contributed to the formulation of a broad model of hillfort development with, it has been assumed, at least regional applicability (Cunliffe 1991, 344–64). In simple terms this represents a three stage chronological progression from slight univallate forms to those of increasing elaboration and size. Large multivallate hillforts, discussed under the heading 'developed hillforts', represent the final stage of this model (see Fig 1.1). Hillforts of developed type, where excavation has demonstrated long sequences of occupation and a high density of internal activity similar in character to Danebury, are known in Dorset and Somerset at Maiden Castle and South Cadbury Castle. Others that have not been extensively excavated can be recognised from the form of the defensive earthworks (and in some cases the density of internal features surviving as earthworks) elsewhere in Wessex (for example at Yarnbury Castle, Wilts; Fig 1.5).

The dating of the construction and occupation histories of the other hillforts in the Danebury area is based on the presence of pottery styles comparative to those present at Danebury. Here the various phases of the hillfort, spanning the Late Bronze Age to the early Roman period, are defined by characteristic changes in pottery form and style (ceramic phases 1–7) that have been tied to a sequence of radiometric dates. It is therefore possible to arrive at a broad date range for a given hillfort based on the range of pottery styles present on the site. In some cases gaps in the ceramic sequence suggest periods of abandonment followed by reoccupation – commonly linked to refurbishment of defences or redefinition of enclosing ditches – in a later period. A long uninterrupted sequence of changes in ceramic style indicates continuity and longevity of occupation comparable to Danebury. By contrast a limited range of pottery generally indicates a single, probably short-lived phase, of activity uncomplicated by any later phases.

How broadly applicable this model is cannot be known without more survey both in the wider Danebury region and farther afield into neighbouring regions that also posses a high density of hillfort sites but have different defining characteristics, such as soils and geology (for example the Jurassic Ridge and west of Cranborne Chase). Comparison of the evidence with neighbouring regions and even other areas of chalkland landscape in central southern Britain is problematic because no other area has been studied with the same intensity as the Danebury area

Fig 1.5
Aerial photograph of Yarnbury Castle, Wiltshire displaying several of the characteristics of a 'developed' hillfort including multiple banks and ditches and a single entrance with elaborate outworks (NRMC; NMR 15406/15, SU 0340/149).

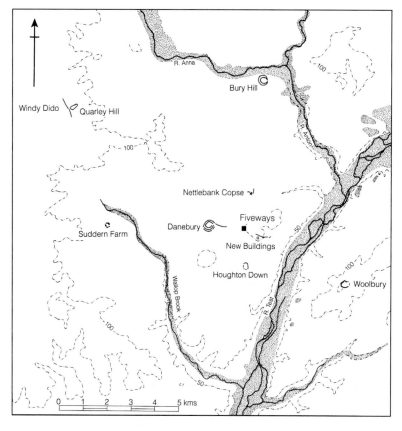

Fig 1.6

Hillfort sites and other Iron Age enclosed settlements investigated by The Danebury Environs Project in Hampshire from 1989–96 (from Cunliffe 2000).

sification previously developed in the models. While not invalidated, the present models require further elaboration to incorporate the additional variation in hillfort sites now shown to exist. The Wessex Hillforts Survey Project was initiated precisely in order to contribute towards the additional data needed to place the evidence from Danebury and its environs in an ever wider regional context.

In order to provide sufficient background data on the regional setting of the Wessex Hillforts Survey it is necessary at this point to describe in some detail the results of the Danebury Environs Project where it relates to hillforts, as well as the results of a recent study of hillfort distribution in the neighbouring region of Sussex (Hamilton and Manley 1997).

Hillfort development in the Danebury Environs

The Late Bronze Age to Earliest Iron Age

The earliest forms of hillfort recognised in the region are hill-top or plateau enclosures at the site of Balksbury and the outer pre-hillfort enclosure on Danebury Hill (Fig 1.7 and *see* Fig 1.3). Although there is some disparity in the structural form of these two sites, both seem to have been established in parallel with systems of linear earthworks that indicate a growing emphasis on boundaries, enclosure and barriers at the end of the Bronze Age, thereby transforming the previously open landscape of the Early Bronze Age.

Both enclosures were protected by simple earthworks and show only minor traces of internal activity in the form of post-settings. At Balksbury, a bank and ditch defined a roughly triangular enclosure of some 18 hectares in extent (Wainwright and Davies 1995). Three distinct phases of construction have been identified, beginning with a slight ditch with a low un-revetted bank on one side, the ditch being twice recut. At the one entrance, located at the south-eastern corner, three phases can also be seen in the timber revetment of the entrance passage. Although a considerable area of the inside of the enclosure was thoroughly excavated (*see* Fig 1.3), a number of four- or five-post buildings of the kind conventionally regarded as 'granaries' (or platforms for storing hay or other fodder) and possibly three circular post-built houses found in the southern part of the site were the only evidence of

(28 seasons of intensive research excavation). Partly as a result of environmental factors, Iron Age sites in northern England generally produce far less ceramic material with little variation in form over time, rendering the construction of detailed chronologies in these areas far more difficult in comparison to Wessex (Haselgrove 1999, 114).

The earlier model for Wessex, based on excavations at Balksbury (Wainwright and Davies 1995) and Danebury (Cunliffe 1984a, Cunliffe and Poole 1991) in Hampshire, has been considerably refined by the work of the *Danebury Environs Project* (Fig 1.6) and the resulting publication (Cunliffe 2000) has provided the greatest insight yet into the history of hillfort development and occupation within a region of central-southern England. The extended research on neighbouring hillfort sites, other enclosed settlements and linear boundaries in the Danebury Environs has highlighted the complexity in the archaeological record and the danger of over simple generalisations about hillfort origins, development and function. Although the three-phase model of hillfort development is still broadly applicable and has by no means been discredited by this new work, it is now evident that the archaeological reality defies the simple clas-

activity in the Late Bronze Age phase of the site. A well defined pottery assemblage of Late Bronze Age date was also recovered. The defensive enclosure at Balksbury appears to have been abandoned and ceased to function as a communal focus after c 9–800 BC, although it was later used as the site of an un-enclosed farmstead from the Middle Iron Age through into the Roman period. This later nucleus of activity

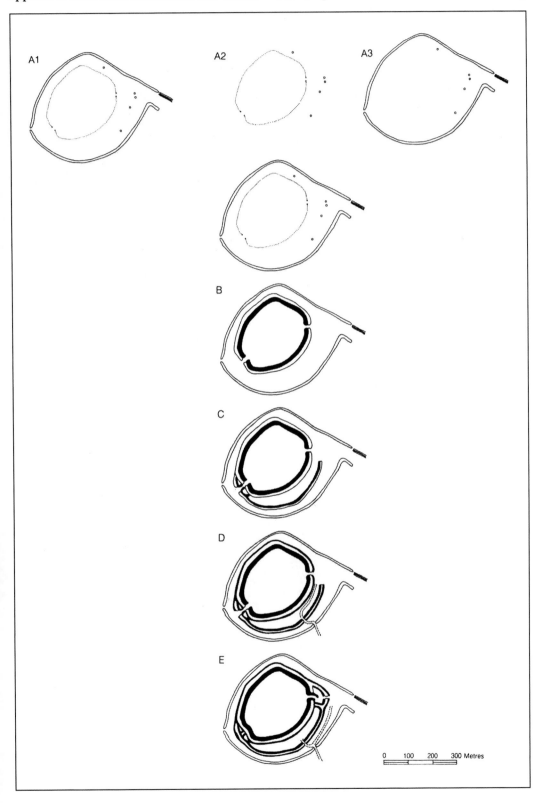

Fig 1.7
The main phases in the development of Danebury hillfort (from Cunliffe 1995).

within the abandoned former defences was concentrated in a comparatively restricted area of the old enclosure.

At Danebury (Fig 1.7), 16.2 hectares of the hilltop were enclosed by a slight ditch, possibly with two entrance gaps, almost entirely recut on a more substantial scale in the Middle Iron Age (the Outer Enclosure). The north-eastern side of the enclosure ditch joins with a linear earthwork (the Danebury Linear), possibly a later addition. Internal features of the enclosure in this period consisted of some large pits, which may have held timber uprights (possibly with some ritual function), and a group of four-post structures. (Although common in the later hillfort, these examples were shown to predate the first phase of hillfort defences.) A small assemblage of Late Bronze Age pottery was also recovered from contexts predating the construction of the later hillfort.

Other possible examples of the type of site represented by the Late Bronze Age enclosures at Balksbury and Danebury have been tentatively identified at Beacon Hill, Harting (West Sussex); Martinsell Hill, Wiltshire and Walbury Hill, Berkshire on the basis of the form of the enclosing earthworks and the size of the enclosures. The latter two sites were included in the programme of geophysical exploration carried out for the Wessex Hillforts Survey and the results are presented in Chapter 2 of this volume.

Early Iron Age

Of the two sites enclosed in the Late Bronze Age, only Danebury remained a significant location and was redefined by a stronger rampart and ditch, possibly towards the end of the 7th century BC (Fig 1.7). Bury Hill (fort number 1 or Bury Hill I) – a hillfort 10 hectares in extent defined by a chalk rampart fronted by a timber palisade – probably replaced Balksbury as the main communal enclosure in the Danebury region in the late 7th–6th-centuries BC. A similar enclosure dating to the same period is known at Winklebury, to the north-east near Basingstoke (Smith 1977). Both sites are apparently largely devoid of evidence of internal activity (based on limited areas of excavation and magnetometer survey). The first phase of hillfort defences at Danebury (enclosing a smaller area of 5.3 hectares within the earlier outer enclosure) was also established at some time during the 6th century BC using a

box-timber form of construction. The first hillfort ramparts, given their style of construction, are probably broadly contemporary with the timber revetted hillfort ramparts at Bury Hill I and Winklebury.

At a slightly later date (probably during the early 5th century BC) several more hillforts were built in the Danebury area at Figsbury, Quarley Hill and Woolbury (Fig 1.6). These sites are all remarkably comparable in size, structure and date: contour works enclosing similar areas with dump constructed ramparts (but no evidence for timber framed or revetted construction) with two opposed entrances. There is no evidence of extensive debris-generating activities at Quarley, Figsbury, Woolbury and Bury Hill I in this period, suggesting very low levels of internal occupation activity. This interpretation is backed up by the results of magnetometer surveys at Bury Hill and Woolbury (this volume) which suggest an almost total absence of internal structures.

While it may have had exactly the same range of functions as the other early hillforts at the beginning of the 5th century BC, Danebury differed from them in that the enclosure was used extensively for the construction of storage pits (which were concentrated in the centre around a focus of rectangular structures that may have been shrines) and for the building of circular houses occupying a peripheral zone in the lee of the rampart. Four-post storage buildings and a dendritic pattern of roads completed the plan. Once established, occupation seems to have been continuous, extending throughout the 5th and 4th centuries. The implication of this is that, in addition to its social and religious functions, Danebury served as a focus for a population who occupied the site either permanently or for a significant period during each year. It is interesting to note that this change to resident occupation seems to have taken place at about the time that the forts of Quarley, Figsbury and Woolbury were constructed – events that may be related. By the end of the 5th century BC, Danebury was a defended settlement of considerable extent with an exceptional storage capacity and a cluster of centrally placed communal structures, while the countryside around was quite densely scattered with farmsteads. Towards the periphery of what could be regarded as the core territory of Danebury, hilltop fortifications of comparable size were being erected at Figsbury, Quarley and Woolbury. The lack of occupation within these sites suggests that they may have been created as strategic points to command the perceived boundaries of a territory centred upon Danebury.

Developments from the end of the 4th century bc (300–100 bc – The Middle Iron Age)

On the basis of the distribution of pottery styles in the region, it seems likely that the political geography of Wessex changed in the early 3rd century BC. It was at this time, after a diminished level of use, that Danebury underwent a major phase of reconstruction and took on many of the defining characteristics of a developed type of hillfort (*see* Fig 1.7). The south-west gate was blocked and the rampart was augmented with material from internal quarries immediately inside the rampart. Finally a corridor approach and projecting hornworks were added to the single remaining entrance. For the next 200 years or so the interior was heavily utilised. A massive storage capacity in the form of rectangular post structures and below-ground silos was maintained; close packed circular houses in the lee of the rampart were rebuilt every 20–30 years and a religious focus continued to develop towards the centre of the fort. The intensity of activity measured in terms of material discarded was greatly increased from earlier periods. While the contrast to the earlier period is dramatic it is one of intensity rather than range. The layout and the structures were not significantly different, but the quantity and variety of material deposited in the later period is strongly suggestive of a greatly increased level of activity (or different attitudes to the disposal of material) and also a greater range of functions (including a centre of craft production and a place where exchange systems were articulated).

There is no evidence that the neighbouring hillforts in the area (Figsbury, Quarley and Woolbury), established in the Early Iron Age, were still in use after the end of the 4th century BC. All retained their simple entrances of undeveloped form. The situation at Bury Hill was quite different. Here the early, long abandoned hillfort was refortified, though the area enclosed was reduced. The new defences (Bury Hill, fort number 2 or Bury Hill II) differed from the traditional form of Middle Iron Age defences in that they were composed of two massive concentric ramparts with a single ditch in between and are therefore multivallate in form. It is clear from the excavated

sample of Bury Hill II that although the new defences had enclosed a settlement, the duration of the associated occupation was relatively short (limited to the period defined by ceramic phase 7 at Danebury). In chronological terms this could well have been restricted to the early part of the 1st century BC, placing Bury Hill II in the Late Iron Age.

In summary, the evidence from the hillforts in the region supports the view that during the 3rd and 2nd centuries only Danebury remained in use and with a greatly enhanced level of activity, until the construction of a new hillfort at Bury Hill late in the occupation history of Danebury. Occupation within the newly constructed hillfort ran parallel with the last stages of occupation at Danebury.

The Late (immediately pre-Roman) Iron Age (100 bc–ad 50)

The hillforts at Danebury and Bury Hill II (both in active occupation at the turn of the century (100 BC)), were abandoned by the end of the first half of the 1st century BC. The end of the occupation at Danebury may be linked to the firing of the gate structure; once this occurred only a very low level of occupation persisted into the period following 50 BC. By the very end of the Iron Age, some of the site was being put to agrarian use (comparable with Cissbury in West Sussex). Once the hillforts were finally abandoned other enclosed settlement sites in the region re-emerged, such as Suddern Farm and Houghton Down (Cunliffe and Poole 2000c, 2000e), which continued in occupation into the Roman period (*see* Fig 1.6). A number of the earlier disused hillfort sites, such as Woolbury, were also reoccupied by farming communities (often defined by small paddocks and enclosures) at this time, again continuing into the Roman period.

The overall pattern

In the Danebury area, the desire for hilltop enclosure began with the construction of Balksbury and the Outer Enclosure at Danebury and continued throughout the 1st millennium BC, culminating in a spate of hillfort building in the 5th and 4th centuries BC. Thereafter the dominance of Danebury suggests that some unified authority had emerged only to be challenged some two centuries later by a polity setting up fortifications at Bury Hill. After a period of transition in the early 1st century BC, the emergence of new ditched enclosures – no longer on dominant hilltops – points to a new socio-political grouping, but one that still adhered to the massive enclosing ditch as a symbol of authority.

Cunliffe identifies Sidbury and Yarnbury in Wiltshire (18km and 28km from Danebury respectively) as possible candidates for developed hillforts functioning in a similar way to Danebury during the 3rd and 2nd centuries and controlling neighbouring territories. No dating evidence has been obtained from Sidbury, but the form of the earthworks suggests it is of the developed variety. Other excavated hillforts farther afield in Wessex that conform with the developed model (defined by such characteristics as elaborate defensive earthworks and entrance approaches and occupied intensively over long periods of the Iron Age) are Maiden Castle in Dorset and South Cadbury Castle in Somerset.

The growth of Danebury, after its major phase of re-defence in *c* 270 BC, when the hillfort became a major focus of intense activity, was directly related to the abandonment of all other sites within a radius of up to 10km (based on the absence of ceramic phase 7 pottery from settlements in the environs of the hillfort). A similar situation has been noted around the hillfort of Maiden Castle at this time (Sharples 1991, 260).

Table 1 Summary of the sequence of hillfort development in the Danebury Environs from 800 BC–AD 50

1. Large Late Bronze Age hill-top/plateau enclosures (Danebury and Balksbury).
2. Simple univallate hillforts initially with timber framed or revetted ramparts succeeded by later univallate hillforts defined by dump ramparts frequently built at focal points on the system of earlier linear boundaries. With the exception of Danebury none of these new forts show evidence of significant internal occupation and the upkeep of the defences is generally short-lived. One interpretation of these sites is that they are peripheral markers of a territory centred upon Danebury, explaining the low level of use in comparison to Danebury.
3. The defences at Danebury are continuously augmented and the site develops into a major centre of population with evidence of intensive occupation from the 5th century until the late 2nd/early 1st century bc.
4. The latest hillfort development in the region takes place at Bury Hill II with the construction of multivallate fortifications on the site of the earlier abandoned hillfort. This development possibly represents the emergence of a rival polity challenging the territorial control of Danebury.
5. Abandonment of the remaining two hillforts in the region at Bury Hill II and Danebury to be replaced by other forms of settlement including banjo enclosures, Suddern Farm-type enclosures bounded by impressive ditches and clustered enclosure settlements. Areas within some earlier hillforts continue to be occupied by small farming communities from the Late Iron Age into the Roman period.

Taken together, the evidence from the three hillforts and others in the Danebury region has enabled the construction of a coherent picture, showing for the first time something of the complexity of the situation at this level in the settlement hierarchy. It is now clear – from the Danebury region at least – that many hillforts should be seen as successors of earlier hillforts. The settlement pattern is constantly shifting from one location to the next and the distribution pattern of hillforts that we see in the landscape today is therefore the culmination of a series of developments over a considerable period of time and does not represent a group of sites all in contemporary use. The result is considerable complexity in the surviving archaeological record – borne out by the work in the Danebury Environs.

The pattern in neighbouring regions

The hillforts of Sussex

Hamilton and Manley (1997) have recently attempted analysis on a regional scale of the pattern of hillfort distribution in the two counties of Sussex (Fig 1.8). Three main groupings have emerged, reflecting three main phases of hillfort development in successive periods. A striking aspect of the re-analysis of the dating of later prehistoric enclosures is that the greatest proportion of the sites belongs to the Late Bronze Age. A particular emphasis of the paper in *Sussex Archaeological Collections* is to consider how a greater appreciation of the topographical position of the sites might enlighten our interpretation of them.

The Sussex hillfort sites are classified simply into three divisions by period (based on available dating evidence, which is often

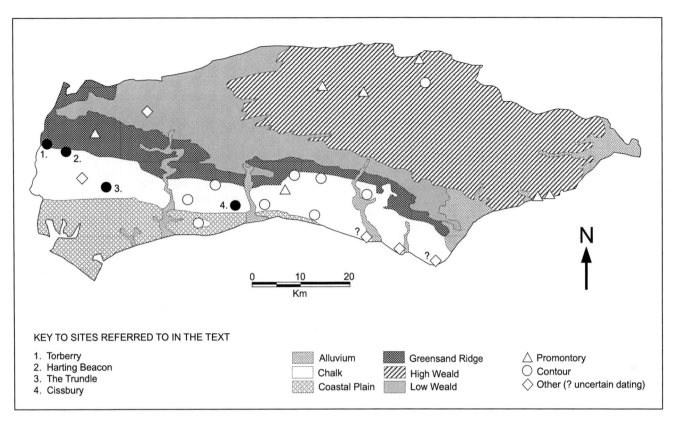

KEY TO SITES REFERRED TO IN THE TEXT

1. Torberry
2. Harting Beacon
3. The Trundle
4. Cissbury

▨ Alluvium   ▨ Greensand Ridge   △ Promontory
□ Chalk   ▨ High Weald   ○ Contour
▨ Coastal Plain   ▨ Low Weald   ◇ Other (? uncertain dating)

limited), and hillforts of several different forms, size and type are present in each of the periods. Under this scheme there is no distinction made between large hilltop enclosure type sites and smaller univallate forms of hillfort in the Late Bronze Age to Early Iron Age. Distinct geographical patternings of hillfort distribution can apparently be observed in each of the three periods and, like Wessex in the middle period (corresponding to the Middle Iron Age), hillforts seem to be fewer in number but exhibit intensification of internal activity.

Discussion on the function of the sites revolves around their topographical position and the tendency for them to favour particular topographical positions at different periods. This leads the authors to suggest that they may have functioned differently in each of the three phases identified. They believe it is inappropriate to explain sites in terms of continuums of development, such as increasing socio-economic centralisation and developing hierarchies (models that have been applied in the past to Danebury), and that the successive phases of hillfort construction are linked more to position in the landscape, reflecting aspects of symbolism and territoriality.

By far the largest number of sites belong in the first phase, spanning the Late Bronze Age and Early Iron Age periods, including small forts 1–2 hectares in area (for example Chanctonbury, Hollingbury, Thundersbarrow and Wolstonbury) plus some large forts comparable to hilltop enclosures in Wessex (Harting Beacon and Bell Tout). There is a tendency for these sites to occupy peripheral downland locations (possibly to observe outwards the landscape and people in the surrounding area). The enclosures in this period, being sited on the boundaries between different geological and environmental zones, are also suitably placed to access a varied range of natural resources both downland and river valley. The enclosing earthworks consist of a mixture of timber-revetted and dump-style rampart construction similar to the techniques employed in the Danebury Environs and on the Ridgeway Hillforts (Chapter 2, this volume). Evidence of domestic use of the sites is generally lacking. Few if any of the sites are known to contain internal features, such as pits, and associated artefact finds are normally few in number. Despite a reasonably large area excavation of the interior at Chanctonbury Ring, very few features were uncovered, suggesting that the site was not primarily used for occupation (Bedwin 1980). Harting Beacon is known to

Fig 1.8
Distribution of hillforts in Sussex related to geological zones (based on Hamilton and Manley 1997).

contain four- and six-post structures similar to hilltop enclosures in Wessex (Bedwin 1978, 1979). Highdown Hill and Hollingbury do show signs of occupation – including the presence of round houses, metalwork hoards, fine-ware pottery and other occupation debris.

The number of hillfort type enclosures in Sussex is dramatically reduced in the Middle Iron Age. Only four sites are present (the Caburn, Cissbury, the Trundle and Torberry) spaced at even intervals and located centrally within each major block of downland defined by the north–south rivers of the Sussex Downs. A greater intensity of activity took place within these sites compared to the Late Bronze Age/Early Iron Age enclosures, as evidenced by large numbers of internal pits. As is also generally the case in Wessex, most of the Sussex Middle Iron Age forts were preceded by Late Bronze Age or Early Iron Age activity. In some cases the defences of the enclosures were subsequently substantially remodelled in the Middle Iron Age, as at Torberry (Cunliffe 1976). This reconfiguration has traditionally been seen as relating to the emergence of central places (the former Danebury model) which replaced socio-economic functions previously dispersed across several enclosures, but Hamilton and Manley argue for a function as territorial landmarks or 'landmark enclosures' situated in prominent central downland positions to be seen from a distance all around. The substantial ramparts that define this group of sites emphasise them from afar (a trend continued into east Hampshire at the hillforts of Old Winchester Hill and St Catherine's Hill). Hamilton and Manley suggest that the sites in this period may not have been primarily defensive nor settlements in the conventional sense. The pits that have been found inside the sites need not necessarily imply a settlement function. Instead the sites could have acted as foci for selective, patterned deposition. The point is also made that the elaborate entrances at some of the sites may be as much to do with the 'theatre of presentation and approach' as protection from attack.

In the Late Iron Age (the final phase) in Sussex, enclosure activity shifts away from the chalk downland and concentrates in the Weald, suggesting involvement with iron working and the importance of the natural iron resources of the area. The differing functions of the Sussex sites in successive periods are seen as being reflected in a shift in their topographical position and location in relation to valued resources, such as land suitable for a mixed range of agriculture and industrial raw materials in the case of the Late Iron Age pattern.

The Jurassic Ridge

The pattern of development in Wessex outlined by Cunliffe (Cunliffe 1991) would appear to hold true for the hillforts of the Jurassic Ridge bordering Wessex to the north and north-west including the Cotswolds and parts of Gloucestershire, Oxfordshire, Northamptonshire and Worcestershire.

Large enclosed sites that appear to share similar characteristics with the early hilltop enclosure class of site in Wessex have been recognised at sites such as Norbury Camp and Nottingham Hill, Gloucestershire. As in Wessex, early hillforts seem to be prolific while far fewer developed hillforts of the Middle Iron Age have been identified. The excavated site of Crickley Hill (Dixon 1976, 1994) is the best known example in the region of an Early Iron Age hillfort, with a construction date for the first phase of defences (a massive timber-laced rampart with an external stone facing) in the 7th or 6th century BC. The main features within the fort at this time were rectangular post-built structures (either dwellings or rows of storage buildings). In the late 6th or early 5th century BC the defences were reconstructed and the earlier rectangular buildings replaced by circular timber buildings.

Conderton (or Dane's) Camp, in Worcestershire (Thomas 2005) and Hunsbury in Northamptonshire (Fell 1937) share certain features in common with those Wessex hillforts that originated in the Early Iron Age period but continued to be occupied on a more intensive scale during the Middle Iron Age (the so called developed form of hillfort). The small 1.5 hectare hillfort at Conderton Camp on Bredon Hill, Worcestershire displays a relative paucity of internal activity in the period following its initial construction in the earlier part of the Middle Iron Age (c 300 BC). In the succeeding period the defences were remodelled and strengthened, the enclosed area was retracted and one of the two opposed entrances was blocked (a development paralleled at Danebury). The second period of the hillfort is associated with dense internal occupation activity suggested by a row of tightly packed circular houses (possibly with several successive phases of construction) in the eastern half of the fort and an area given over to a very dense grouping of as many as 100 storage pits in the western half. This interpretation of the site is based on limited excavation carried out at the end of the 1950s and more recent geophysical survey (*see* Thomas forthcoming). Artefacts recovered from the interior, such as iron currency bars, are also indicative of the developed status of the site.

The multivallate hillfort at Hunsbury near Northampton (Fell 1937), possessing evidence of intensive occupation in the Middle Iron Age and a range of finds suggesting craft and exchange functions, is another possible contender for developed hillfort status in the region.

Prospecting techniques in hillfort archaeology

Hillforts in the landscape

It is now appreciated that hillforts are only a single element in a complex and changing pattern of landuse in the 1st millennium BC that encompassed many other forms and types of settlement both enclosed and unenclosed. An understanding of hillforts cannot truly be achieved without some appreciation of the wider systems in operation, necessitating research into the interaction and chronological relationship of a particular hillfort with contemporary non-hillfort sites (including field systems, boundaries and trackways) as well as neighbouring hillforts and other enclosed settlements in the surrounding landscape.

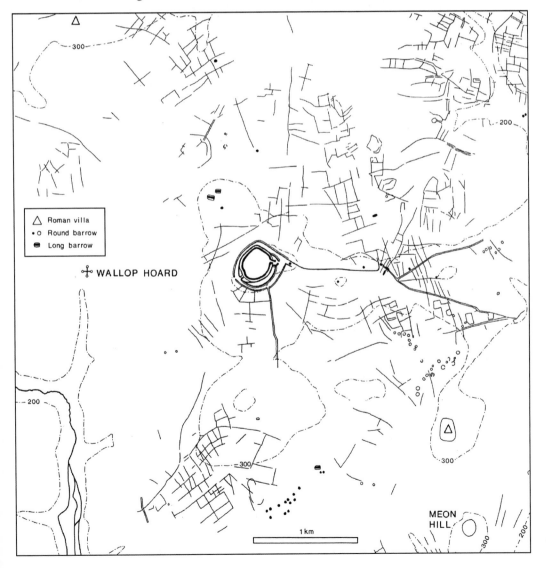

Fig 1.9
The hillfort of Danebury in its landscape context based largely on aerial photographic evidence (from Cunliffe 1986).

To understand the role of a hillfort in society it is necessary to understand how it relates to the surrounding settlement pattern. Intensified activity within a hillfort at a given point in time may be reflected in the simultaneous abandonment and depopulation of settlements in the surrounding landscape. This might be interpreted as the consequence of a time of crisis or the hillfort taking on the role of a semi-urban central place (Danebury and Maiden Castle).

The Maiden Castle Project in Dorset (Sharples 1991) and the Danebury Environs Project in Hampshire (Cunliffe 2000) are notable examples of projects that have in recent decades attempted to achieve this greater understanding using the systems approach. The theme of studying the hillfort in its chronological and landscape context has been continued in recent years by the South Cadbury Environs Project in Somerset centred on the hillfort of South Cadbury Castle (Coles *et al* 1999; Leach and Tabor 1997; Tabor and Johnson 2000) and at Castle Hill, Wittenham Clumps, Oxfordshire (Oxford Archaeology 2003, Payne 2002b, 2002c). Aerial photography was used to great effect in the 1980s to provide detailed evidence of archaeological sites in the environs of Danebury hillfort (Fig 1.9; Palmer 1984), but in more recent years the use of ground-based archaeological prospecting has proved to be as important in studies of this nature, particularly in areas such as the South Cadbury Environs where the value of aerial photography is restricted due to both predominantly pastoral land use and a limited archive of available aerial photographic material. Recently, magnetometer survey has begun to provide a rich archaeological context for the hillfort of South Cadbury of similar quality to the results achieved from aerial reconnaissance in the mainly arable landscape (favourable to the formation of crop and soil marks over archaeological sites) around Danebury in Hampshire (Fig 1.9). A programme of aerial reconnaissance undertaken by the National Mapping Programme (Bewley 2001) has recently begun to provide evidence of the contemporary landscape setting of the 'Ridgeway Hillforts' (Segsbury, Uffington Castle and Alfred's Castle) on the North Berkshire (or Lambourn) Downs, although most of this data has yet to be published.

The role of geophysical survey

The original excavations at South Cadbury in the 1960s (Alcock 1968a, 1968b, 1969, 1970, 1971) were some of the first archaeological projects to employ geophysical methods on an ambitious scale not only as a predictive method to assist targeting of excavation but also to provide a wider context within which to interpret the excavations (Musson 1968; Tite 1972). Similar, equally successful, exercises linked to sample excavation were carried out during this period at Conderton Camp, Worcestershire and Rainsborough Camp, Northamptonshire (Aitken and Tite 1962; Tite 1972). These projects were a successful early demonstration of the effectiveness of magnetometry for exploring hillfort interiors and characterising the relative density of occupation features they contained. What was lacking was the ability to collect sufficiently high resolution data-sets, due to the slow mode of operation of the instruments, and the means to manipulate the data subsequently to produce easily interpretable visual representations. The approach first pioneered in the experiments of the 1960s at sites such as South Cadbury was not repeated until the early 1980s at Maiden Castle in Dorset, by which time geophysical techniques in archaeology were coming of age with the arrival of routine digital data recording and computerised plotting of the data. The complete magnetometer survey of Maiden Castle, undertaken by the Ancient Monuments Laboratory (AML) between 1984 and 1985 (Balaam *et al* 1991, Payne 1996) was a striking reaffirmation of the benefits of linking large scale overall geophysical coverage with smaller targeted research excavation of hillfort interiors (Fig 1.10). Digital capture of the data from Maiden Castle on portable field computers heralded the routine use of this method with resulting improvements in data presentation. The computer-plotted halftone or greyscale plots that became the norm in archaeological geophysics from the late 1980s onwards, coupled with the development of increasingly powerful information technology, allowed the results of geophysical surveys to be seen in much greater clarity than ever before and enabled the recognition of even the weakest anomalies from features such as ring-gullies. As the number of geophysical surveys of hillfort sites increased during the 1990s it gradually became apparent that, largely due to the technological improvements of the preceding decade, archaeological geophysics had the power to contribute much to our understanding of hillfort interiors.

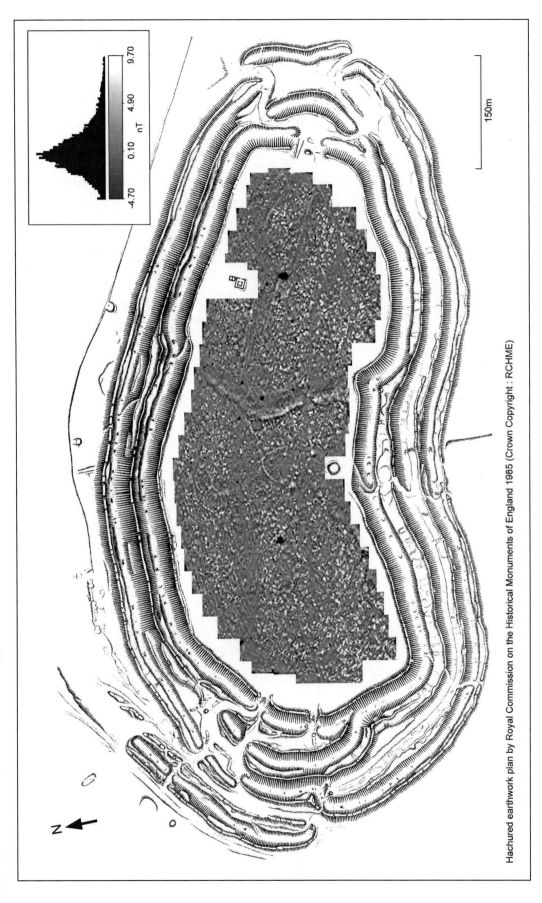

150m

nT
9.70
4.90
0.10
-4.70

Z

Hachured earthwork plan by Royal Commission on the Historical Monuments of England 1985 (Crown Copyright : RCHME)

Fig 1.10
The magnetometer survey
of Maiden Castle in Dorset
carried out by EH prior to
excavation in 1985 (from
EH, Ancient Monuments
Laboratory).

Fig 1.11

Oblique aerial photograph of Old Winchester Hill, Hampshire. The site is crossed by several long-distance footpaths and is managed primarily as a nature reserve by English Nature. Footpath and track erosion converges on the triangulation pillar and along the ramparts (NMRC; NMR 15393/23, SU 6420/53).

Geophysical survey in the 1990s as an aid to site management

Overall responsibility for the conservation of hillfort sites – the majority of which have statutory protection as scheduled ancient monuments – is the duty of English Heritage. A problem to date has been the lack of extensive data on hillfort interiors, which has deprived English Heritage of even the most basic information on the archaeological content of many hillforts – a prerequisite of informed conservation management. Although an increasing number of sites are now sympathetically managed in favour of preserving any buried archaeological features present inside them, a considerable number still face pressure from gradual degradation by agricultural activities such as ploughing, grazing and arboriculture, as well as burrowing and visitor erosion. The need to improve our understanding of the internal layout of hillforts, both for practical reasons of site management and in order to

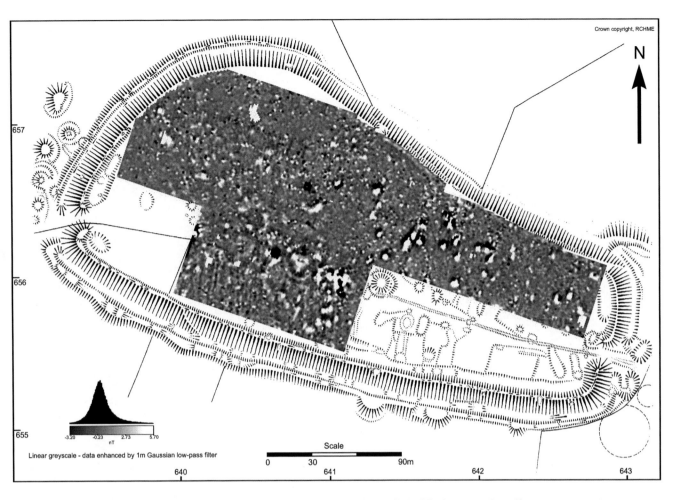

Crown copyright, RCHME

Linear greyscale - data enhanced by 1m Gaussian low-pass filter

Scale

0   30   90m

continue to improve our academic comprehension of the role and functions of this class of monument without resorting to costly and undesirable ground disturbance, were the two main underpinning reasons for the development of the programme of largely geophysical survey-based research described in this volume.

The understanding of hillfort development in central-southern England applicable to the Danebury region is based on limited information derived from relatively small scale sample excavations (Cunliffe 2000), but it was believed that it could be markedly enhanced, refined and extended by access to the level of information that geophysical survey was potentially capable of providing. During the early 1990s, geophysical surveys had been undertaken by the Ancient Monuments Laboratory of English Heritage on several hillforts in central-southern England, including Buckland Rings and Old Winchester Hill in Hampshire (Figs 1.11, 1.12), Caesar's Camp in Berkshire and Letcombe Castle (Segsbury Camp), Oxfordshire. These surveys were commissioned by the Conservation

Department of English Heritage, primarily to provide information to support casework aimed at stabilising the management of the sites in order to better secure their preservation for the future. The surveys were able to significantly enhance the data available on each of the hillfort interiors and were a successful demonstration of the power and affordability of fluxgate magnetometry to transform knowledge of archaeological sites that may be clearly-visible, well-defined earthworks but are otherwise poorly understood, particularly in terms of their internal archaeological contents and arrangements. The surveys – all carried out in a relatively short space of time – made a significant contribution to furthering understanding of the sites.

The magnetometer survey at Letcombe Castle, linked to a Countryside Stewardship agreement that converted the site from arable to stable grassland, was particularly useful, allowing the characterisation of a hillfort site for which negligible archaeological information had previously been available (Figs 1.13, 1.14). The availability of such data has clear benefits for the

Fig 1.12
Magnetometer survey carried out in 1995 of a sample of the interior of Old Winchester in relation to the RCHME hachured earthwork survey (from EH, Ancient Monuments Laboratory and RCHME).

management of the site: for example, the information provided by the survey is of practical use for determining if a zone that is suffering from erosion due to burrowing or heavy footpath wear also contains vulnerable archaeological features. Mitigation measures can then be taken to decrease the threat of erosion in the vulnerable area (for example by re-routing foot-paths). Other ground disturbance such as the erection of fences and sign-posts can be avoided in areas where the survey has indicated the presence of archaeological features. In addition to the surveys carried out for management purposes, the ability of geophysical methods to help address substantial archaeological questions related to hillforts was also emphatically demonstrated by a succession of surveys in support of the Danebury Environs and Uffington White Horse Hill Projects between 1989 and 1991 (Cunliffe 2000, Miles *et al* 2003).

Because of the degree of overlap, it is necessary at this point to provide a brief review of geophysical survey of hillfort sites in southern England that led up to the development of the Wessex Hillforts Survey programme. These surveys, carried out between 1989 and 1995, were a major influence on the design of the subsequent project carried out between 1996–8.

The hillforts of the Lambourn and Marlborough Downs (or the Ridgeway group)

The survey at Segsbury Camp (or Letcombe Castle) carried out from 1993–5, provided the clearest illustration of the considerable academic potential of geophysical methods in hillfort research (Fig 1.14). Letcombe is one of the grouping often referred to as the Ridgeway Hillforts which, with the exception of Uffington Castle, had been subject to very limited investigation before 1993 (some excavation by the Hillforts of

*Fig 1.13
Oblique aerial view of
Letcombe Castle or
Segsbury Camp,
Oxfordshire (Copyright
reserved Cambridge
University Collection of
Air Photographs, BIT 36,
1972).*

*Fig 1.14 (opposite)
The original trial
magnetometer transect
across Letcombe
Castle/Segsbury Camp
undertaken in 1993
(from Ordnance Survey
and EH, Ancient
Monuments Laboratory).*

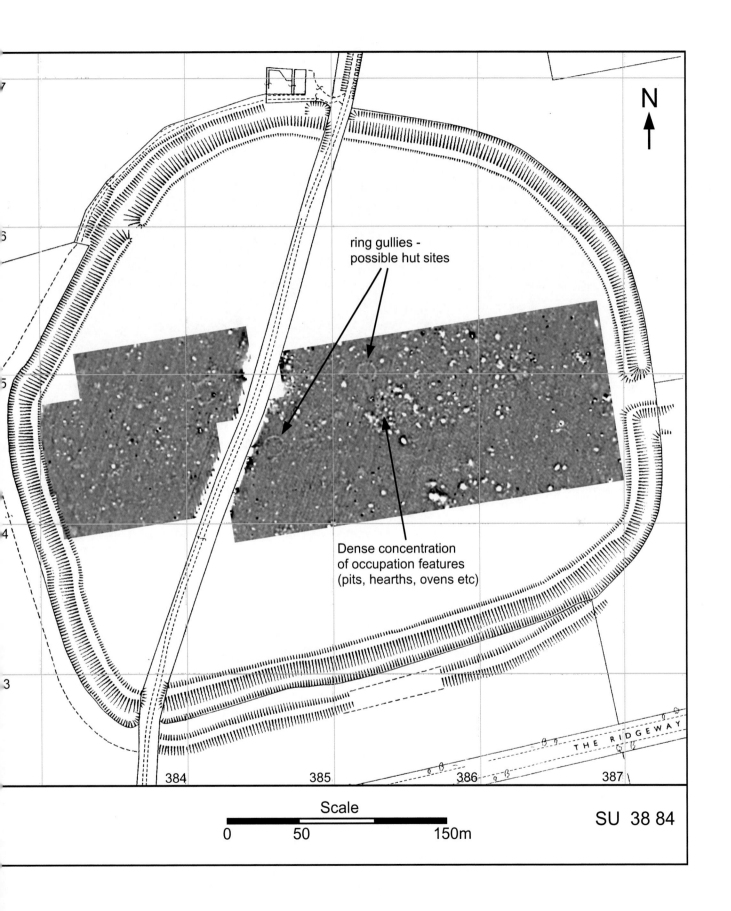

N

ring gullies -
possible hut sites

Dense concentration
of occupation features
(pits, hearths, ovens etc)

THE RIDGEWAY

384   385   386   387

Scale

0   50   150m

SU 38 84

Fig 1.16 (opposite)
Plan of the hillfort of
Uffington Castle with the
interpretation of the
magnetometer data (from
EH, Ancient Monuments
Laboratory).

the Ridgeway Project has since taken place). Nevertheless, they excited considerable speculation about their function within the Iron Age settlement pattern of the region. Nothing was known of the interior layout of Segsbury prior to the initial magnetometer survey transect in 1993 (Payne 1993b). Now, with total survey coverage and evidence for at least 20 circular structural features within the hillfort combined with large agglomerations of pits (Chapter 2, this volume), we can confidently attribute Segsbury to the class of Danebury-style developed hillforts with probable functions as a centre of population and an enhanced storage capacity (Payne 1996). This emphasises that our perception of what constitutes a developed hillfort should be as much about the evidence inside the defences as features such as multivallate ramparts and elaborate entrances traditionally associated with such sites but less recognisable at Segsbury.

In 1989 a magnetometer survey was carried out by the AML, inside the neighbouring hillfort of Uffington Castle, Oxfordshire (Figs 1.15, 1.16) in support of the White Horse Hill Project (Miles *et al* 2003). The overall objective of the project was to enhance understanding of the

various scheduled monuments on White Horse Hill, by means of limited excavation, to help inform their future management and public presentation by English Heritage and the National Trust who share joint responsibility for conserving the sites. As the archaeological excavations carried out by the Oxford Archaeological Unit had to be small in scale to disturb as little of the monuments as possible, the wider use of geophysical survey was an important additional component of the project. A very similar approach was adopted by the Danebury Environs Project for the internal investigation of the hillforts of Woolbury and Bury Hill during 1989–90 (*see below*). The Uffington Castle survey (Fig 1.16) was carried out to provide information on the archaeological content of the hillfort interior to augment a limited archaeological investigation through the surrounding perimeter earthworks. The purpose of the excavation was to recover information on the origins and development of the hillfort with minimal disturbance to the site; the excavated section therefore exploited an existing breach through the ramparts. Exploration of the hillfort interior was limited to non-intrusive investigation by

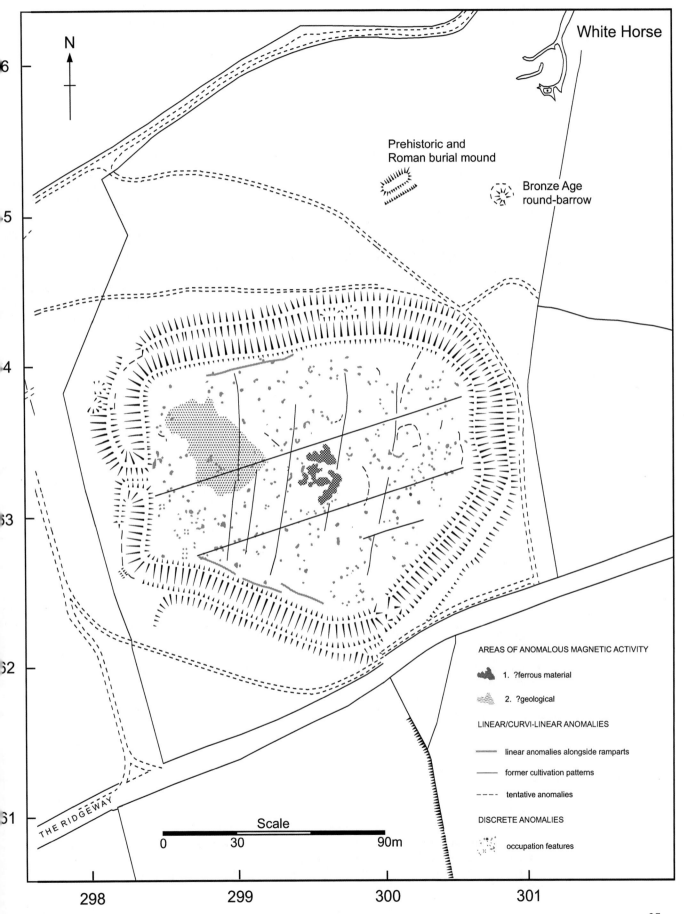

White Horse

Prehistoric and
Roman burial mound

Bronze Age
round-barrow

AREAS OF ANOMALOUS MAGNETIC ACTIVITY

1. ?ferrous material

2. ?geological

LINEAR/CURVI-LINEAR ANOMALIES

linear anomalies alongside ramparts

former cultivation patterns

tentative anomalies

DISCRETE ANOMALIES

occupation features

THE RIDGEWAY

Scale

0   30   90m

298   299   300   301

magnetometer survey (*see* Payne 2003a). Despite the availability of numerous aerial photographs of the site, few of them had revealed any detail of archaeological features within the hillfort except for traces of Medieval or Post Medieval strip cultivation. Magnetometer survey, therefore, had an important role in mapping the density and layout of any buried archaeological features present underneath the relatively blank physical topography of the hillfort interior. The pattern of discrete magnetic anomalies mapped by the survey (Fig 1.16) suggests that the site contains a moderate density of pits dispersed fairly evenly across the interior, with some loose clusters of pits and closely paired pits in places but otherwise few indications of any other forms of occupation (such as ring gullies).

Subsequently during 1994–5 some small-scale excavation took place inside Uffington Castle as part of the Hillforts of the Ridgeway research project undertaken by the Oxford University Department of Continuing Education (Miles *et al* 2003). The areas of the hillfort interior that were opened up were carefully positioned to investigate areas containing geophysical anomalies mapped by the earlier 1989 survey. Of the sample of magnetic anomalies investigated by excavation, ten were shown to represent pits with fills containing Iron Age and Romano-British material and another one was found to be an oven of Romano-British date. The availability of the geophysical data was crucial for enabling the precise targeting of small excavation areas (strictly limited in extent by the terms of the Scheduled Monument Consent to excavate) onto features of interest, thus avoiding unnecessary ground disturbance and wasted effort on opening up unrewarding trenches. The relative paucity of features inside Uffington Castle (*see* below) compared to other hillforts with long sequences of habitation (such as Danebury and Maiden Castle) presented the very real danger of opening up blank areas and missing the archaeological features that were being sought to provide material evidence for the occupation history of the site. The magnetometer survey and subsequent excavation at Uffington demonstrated that large and medium sized pits were easily detectable with a traverse separation of 1.0m and a reading interval of 0.25m along traverses (1.0×0.25), but smaller post-hole type features generally failed to register appreciable anomalies, even when the traverse interval was reduced to 0.5m (Payne 1996).

The conclusion drawn from the geophysical results from Uffington (based on the density and range of features mapped within the hillfort) was that it had only been occupied for a relatively short period of time during the earlier Iron Age. Excavation has now demonstrated further activity on the site during the Roman period that resulted in the incorporation of material of Roman date in the partially filled up earlier Iron Age pits. In this respect the site parallels other hillforts in the region, such as Woolbury, which after a period of disuse when the defences were no longer maintained (often lasting many centuries) were reoccupied by farming communities from the Late Iron Age into the Roman period. Liddington Castle, sited in a similar position to Uffington above the northern scarp of the Marlborough–Lambourn Downs, probably also had a similar history of occupation, as suggested by finds of early Iron Age and Roman material (Bowden 2000; Hirst and Rahtz 1996).

Hampshire hillforts

Although no large scale geophysical survey took place at Danebury itself, during the early 1990s the Ancient Monuments Laboratory (AML) took part in the subsequent research on the Danebury Environs (*see* Fig 1.6), providing a series of fluxgate magnetometer surveys on several of the neighbouring hillfort sites to Danebury (Cunliffe 2000). The aim of the Danebury Environs Project was to arrive at a broader understanding of the interaction of the hillfort with its contemporary environment by studying the development of settlement and contemporary systems of land allotment in its locality from the end of the Bronze Age to the beginning of the Roman period. The eventual objective was to understand the role of the hillfort in the context of the changing social and economic systems in the wider Danebury area during the 1st millennium BC.

As a first step in the study it was clearly crucial to examine the several other hillforts in the immediately surrounding area to assess their development relative to Danebury (addressing questions such as: when they were established, how long they were occupied for, how many phases of occupation were represented and when did they go out of use?). Magnetometer surveys played an integral part in this process.

The nearest hillfort to Danebury, located 4 miles (6.4km) to the south-east, is at Woolbury near Stockbridge, Hampshire (*see* Fig 1.6 and Fig 2.30). Woolbury appeared, on the basis of the surviving earthwork remains, to represent an example of a simple, Early Iron Age hillfort, constructed at about the same time as the first phase of hillfort defences at Danebury (in the 5th century BC). The straightforward construction of the ramparts suggested however, that, unlike Danebury, it was potentially unencumbered by Middle Iron Age occupation. The results of the fluxgate magnetometer survey carried out by the AML between 1989 and 1990 clearly indicated a low level of magnetic activity inside the hillfort, suggesting that settlement activity within Woolbury was of a much lower intensity than at Danebury. This interpretation was subsequently confirmed by excavation, which revealed that, unlike Danebury, Woolbury did not develop as a major focal point of habitation (Cunliffe and Poole 2000a). The magnetometer survey also confirmed the location of the missing eastern section of the hillfort ditch, which later excavation showed had been gradually infilled and levelled by cultivation during the late Iron Age and Roman period, when a small farming community was established in the abandoned hillfort. This farmstead, which consisted of a series of enclosures defined by narrow ditches, was detected by the magnetometer as a group of linear anomalies in the eastern part of the survey area.

In 1990, the second year of the Danebury Environs Project, at Bury Hill (4 miles (6.4km) north of Danebury on the outskirts of Andover), it was again critical to define the status and development of the hillfort in relation to the neighbouring forts in the area at Balksbury, Danebury and Woolbury (*see* Fig 1.6). Bury Hill (*see* Fig 2.13) had been interpreted as the remains of two hillforts (Hawkes 1940) – a smaller, strongly fortified bivallate enclosure (Bury Hill II) superimposed on a larger, more lightly defended fort with a single rampart (Bury Hill I). The earthworks of Bury Hill I are now understood (Cunliffe and Poole 2000b) to represent the remains of an Early Iron Age hillfort which, after a long period of disuse, was succeeded by the fortification of Bury Hill II. In 1990 the AML carried out fluxgate magnetometer surveys in each of the forts, covering 47 % of the area enclosed by the inner fort (Bury Hill II) and a more limited area of the remaining part of the earlier outer enclosure (Bury Hill I). It was hoped that magnetometer survey would be able to demonstrate the relative intensity of occupation in each fort by surveying sufficiently large areas to show contrasting or recurring patterns of activity. The results suggested that the early fort was largely devoid of significant features, in sharp contrast with the later fort, which appeared to contain a moderately high density of pits of various sizes scattered evenly across the area surveyed. Following the survey, excavation in the two forts showed that Bury Hill I was probably never used intensively, whereas there was plentiful evidence of high status activity (of the Late–Middle Iron Age) within the defences of Bury Hill II (Cunliffe and Poole 2000b), fully confirming the initial expectations based on the magnetic data.

Magnetometer survey of a sample of the interior of Old Winchester Hill hillfort (*see* Figs 1.11, 1.12) carried out by the AML in 1995 – again for the purposes of improving management and presentation of the site (in a publicly accessible nature reserve) to visitors – produced very similar results to those obtained from the hillfort of Woolbury. On the evidence of the magnetic data, Old Winchester appears to contain only thin scatters of pits interspersed with empty areas, although features associated with a linear group of round barrows occupying a central position within the later fort were also detected.

Off-chalk sites

The results of magnetometer surveys at Buckland Rings (Hampshire) and Caesar's Camp (Berkshire) in 1993 and 1995 (Payne 1993a; Linford 1995) were less informative than those obtained from hillforts on chalk geology or chalk plateau drift, possibly reflecting less than optimal geology for magnetic prospection. Buckland Rings (NGR SZ 31 96) lies off the chalk on a spur of Pleistocene plateau and river terrace gravels deposited over Tertiary sands of the Bagshot Beds on the south-east edge of the New Forest near the coastal town of Lymington. Caesar's Camp in Windsor Forest (NGR SU 864 657) is situated on similar geology consisting of plateau gravel over sands of the Barton Beds.

The results of the magnetometer survey at Buckland Rings were poor by comparison with some of the forts surveyed in the years previously on the Hampshire chalkland to the north. With the exception of sections of the defences, the position of the entranceway plus evidence for a former archaeological intervention detected along the eastern degraded side of the fort (Hawkes 1936), anomalies that could relate to archaeological

Fig 1.17 (opposite)
The location of the Wessex
Hillforts Survey area
indicating the sites included
in the project and other
main hillfort sites in central
Southern England.

features in the interior were all but absent. Magnetic susceptibility (MS) values from the topsoil were low, suggesting geological conditions unfavourable to the detection of features such as pit fills. The apparent absence of magnetic anomalies indicative of archaeological features inside the hillfort could therefore reflect the local geology rather than a genuine lack of internal activity. Despite the uncertainty over the internal character of the hillfort, the survey still provided valuable information for informing the future management of the site, in particular by identifying the position and form of the main eastern entrance through the defences into the hillfort along part of the defensive circuit where the earthworks are poorly preserved.

In 1995, a survey of a sample of Caesar's Camp carried out by the AML (Linford 1995), succeeded in detecting an internal quarry ditch inside the line of the inner rampart and a thin scatter of possible pits together with an aggregate of pits in the interior. Magnetic susceptibility (MS) was highest in the vicinity of the ramparts (suggestive of occupation concentrated in the area close to them) but MS values recorded over the rest of the site were very low (suggesting a lack of iron rich minerals in the topsoil developed over the site). Assuming that the magnetic evidence is a reliable indication of the buried features present within the fort, the results from Caesar's Camp suggest a relatively sparse degree of activity within the area sampled and provide little evidence for sustained occupation or a wealth of interior structures. However, as was the case at Buckland Rings, it was thought that the identification of subtle magnetic anomalies would be unlikely on a site with such extremely low topsoil and subsoil MS values.

Although in the first half of the 1990s geophysical survey on hillfort sites in southern England was targeted on a largely piecemeal basis according to management priorities, magnetometer survey in particular proved capable of making a substantial contribution towards the study of hillfort sites. In the majority of cases, geophysical survey provided the means of assessing the distribution and intensity of settlement activity within the interior of a particular hillfort, thus providing an insight into the length of occupation of the site, how space was organised and where different activities were carried out in the enclosed space. There clearly was, then, scope to undertake a strategic programme of geophysical survey, in order to extend the potential shown by the earlier surveys to explore the diversity of hillfort settlement patterns at a regional level.

The development of the Wessex hillforts survey programme

In the wake of all the relatively unstructured activity described above, came the realisation that non-destructive geophysical survey techniques could make a wider contribution to broadening knowledge of hillfort origins, function and development in central-southern England. The result was a proposal for a more ordered and wide-ranging thematic survey project on hillforts focusing on the chalk downland of Wessex (Fig 1.17), where a sound database of knowledge of Iron Age archaeology was already in existence, acquired over many years through the research by Cunliffe on Danebury and its environs and earlier archaeologists such as Hawkes and Cunnington. This programme of survey was christened the *Wessex Hillforts Project* or *Wessex Hillforts Survey*. Unlike most earlier hillfort related projects in southern England, the study was designed to be more ambitious in scale, investigating hillforts spread across a wide region but at a relatively coarse level of detail, rather than examining groups of sites in a smaller locality in some considerable detail as had already been done by the Danebury Environs Project. Although magnetometry is only capable of providing a relatively coarse level of detail of the buried archaeological features present in a given hillfort, compared to what can be achieved by intrusive means, a large number of sites can be covered economically and in a short space of time. The project was designed to bridge the gap between these two levels of investigation and extend the study of hillforts into the areas immediately beyond the Danebury Environs, drawing upon the backdrop of previous detailed research to provide a context within which to interpret the results from the new sites. One of the principals of the project was to include as many different types of hillfort (in terms of size of area enclosed and the form of the defences) as possible, in order to obtain a representative sample of the diverse range of hillfort sites present in the area (*see* Fig 1.1). This was a particularly important aspect of the project, designed to enable the possible interrelationship of hillfort form and function to be examined. The fact that the project was based entirely on non-invasive

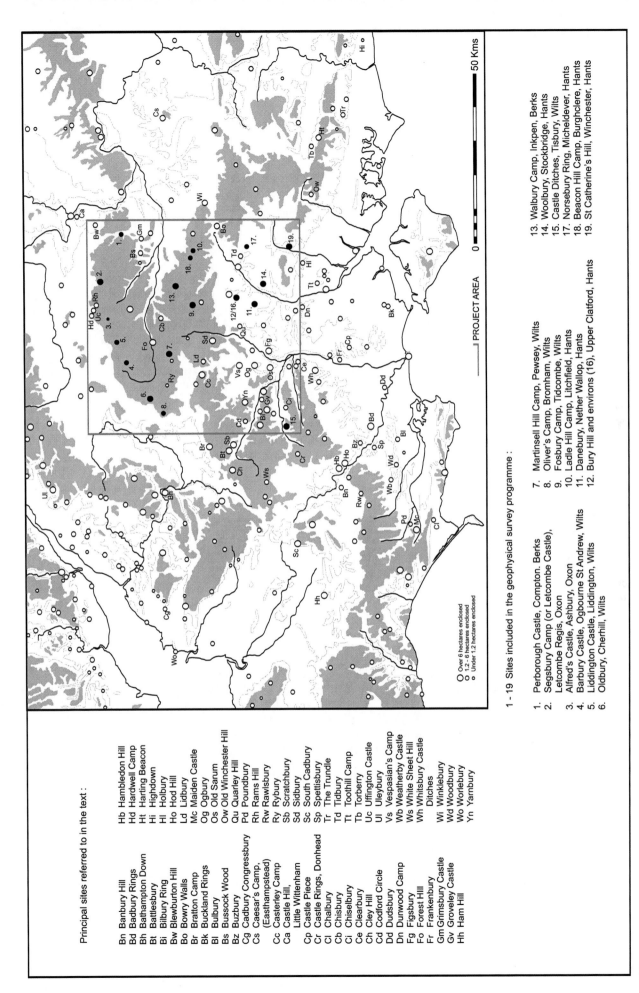

Principal sites referred to in the text:

Bn	Banbury Hill	Hb	Hambledon Hill
Bd	Badbury Rings	Hd	Hardwell Camp
Bh	Bathampton Down	Ht	Harting Beacon
Bt	Battlesbury	Hi	Highdown
Bi	Bilbury Ring	Hl	Holbury
Bw	Blewburton Hill	Ho	Hod Hill
Bo	Bowry Walls	Ld	Lidbury
Br	Bratton Camp	Mc	Maiden Castle
Bk	Buckland Rings	Og	Ogbury
Bl	Bulbury	Os	Old Sarum
Bs	Bussock Wood	Ow	Old Winchester Hill
Bz	Buzbury	Qu	Quarley Hill
Cg	Cadbury Congressbury	Pd	Poundbury
Cs	Caesar's Camp,	Rh	Rams Hill
	(Easthampstead)	Rw	Rawlsbury
Cc	Casterley Camp	Ry	Rybury
Ca	Castle Hill,	Sb	Scratchbury
	Little Wittenham	Sd	Sidbury
Cp	Castle Piece	Sc	South Cadbury
Cr	Castle Rings, Donhead	Sp	Spettisbury
Cl	Chalbury	Tr	The Trundle
Cb	Chisbury	Td	Tidbury
Ci	Chiselbury	Tt	Toothill Camp
Ch	Clearbury	Tb	Torberry
Cy	Cley Hill	Uc	Uffington Castle
Cd	Codford Circle	Ul	Uleybury
Dd	Dudsbury	Vs	Vespasian's Camp
Dn	Dunwood Camp	Wb	Weatherby Castle
Fg	Figsbury	Ws	White Sheet Hill
Fo	Forest Hill	Wh	Whitsbury Castle
Fr	Frankenbury		Ditches
Gm	Grimsbury Castle	Wi	Winklebury
Gv	Groveley Castle	Wd	Woodbury
Hh	Ham Hill	Wo	Worlebury
		Yn	Yarnbury

1 - 19 Sites included in the geophysical survey programme :

1. Perborough Castle, Compton. Berks
2. Segsbury Camp (or Letcombe Castle), Letcombe Regis, Oxon
3. Alfred's Castle, Ashbury, Oxon
4. Barbury Castle, Ogbourne St Andrew, Wilts
5. Liddington Castle, Liddington, Wilts
6. Oldbury, Cherhill, Wilts
7. Martinsell Hill Camp, Pewsey, Wilts
8. Oliver's Camp, Bromham, Wilts
9. Fosbury Camp, Tidcombe, Wilts
10. Ladle Hill Camp, Litchfield, Hants
11. Danebury, Nether Wallop, Hants
12. Bury Hill and environs (16), Upper Clatford, Hants
13. Walbury Camp, Inkpen, Berks
14. Woolbury, Stockbridge, Hants
15. Castle Ditches, Tisbury, Wilts
17. Norsebury Ring, Micheldever, Hants
18. Beacon Hill Camp, Burghclere, Hants
19. St Catherine's Hill, Winchester, Hants

Over 6 hectares enclosed
1.2 - 6 hectares enclosed
Under 1.2 hectares enclosed

PROJECT AREA

0   50 Kms

29

methods was another element in its favour, and the project represented a rare opportunity to demonstrate that geophysical fieldwork was capable in its own right of making a contribution to solving substantive archaeological problems without the need for any disturbance to the sites.

Broad issues that it was hoped geophysical survey would potentially be able to resolve included such questions as:

- Are all large, slightly defended early Iron Age enclosures actually largely devoid of settlement activity – as the few excavated examples suggest?
- Which hillforts appear to exhibit comparable densities of occupation to developed hillforts such as Danebury and Maiden Castle?
- Where a series of hillforts have been postulated as the largely contemporary centres of adjacent territorial blocks (such as those on the Ridgeway and the South Downs), do they exhibit a similar density and character of occupation?
- Where two or more hillforts are in unusually close proximity, do they exhibit similar densities of occupation? or does one appear to be more intensively occupied?
- Does occupation commonly occur outside hillforts?

In addition, site-specific issues could be examined, for example: Does the frequently referenced 'unfinished' hillfort at Ladle Hill actually contain a settlement?

The survey area

The area chosen for the study was the eastern half of Wessex, comprising three main blocks of undulating chalk downland broken by river systems, including the Hampshire Downs, the North Berkshire Downs and the eastern part of Salisbury Plain (*see* Fig 1.17). The area contains at least two major groupings of hillforts: those of the Danebury region studied by the Danebury Environs Project and the 'Ridgeway hillforts' of the Marlborough and Lambourn Downs on the edge of the chalk escarpment overlooking the Vale of the White Horse to the north. The area is bounded by the Upper Jurassic geology of the Vale of the White Horse and the Thames Valley to the north and the Tertiary deposits of the Hampshire Basin to the south. In contrast to the northern and southern limits of the project area, the eastern and western boundaries are not defined by any natural physical features such as geological boundaries or major river valleys. The eastern boundary follows a north–south line across chalk downland approximately parallel with and just to the east of the A34 main trunk road from Winchester to Newbury as far as the Goring Gap. This line places the Tertiary deposits of London Clay and Bagshot Beds east of Basingstoke and Newbury largely outside the eastern boundary of the project. The south-east corner of the study area coincides approximately with the city of Winchester. The western edge of the project area runs in a north–south line through the middle of Salisbury Plain, 10km east of the towns of Shaftsbury and Warminster up to Devizes in the north-west corner of the study area. In total the study area covers approximately 6,000 sq km and includes parts of the counties of Berkshire, Hampshire, Oxfordshire and Wiltshire.

Collis (1994) has recently stressed the pre-eminence of Wessex for British Iron Age studies, and it was clearly important that a pilot project involving the large scale geophysical survey of hillforts should take place against as comprehensive a backdrop of interpretative data as possible. In addition, the efficacy of geophysical techniques on chalk substrates has been amply demonstrated (David and Payne 1997, Payne 2000a) and the selection of primarily chalkland sites was a deliberate attempt to maximise the probability of achieving successful results.

The diversity of hillfort sites in the area would allow the study of hillfort interiors relative to the area enclosed and the complexity of the defences, enabling possible relationships between site form and internal layout to be recognised. Although a wide range of hillfort types are represented in the area (*see* Fig 1.1), few have yet been excavated on any scale and therefore the internal characteristics of the majority of the sites, and the variation in these between sites, largely remained a mystery.

The area also possesses the potential for integrating geophysical survey with access and management schemes in association with a number of countryside and environmental agencies such as The National Trust, English Nature, local authorities and the Countryside Commission who own or are involved with the management of several hillfort sites in the region, with scope for informing the public about the archaeological significance of the sites. Hitherto the lack of data has prevented these agencies from doing this at more than a very basic level. Furthermore, there was a pressing need to identify sites with high archaeological potential presently in unsympathetic management in order to help prioritise and target conservation initiatives aimed at securing the preservation of sites where archaeological information was potentially being gradually degraded over time through lack of intervention.

The sites included in the project and selection criteria

The sites selected for survey make up a representative sample of the various hillfort types identified in the region. For reasons of cost and because of practical considerations such as tree cover on some sites, it was not possible to attempt a systematic and exhaustive study of all the hillforts in the project area. Two hillforts in close proximity to one another just north of Newbury at Bussock Wood and Grimsbury Castle had to be omitted from the sample because both are currently in wooded areas. Other hillforts close to expanding towns such as Andover, Basingstoke and Southampton had not escaped being built over by housing and road development. Because of the constraints of such land use on the effective application of geophysical methods an initial selection process was operated whereby a short-list of the most suitable sites for survey was prepared from English Heritage management sources. The selection of sites also reflected management priorities based on perceived threats to the sites such as pressures arising from cultivation and other forms of erosion. The short-list of sites included in the survey programme (*see* Fig 1.17, Sites 1–19) was arrived at by the following means:

1. Surface conditions were required to be suitable for survey with minimal surface obstruction from vegetation or modern ferrous contamination.
2. The underlying geology should be favourable for magnetometer survey and reasonably consistent across the total sample (chalk, greensand or clay-with-flints).
3. Where sites were under grassland, priority was to be given to sites in public management (such as Barbury Castle) or with extensive public access.
4. Sites with existing adequate geophysical survey coverage (such as Uffington Castle) were excluded.

Surveys could only be carried out with the full consent of the landowners and in one case (Tidbury Ring, Hampshire) permission was not forthcoming requiring the substitution of an alternative site (Fosbury, Wiltshire).

The resultant list of sites was then considered in terms of its methodological and academic integrity. In methodological terms it was important that the sample contained a balance of sites with surviving earthwork remains in the interior (for example Beacon Hill) and sites under permanent cultivation with largely plough flattened interiors (for example Norsebury Ring). In addition it was proposed to survey an unexcavated area inside Danebury to provide a control method for assessing how representative geophysical data is of the full archaeological content of a hillfort where it is known from excavation.

In academic terms the sample was checked and, where necessary, augmented to ensure that it included the following:

1. Examples of recognised hillfort types such as large hilltop enclosures, eg Walbury, Martinsell; univallate contour hillforts, eg Liddington Castle, St Catherine's Hill; multivallate hillforts, eg Barbury Castle, Castle Ditches; and small hillforts, eg Oliver's Camp, Alfred's Castle
2. Examples from previously suggested 'groupings' of hillforts, eg the 'Ridgeway forts' (Barbury Castle, Liddington Castle, Uffington Castle and Letcombe Castle (Segsbury Camp))
3. Examples from the Danebury Environs (Bury Hill and Woolbury)
4. Examples of hillforts in unusually close proximity (eg Danebury and Woolbury; Beacon Hill and Ladle Hill)
5. Examples of special interest (eg the 'unfinished' hillfort at Ladle Hill).

After this procedure was carried out, the total internal area of all the sites selected was calculated and an attempt made to match the amount of survey coverage required to the budget available. The short-list was finally adjusted to include the widest possible range of hillfort types including some of the larger examples, such as Walbury Hill Camp in Berkshire, within the budgetary constraints. This allowed a total of 18 sites to be included in the project with an additional external survey area at Bury Hill in Hampshire.

Of the 18 hillfort sites selected for study by the project, excavation had only previously been carried out inside five (excluding Danebury): Bury Hill and Woolbury for the Danebury Environs Project (Cunliffe 2000); earlier work by C F C Hawkes at Bury Hill and St Catherine's Hill (Hawkes 1940 and 1976); Liddington Castle in 1976 (Hirst and Rahtz 1996) and an excavation at Oliver's Camp near Devizes by M E Cunnington, published in 1908. All of these documented interventions were small-scale and based on a single season of excavation.

Seven out of the 18 sites selected for survey under the project possessed scope for improved interpretation in their management as public open spaces.

Wherever practical, 100% samples of the interior of each hillfort were surveyed. In some cases this was not possible due to partial tree cover or other unsuitable terrain such as quarried areas.

The aims and objectives of the project

In his 1976 introduction to *Hillforts: Later Prehistoric Earthworks in Britain and Ireland,* Avery writes:

> We need the exploration of the interiors of both major and minor forts, and also the exploration of nearby settlement sites, on a scale large enough to throw light on the population, social structure and economy of these sites. Just as no two sites reflect identical approaches to tactical defence, so all sites will vary in social structure and economy. The task of the next 40 years must be to create sound data, and a sound chronology, as the basis for an understanding of these aspects.

The Wessex Hillforts Project was initiated in an attempt to contribute to this long process of broadening understanding. To date our knowledge of hillforts in general has been reliant on a limited number of intensively studied sites such as Danebury, while the bulk of sites remained poorly understood. The Wessex Hillforts Project was designed to help right this imbalance, therefore allowing a more synthetic approach to hillfort study.

In a recent collection of papers entitled *Science in Archaeology: an agenda for the future* (Bayley 1998; Gaffney *et al* 1998) the Wessex Hillforts Project is described as an example of a site-based project that employed geophysics as the prime methodology (as opposed to more traditional and costly intrusive techniques) for the investigation of hillfort interiors. Using a planned sampling strategy (involving a selection of representative hillfort types), the project attempted to rectify not only the historic excavation bias towards hillfort defences, but also combined investigations into the nature of early and developed hillforts, spatial differentiation of function, regionally and at an intra-site level. Also included in the research design (Trow *et al* 1996) was the exploratory assessment of a number of methods including magnetic susceptibility and digital terrain modelling, for rapid characterisation of hillfort interiors and settlement intensity. This approach represented a measured response to archaeological problems that might otherwise have demanded a massive investment in traditional excavation, but without being directly threatened by development the sites included in the project were unlikely to see such an investment in the foreseeable future. The project was designed to solve substantive archaeological problems explicitly using geophysical data and data from other non-invasive sources.

The over-arching aims of the project were to provide data for improved management and interpretation as well as widening academic comprehension of the diverse hillfort types in Wessex, particularly in terms of their relative socio-economic function and varying occupation histories as reflected in their internal layout.

The specific objectives of the project as set out in the 1996 Project Design (Trow *et al* 1996) were designed to address the following research questions and academic issues relating to hillfort sites in southern England:

i) To support English Heritage casework relating to the conservation and management of hillforts in the South East and South West Regions by providing high quality, wide-ranging and detailed data on the internal archaeological content of hillforts to assist the putting in place of appropriate management measures at each of the sites starting from an informed basis. This aim stemmed from the premise that it is difficult to effectively protect a site if you are largely ignorant of the range of archaeological features that are preserved within it.

ii) To obtain information on the internal arrangements of hillforts that might otherwise be gradually lost over time as a result of agricultural erosion. Obtaining such information by excavation would be prohibitive in terms of cost due to the quantity and scale of the sites in unsympathetic land use.

iii) To contribute to improved on-site interpretation for visitors to the monuments, to promote increased public understanding, awareness and enjoyment of the archaeological heritage.

iv) To broaden academic understanding of the diverse hillfort types in Wessex, particularly in terms of their socio-economic function as reflected in their internal layout. On completion of the data collection it was hoped that it would be possible for the first time to understand:
- The nature of the internal arrangement of early hill-top enclosures
- The range of internal patterns exhibited by early hillforts
- The consistency of dense internal activity within the category of developed hillforts
- The functions of small hillforts and their difference from, or similarity to, enclosed settlements (numerous examples of which have been surveyed in Hampshire and Wiltshire and a smaller number in adjacent Gloucestershire and Oxfordshire; Source: English Heritage Geophysical Survey Database)
- Recurring patterns of spatial organisation.

v) To assist the design and development of appropriate methodologies for the non-intrusive archaeological assessment of major earthwork monuments under different landuse regimes and pressures.

vi) To demonstrate the potential of thematic programmes of non-destructive survey in the development of regional research frameworks.

Given the historically proven effectiveness of aerial archaeology on the Wessex chalkland, it was decided that understanding of the individual sites largely based on the geophysical data could be markedly enhanced by a study of the existing aerial photographic (AP) record, held in the National Monuments Record (NMR) at Swindon, from the locality of each hillfort site. The decision was taken to examine the AP evidence within a 2km radius of each site and assess its archaeological significance and possible relation to the actual hillforts centred on. This data is presented in Chapter 2 together with discussion of the topographical siting of each hillfort, the interrelationships between sites and the ground plan and surface morphology of each site.

The methods employed by the project

Survey techniques

Fluxgate magnetometer or gradiometer survey (Fig 1.18)

Magnetometer survey is the preferred geophysical method for the initial location or general planning of archaeological sites (English Heritage 1995) and for this reason was the principal geophysical survey technique adopted for the project. Rapid ground coverage (at a rate of around 1.5 hectares a day) and the ability, under suitable conditions, to detect a wide range of buried archaeological features are the principal advantages of the technique.

Magnetic surveying is a passive geophysical technique involving the measurement of minute variations in the magnitude or gradient of the Earth's magnetic field at close intervals (1.0m or less) across the ground surface (English Heritage 1995; Clark 1996). Modern magnetometers are capable of detecting magnetic variations or anomalies over 50,000 times weaker than the natural ambient field strength. Magnetic anomalies occur in association with archaeological features due to magnetic susceptibility differences between their composition and the surrounding deposits that occur when iron-rich

Fig 1.18
Magnetometer survey in progress using a Geoscan FM36 Fluxgate Gradiometer (from Archaeometry Branch, EH, Centre for Archaeology).

minerals in the soil form more strongly ferro-magnetic materials such as magnetite or magheamite. This magnetic enhancement is usually related to burning, although more subtle inorganic and bacterially controlled mechanisms may also play a part under suitable soil conditions. Such conditions occur naturally in most topsoils, providing a source of magnetically enhanced material that becomes incorporated in archaeological features and so produces almost indelible magnetic signatures, even where features have been all but erased by intensive agriculture. Magnetometers also respond to the strongly magnetic signals produced by heavily fired structures that have become permanently magnetised as a result of intense heating. This permanent thermo-remanent magnetism is found in domestic and industrial features containing fired clay such as hearths, kilns, furnaces and ovens, and in some cases burnt stone structures (Aitken 1974, 141–7).

Magnetometry, coupled with aerial photography, has been recognised for many years on the Wessex chalkland as a powerful method for planning prehistoric settlements and landscapes. The series of surveys carried out for the Danebury Environs Project from 1989–96 (Payne 2000a) demonstrated that the technique is particularly effective on the chalk and chalk plateau drift of this region, where anomalies, caused by higher magnetic susceptibility of the soil concentrated in buried archaeological features (primarily the infilling of features cut into the chalk such as ditches and pits), stand out clearly against the relatively much lower magnetic background from the surrounding natural substrates.

All of the magnetometer surveys carried out for the Wessex Hillforts Project employed Geoscan FM36 Fluxgate Gradiometer type instruments with built-in data-logging facilities enabling digital data capture of about 16,000 readings in a two hour survey session. The instruments are sensitive to changes in magnetic flux density of a tenth of a nanotesla (nT). In all cases the data were collected on a 30m grid, at 0.25m intervals, along traverses spaced 1.0m apart. This represents a compromise, by which larger area coverage was achieved at the expense of possibly missing smaller archaeological features that might have been detected by narrower instrument traverses (halving the separation between traverses from 1.0m to 0.5m, for example). Data processing involved the initial elimination of the effects of thermally induced instrument drift,

showing as bunching or striping of alternate lines of data (by equalising the mean of each line of readings). In some instances the data were also smoothed slightly, to improve the definition of archaeological anomalies greater than a metre in width, by the use of a Gaussian low-pass filter with a radius of 1.0m (Scollar et al 1990).

The range of archaeological features generally detectable by magnetometry at hillfort sites of Bronze Age and Iron Age date on chalkland geology includes: infilled ditches defining internal enclosures or divisions and other earth-filled features including silo and rubbish pits, irregular quarries or scoops, and shallow 'working hollows'. Annular gullies defining the former positions of round houses of Iron Age date were detected at Segsbury Camp and subsequently confirmed by excavation. Numerous other examples exist at hillfort sites both in Wessex and farther afield including South Cadbury Castle, Somerset and Conderton Camp, Worcestershire. Ovens, furnaces and hearths, both of industrial and domestic type, would also be expected to register appreciable magnetic anomalies. One noteworthy example of a large oven of key-hole shaped plan, detected by magnetometry and subsequently confirmed by excavation, occurred at Uffington Castle (Payne 2003a).

It would be misleading to suggest that magnetometry can provide a complete picture of all the activity and occupation within a hillfort. Some important categories of features can be missed. This applies in particular to some smaller, shallow and less substantial features such as gullies and post-holes (especially where truncated by ploughing), and also some pits and graves, which may only offer a poor magnetic contrast between their fill and the surrounding natural chalk (for example a pit filled with chalk rubble).

Comparison of the geophysical data from the excavated samples of Uffington Castle and the inner camp at Bury Hill provides a clear example of these limitations (Payne 2000a, 2000c, 2003a). Generally only the larger pit-type features (and in the case of Uffington, the oven) were represented in the magnetic data, while the majority of the smaller features recorded during excavation were not visible. The application of more sensitive caesium magnetometers in recent years is now improving the detection rate of narrow circular gullies and slots and post-hole structures within Iron Age settlement complexes (Payne 2004).

General experience of magnetic prospecting on chalk in southern England using fluxgate gradiometers has shown that they are rarely equal to the task of locating smaller post-holes (typically 0.3m in diameter and 0.3m deep), regardless of the sampling interval being used (*see* Payne 1996). Therefore, remains of stake-built structures (such as some common forms of Iron Age round house) are unlikely to be detectable except where associated features such as hearths, surrounding gullies or deposits of burnt daub are present.

This was shown to be the case at an Early Iron Age enclosed settlement at Houghton Down near Danebury, surveyed in 1994 in advance of excavation (Payne 2000a, 2000d). Here, the round houses associated with the earliest Iron Age phase of the site, discovered in the process of excavation, were invisible in the magnetometer data. If generally applicable, this situation would unfortunately result in important categories of activity at Iron Age sites being under-represented in standard fluxgate magnetometer surveys – a limitation that should always be borne in mind in the interpretation of the data. Larger than average post-holes (such as those constructed to retain the doorframe posts of timber houses or the foundation sockets of large four-post structures) are comparable to small pits and therefore more easily detectable even at standard 1.0m × 0.25m sample intervals. A few isolated examples of possible four-post structures detected by magnetometer survey have tentatively been identified at Uffington Castle and Perborough Castle in Oxfordshire (Chapter 2 this volume) and at Conderton Camp in Worcestershire (Chapter 3 this volume and Payne 2005. The latter site is situated on particularly favourable geology for magnetic prospection (Middle Jurassic Inferior Oolite) and in these conditions post-hole type structures would be expected to be easier to resolve than similar features on chalk.

In areas of predominantly chalk geology, features of geomorphological origin may sometimes register in a magnetometer survey, particularly in areas where the superficial geology is variable, or has been influenced by periglacial conditions. The influence of scoring and fissuring of the surface of the chalk has been noted in magnetometer surveys of several sites in the Danebury environs, including Bury Hill and New Buildings. The fluxgate gradiometer is sensitive only to localised soil changes, so a response to larger-scale variation in solid or drift geology (for example an area of plateau drift as on the hill occupied by the hillfort of Woolbury) does not normally occur. However, the partially clay-capped hill occupied by Woolbury hillfort shows a more confused magnetic background compared to those sites where the geology is more uniform (Payne 2000b). The problem would appear to be particularly severe in the case of Walbury Hill on the northern scarp of the Hampshire Downs and at the highest point of the chalk geology in southern England. Purely natural pockets of clay-with-flints are known to occur within the chalk at the hillforts of Segsbury and Uffington Castle and produce anomalies similar to those associated with man-made features such as pits and quarries. There is therefore a potential danger of misinterpreting natural features of the geology as archaeological features. Geological features might be expected to exhibit more irregular form and more random patterning than archaeological features, but experience shows that it is not always possible to differentiate reliably between the two.

Magnetic susceptibility survey (Fig 1.19)

Detailed magnetic susceptibility (MS) surveys were carried out at two of the hillforts with ploughed interiors – Norsebury Ring and Castle Ditches – where the results of the magnetometer surveys proved particularly interesting. The magnetic susceptibility surveys were designed to provide additional information to support the interpretation of the magnetometer surveys.

Different materials become variably magnetised in the presence of the Earth's magnetic field. The degree to which soils become magnetised in the presence of this external induced magnetic field is known as the magnetic susceptibility (MS) and depends on the concentration of naturally occurring iron oxides they contain, and the extent to which these have been modified to more magnetic forms by various mechanisms. These are not as yet wholly understood but seem to be linked with a past human presence on a site (Tite and Mullins 1971; Clark 1996, chapter 4). Concentrations of soils that have become artificially magnetically enhanced (increasing their MS) as a product of human occupation can be defined by topsoil magnetic susceptibility measurement. A susceptibility survey may, therefore, supplement and confirm the findings of a magnetometer survey by indicating the areas within a hillfort where features and debris of domestic and possibly industrial origin are most concentrated. This is of particular interest within hillforts such as Norsebury and Castle Ditches that exhibit signs of internal divisions or smaller internal enclosures. In such cases, MS survey may be capable of defining any concentrations of activity associated with these discrete areas, therefore helping to shed light on their function or the nature of the activities carried out in particular zones of the hillfort.

Two alternative procedures are commonly used in archaeological magnetic susceptibility surveys, the first of which is to collect volumetric susceptibility readings on *in-situ* soil using the Bartington MS2 meter and MS2-D field sensor (Fig 1.19). This method allows rapid ground coverage, but for accuracy it requires close contact between the ground surface and the detector coil. It may therefore produce a slightly different response to the alternative method of taking readings in the laboratory directly on soil samples collected from the site. Laboratory samples are air dried, weighed and measured using the Bartington MS2-B sensor, and mass specific susceptibility values can then be calculated by standardising the instrument readings to a 10g sample weight. The even surface of the rolled plough-soil inside the two hillforts provided suitable ground conditions for the acquisition of good quality MS data using the field measurement technique (Fig 1.19), allowing good contact to be made between the field sensor loop and the soil. This method was

therefore employed on a 5m grid to giv[e] detailed coverage of each site. Additional s[oil] samples were collected at 20m intervals [to] enable laboratory readings to be carried ou[t] as a check on the field measurements and [as] a test of the consistency of the results fro[m] the two techniques. Because of the possibi[l]ity at Castle Ditches of the readings bein[g] affected by stones in the soil samples, a set [of] laboratory readings was also obtained aft[er] sieving the samples through a 2mm mesh.

The results from the MS surveys ar[e] presented in the sections on Norsebur[y] and Castle Ditches in Chapter 2 (Figs 2.2[?] and 2.48).

Digital terrain modelling

by Tom Cromwell, Nick Burton and Andrew Payne

Background

This element of the project was undertake[n] by staff of the former Central Archaeolog[y] Service (CAS) at the request of the Ancie[nt] Monuments Laboratory. The aim was t[o] provide topographic models onto whic[h] geophysical data could be 'draped' for pre[?]sentation and interpretation.

The advantage of digitally modellin[g] detail of the site microtopography is tha[t] the data (providing the resolution i[s] sufficient) can subsequently be manipulate[d] and interrogated to extract information o[n] the most subtle of earthwork feature[s] (*see*, for example, Chapman and Van d[e] Noort 2001; Newman 1997). Thi[s] approach is not possible with a fixed map[?]type view of the traditional hachured kind[,] although hachured plans have clear advan[?]tages of their own, such as indication [of] phasing between earthworks, detaile[d] ground observation during the surve[y] process and a much greater analytica[l] element. When combined with GIS soft[?]ware the digital terrain data can be viewe[d] from different directions and overhea[d] angles in order to highlight specific feature[s] and areas such as recessed building plat[?]forms terraced into the slopes of a hill[.] Vertical exaggeration of height readings ca[n] be applied to enhance the visibility of ver[y] slight earthwork features and light shadin[g] can be applied from various angles an[d] directions to emphasise subtle surface detai[l] by the shadowing effect this generates.

Survey methodology

The survey data was collected on a gri[d] pattern of points. The data points needed t[o]

Fig 1.19 Magnetic Susceptibility survey equipment manufactured by Bartington Instruments (from Archaeometry Branch, EH, Centre for Archaeology).

Fig 1.20
GPS surveying equipment used to produce the three dimensional topographical models of selected hillforts.
a) Trimble Navigation 4600LS post-processing GPS equipment b) Leica Geosystems System 530 real-time kinematic equipment (from EH, Centre for Archaeology and courtesy of Leica Geosystems Ltd).

be very accurate, with maximum permissible error margins of only a few centimetres in Easting, Northing and height in order to create models that were accurate at the scales at which they could be usefully viewed. These models would then be the next best thing to being out on site. To do this, however, meant surveying each hillfort in great detail. The only practical solution was to use GPS – a surveying version of the satellite navigation equipment used in aviation and marine applications. Each site was first divided into convenient sections using a baseline through the middle of the site, and each section then gridded-out using tapes and ranging poles to ensure that data was collected evenly across the whole hillfort. The GPS equipment was then carried along the grid lines, taking readings at fixed intervals to produce an even distribution of data.

As the technique was being used to map topographical detail, only sites with evidence of surface features in the interior were selected, although in retrospect it may have been equally valuable to test the methodology on sites that are more difficult for traditional earthwork survey, in particular those with tall vegetation cover. At such sites the technique may have a particularly useful role for picking up earthworks that can't be seen by eye because they are obscured by vegetation.

The final selection of hillforts for topographical recording was Alfred's Castle, Barbury Castle, Beacon Hill, Ladle Hill and Oldbury. Alfred's Castle was of interest as a very small site, not set on a hilltop, with very pronounced earthwork evidence in the interior. Barbury Castle was of median size, but exhibited a wealth of visible features that

would be quite distinct in a model. Beacon Hill was also of median size with visible features, and its close proximity to Ladle Hill added academic interest. Ladle Hill was included because it appeared to be an unfinished fort, and was thus exceptional. In the case of Ladle Hill the partially constructed defences and associated dumps of rampart material were fully included in the survey. Finally, Oldbury was selected as a very large site with abundant visible features.

In 1996, four of the sites (Alfred's Castle, Barbury Castle, Ladle Hill, Oldbury) were surveyed using Trimble Navigation 4600LS post-processing GPS equipment, with the roving receivers mounted on a two-metre pole that the surveyor carried (Figs 1.20(a), 2.22, 2.36 and 2.45). This equipment required the downloading and processing of data at the end of each day in order to turn the raw data into a set of 3-D coordinates that could be examined and modelled in Computer Aided Design (CAD), a process which made it impossible to see gaps in the data until after the day's fieldwork was complete. The receivers were set to take readings at a fixed time interval, and were then carried along the grid lines at a set pace to get an even rate of data collection. Where significant details were encountered the pace was slowed to capture more points in order to get smoother models. The nominal data interval was 2m between points, with extra data points around any visible breaks in slope such as the edges of sharply defined features, in order to obtain accurate models using Digital Ground Modelling III (DGM3) software that CAS employed at the time. In the event, the post-processing nature of the equipment meant that point intervals averaged closer to 3m in most cases. Beacon Hill, by comparison, was surveyed in 1999 using Leica Geosystems System 530 real-time kinematic equipment (Fig 1.20(b)), which eliminated post-processing by giving Ordnance Survey coordinates instantly through the use of on-board radios and processors. Experience with pole-mounted equipment indicated that height data would not be compromised by a backpack-mounted system, so the backpack-mounted antenna was used and the pole was discarded. Beacon Hill was surveyed at an interval of 1m by setting the receivers to capture data every time they moved more than 1m from the previous reading. The equipment also kept track of the grid lines to be walked, guiding the surveyor along each line without the need for tapes or ranging poles. The results (see Figs 2.11 and 2.12) were faster, and more accurate than the previous surveys, with little wasted time. It should be noted that Trimble Navigation also offers a real-time kinematic system (the 4800 model) with these same benefits.

All of the surveys were plotted relative to the Ordnance Survey grid (OSGB36). For the early sites, this was accomplished by surveying the sites on an arbitrary grid with pegs to mark the baseline, followed by a control survey to tie the pegs into OSGB36 by surveying them relative to a series of local trig pillars. In the case of Beacon Hill, however, there was a trig pillar within the site so the survey grid was established on OSGB36 at the start.

From the outset the project was aimed at modelling the internal 'living space' of each hillfort, corresponding to the area surveyed by geophysics. For practical reasons the topographic surveys were carried up to the top of the ramparts, thus modelling the inner slopes of the defences.

Data processing
All of the point data were imported into AutoCAD for editing and modelling, at which point they could be separated into items such as boundaries and paths. The files were divided into appropriate layers. The first four sites were then modelled in DGM3 to create contour maps and gridded triangular mesh surfaces, but these were subsequently remodelled using Key Terra Firma IV (KTF4) to produce Triangular Irregular Networks (TINs) and contour plots. The fifth site (Beacon Hill) was also modelled in KTF4, and a contour plot cre-

ated. Once the raw data was checked through CAD modelling, the points were exported to ARCINFO or GEOSOFT OASIS MONTAJ to be modelled and draped with the geophysics plots.

The results of the GPS surveys are presented and discussed in the relevant section in Chapter 2.

Documentary research and aerial photographic analysis

The final stage of the project, following the completion of the internal mapping of the subsurface and surface evidence for activity in the hillforts, was devoted to researching the immediate landscape setting and the broader regional context of the sites included in the survey. The first step in this process was to assemble and interrogate existing published sources of archaeological information on each of the sites, and any records of artefactual material they may have produced, in order to attempt to gain some insight (however limited) into relative dates of occupation.

This phase of analysis also involved the study of the morphology of the hillfort and the preparation of a description of the main visible surface characteristics of each of the sites included in the project (including rampart form, entrances and any visible earthwork features in the interior).

In addition, the relationship of each site to the broader pattern of hillfort distribution in Wessex was considered together with location, aspect, relationships with geology and soils, known land allotment patterns in the immediate vicinity and evidence for extra-mural settlement – enclosed and open. The latter component was addressed largely by examination of aerial photographical records. The aerial photographic material from a 2km radius around each site was examined for the presence of other forms of settlement in the vicinity of the hillfort and evidence for field systems, tracks and linear boundary ditches in an attempt to recognise any possible relationships between these various features that would suggest a developmental sequence for the site in question.

The analysis of the surface and documentary evidence relating to each of the sites and their landscape setting is presented under the heading 'morphology and setting' in Chapter 2 followed by discussion of the geophysical evidence from each hillfort. This format was chosen in order to present all the information on each site together in a single unified entry.

2

The Monuments and Their Setting

by Mark Corney and Andrew Payne

The sites examined provide a representative regional sample of those sites traditionally classified as hillforts in the Wessex region. The range of sizes, from small univallate enclosures such as Alfred's Castle and Oliver's Camp, to fully developed multivallate hillforts like Castle Ditches, encompasses the full spectrum of regional morphology. A substantial majority (12 out the 18 sites surveyed) of the hillforts are highly visible monuments located on or close to the limits of chalk, on escarpment with extensive views across 'off-chalk' vales. This locational trend underscores at least one key aspect of many hillforts as centres that, however their function changed through time, appear designed to be seen from a considerable distance and to exploit a range of topographic, economic and social systems.

The sites examined display a wide range of distinctive morphological features. The results of the study are presented below on a site by site basis arranged by County with individual sections on the visible surface characteristics of each site, the landscape setting and the sub-surface evidence derived from geophysical survey. The entry for each site is preceded by a summary of the main site attributes. Broader discussion of all the sites examined at a regional level will be found below on pp 131–43.

Berkshire

Perborough Castle: Cow Down, Compton; NGR SU 520 780

Summary
Date of survey:
23 July to 2 August 1996
Landuse at time of survey:
Rough grassland/set-a-side
Geology:
Cretaceous Upper Chalk (soft white chalk with many flint nodules)
Soil Association:
343h – Andover 1 – shallow well drained calcareous silty soils over chalk on slopes and crests. Striped soil patterns locally.
Approximate area enclosed:
6 hectares (15 acres)
Planform:
Oval
Form of ramparts:
Around most of the circuit the defences consist of a simple scarp sloping down from the interior. The defences are more pronounced or survive better along the northern side of the site where they cross the more level neck of the promontory. Here they consist of a bank, ditch and counterscarp (or secondary outer bank). The defences around the southern and western sides of the site have been largely ploughed out.
Entrance features:
There is a single entrance on the northern side of the fort in the form of a simple gap in the banks and a causeway across the ditch. Other entrances may not be recognisable because of the destruction of two-thirds of the perimeter earthworks by ploughing.
Previous finds:
32 sherds of Early Iron Age pottery (hand made dull red paste containing medium calcined flints, jars with rounded shoulders and finger tip impressions – type identified by Cotton as 'Southern Second A culture'), two fragments of a possible Middle Iron Age ('Southern Second B culture') saucepan pot, Roman pottery (type not identified)
Previous recorded excavation:
c 1839 by 'Matthews'; field observations, Hewett 1844; field survey Wood and Hardy 1962
Scheduled Ancient Monument:
Berkshire 121
County SMR No.:
01026. 01. 000
Project site code:
WHSP Site 1

Morphology and setting

Perborough Castle (Fig 2.1) is a univallate enclosure of approximately 6ha (15 acres) located on a south-east facing spur overlooking the upper reaches of the River Pang.

Immediately north of the hillfort are the extensive remains of a field system remmnants of which still survive as slight earthworks in unploughed grassland. Aerial photography and limited field survey (Wood and Hardy 1962) suggests that this field system pre-dates the hillfort and that it covered an area of at least 70ha (Bradley and Richards 1978, fig 7.6; Richards 1978). The remains consist of regular lynchets running with the contours and cross-contour banks. The fragmentary outlines of about 40 fields each about an acre (0.4ha) in extent and short-oblong in shape are apparent (Fig 2.2). To the north the block of fields appears to be constrained by a series of major linear earthworks in the form of banks bounded by ditches or a ditch between banks. These works may mark the boundary of the field system.

Fig 2.1
Aerial view of Perborough Castle from the east. The field system on Cow Down is visible in the background and the centre right of the photograph (NMRC; NMR 15580/23, SU 5278/14, 1996).

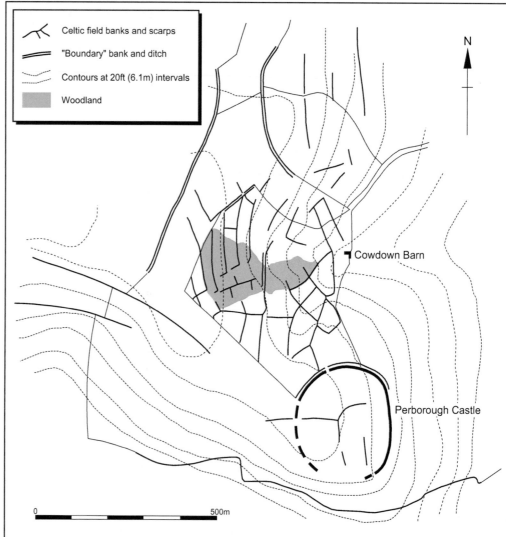

Celtic field banks and scarps

"Boundary" bank and ditch

Contours at 20ft (6.1m) intervals

Woodland

N

Cowdown Barn

Perborough Castle

0   500m

After Wood and Hardy 1962

Fig 2.2
Plan of Perborough Castle and the adjacent field system on Cow Down that partially underlies the hillfort (from Wood and Hardy 1962).

Despite the recent damage to the monument the rampart can be seen to belong to the class of hillfort that is constructed in a series of straight lengths with markedly angular changes of alignment. In the case of Perborough this may be influenced by the presence of the earlier field system (*see below*, page pp 138). On a number of air photographs the remains of a field lynchet within the hillfort can be seen in the interior, set at approximately 90° to a major rampart alignment change on the west side of the circuit (cf NMR SU 5277/2; 15580/24).

Despite the well-preserved nature of the archaeological landscape surrounding Perborough Castle, the hillfort itself is in a very poor condition, the defences having been erased by ploughing around much of the circuit of the enclosure. The defensive circuit is best preserved on the northern side of the site where it runs through an isolated area of unploughed pasture. The interior of the earthwork was deep ploughed in the Second World War and was continuously cultivated until quite recently (Wood and Hardy 1962). Antiquarian records state that prior to the modern ploughing, the interior had contained earthworks suggesting settlement and related features (Hewett 1844). Some caution should be exercised in accepting the 19th-century interpretation, as some of the earthworks are most likely vestiges of the earlier field system that underlies the hillfort. Additionally it must be noted that the magnetometer survey suggests little intensive settlement within the hillfort. It was not possible at the time of the geophysical survey to confirm whether these minor earthwork features are still extant within the fort because of tall vegetation cover, but they might remain observable in more favourable ground conditions. Five large circular hollows visible on the ground inside the hillfort are probably marl pits. Similar hollows occur elsewhere in the locality and are therefore unlikely to be directly associated with the original use of the hillfort.

Pottery recovered from field survey (Wood and Hardy 1962) includes material that would be comfortable in a 6th–5th century BC bracket with little material of later Iron Age date. This would suggest that Perborough Castle falls into the category of an Early Iron Age univallate fort that passed from use by the Middle Iron Age – a trend confirmed by the lack of evidence for intensive settlement in the interior. Romano-British settlement remains and stray finds of this period (including a 4th-century AD coin hoard) are known from Cow Down, 400m north of Perborough Castle (Peake 1931; Richards 1978).

Geophysical Survey (Figs 2.3–2.4)

i) Objectives.

Perborough Castle would appear to represent an example of a simple, medium sized, univallate hillfort of a type commonly constructed in Wessex during the Early Iron Age. The purpose of the magnetometer survey was to attempt to characterise the nature of any internal activity, test for characteristics in common with other neighbouring hillforts in the Ridgeway group of hillforts and identify any recurring patterns of internal spatial organisation associated with such univallate forts. The site is not easily accessible to the public, being privately owned, and therefore possesses little scope for geophysics to contribute to improving visitor interpretation. There were, however, strong arguments for including the site in the survey programme on management grounds because of the long history of ploughing that has contributed to the current degraded state of the monument.

ii) Results.

Across large areas of the site, the magnetic signal is subdued and undisturbed suggesting an absence of archaeological features, but some possible archaeological activity in the form of loose clusters of pit-type features has been detected with a particular concentration around the western to southern periphery of the enclosed area. The central part of the site is distinguished by a relative absence of magnetic anomalies. This may be an indication that a greater amount of agricultural erosion of archaeological layers has taken place in the central area compared to the extremities of the site, but could also be a genuine reflection of the original pattern of occupation. The activity at Perborough is defined by around 100 localised positive anomalies, most of which are likely to represent pits and short lengths of ditch or gully. As at many of the hillfort sites surveyed, some of the pits are clustered tightly together in groups with intervening larger gaps between other pit groups. The density and clustering of pits is quite similar to the patterning seen at other hillforts where occupation was largely restricted to the Early Iron Age and short-lived, such as Uffington Castle and Woolbury. Another similarity with Uffington is the possible presence of some four-poster type structures mapped at several locations inside Perborough. Other examples of such structures may have been truncated by ploughing resulting in a low detection rate. The tendency for the pits at Perborough to concentrate towards the periphery of the enclosure is reminiscent of the magnetometer survey results obtained from Norsebury Ring (this volume), where the central area of the hillfort was likewise largely left free of pits. There is no geophysical evidence for the presence of a ditched enclosure in the south-east corner of Perborough Castle as suggested by Wood and Hardy (1962), although there is a concentration of anomalous magnetic activity within this area.

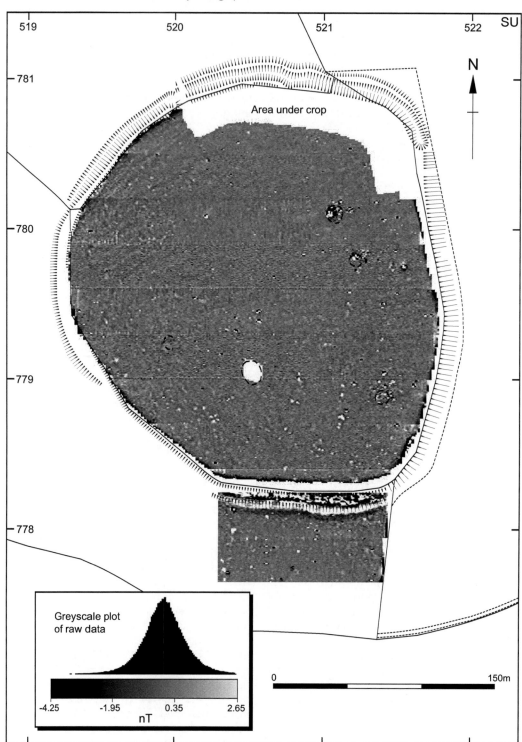

Fig 2.3
Greyscale plot of the
magnetometer data from
Perborough Castle shown
in relation to the plan of
the hillfort earthworks.

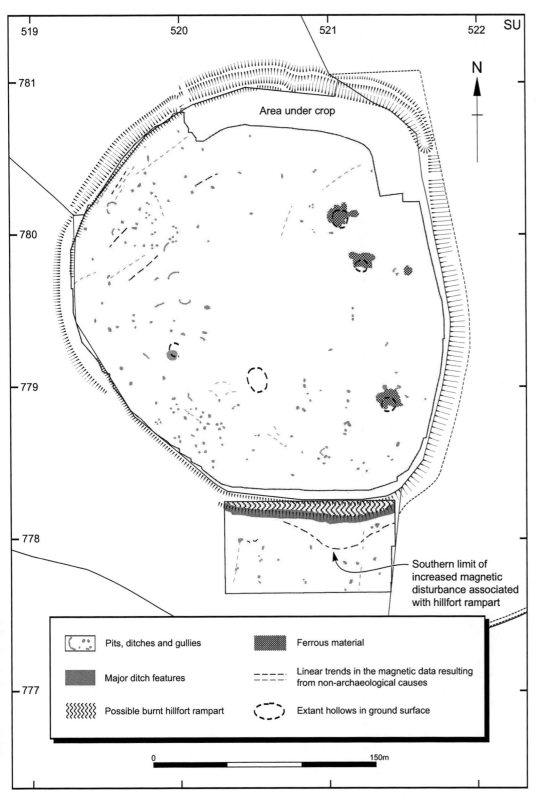

Fig 2.4
Interpretation of the
magnetometer data from
Perborough Castle.

The northernmost part of the hillfort interior had to be excluded from the magnetometer survey due to crop cover. The omission of this area inside the hillfort enabled some additional survey to be carried out immediately outside the hillfort to the south in order to test for the presence of external features (suggested by aerial photographic evidence; for example NMR 7093 929, source: Ashmolean Museum) and to examine a section of the degraded defences. The magnetic signal from the bank and ditch of the hillfort is much higher than would be expected from a chalk or earth built rampart suggesting the presence of considerable quantities of burnt material in the make up of the bank and the fill of the ditch. The positive magnetic signal from the bank ranges from 25–50 nanotesla (nT) bracketed by a negative trough of up to −15nT. The positive component of the anomaly is generally double-peaked, suggestive of discrete parallel structures within the rampart. The anomaly from the adjacent ditch averages at about a 16nT positive deviation from background readings, again unusually pronounced for a chalk cut ditch with a typical infill of weathered material. A possible interpretation of these results is that the defences of the hillfort may have been fired and subjected to intense heating at some time in the past – perhaps in antiquity. The extremely pronounced and variable response over the rampart certainly suggests an element of thermo-remanent magnetisation acquired during an episode of intense heating. An area of generalised magnetic disturbance extends for a distance of up to 20m south from the hillfort ditch, suggesting the incorporation of redeposited burnt material from the rampart and ditch into the topsoil in the field beyond the rampart by ploughing. This hypothetical burning of the defences would merit further investigation by magnetic susceptibility and perhaps archaeomagnetic measurements. The presence of a possible burnt rampart has also recently been recognised at the hillfort of Cissbury Ring in West Sussex, also based on evidence provided by a magnetometer survey (Payne 2001). Crickley Hill provides an excavated example of a fired rampart in Southern Britain (Dixon 1994). The new evidence from Perborough Castle raises the possibility that burnt ramparts are more common in this area than has previously been appreciated.

In the sample of the field to the south of the hillfort defences, a number of localised positive magnetic anomalies are present. Those to the south form an alignment suggesting a response to a former field boundary but overall there is not any coherent pattern. The majority of the anomalies could indicate more pits cut into the subsoil but could equally represent natural pockets of clay within a chalky matrix. The density of the anomalies in the area outside the hillfort defences is not significantly lower than inside the hillfort, and if they do represent archaeological activity might indicate a spread of occupation not constrained to the hillfort and possibly pre-dating the construction of the hillfort defences. Pre-hillfort phases of unenclosed occupation activity have already been recognised at St Catherine's Hill and to a lesser extent at Danebury.

Conclusions

The magnetometer survey has produced clear evidence of occupation within the fort, although judging from the density of the features mapped this does not appear to have been particularly intense or prolonged. This would fit with the pottery evidence which suggests that the main episode of occupation was limited to the Early Iron Age with perhaps more sporadic use in later periods. This interpretation is supported by the smaller quantities of later Iron Age and Roman material recovered from the site and the probable presence of Romano-British settlement on the adjacent area of Cow Down to the north of the hillfort.

Walbury Camp: Coombe/Inkpen; NGR SU 375 618

Summary
Date of survey:
18 to 29 August 1997
Landuse at time of survey:
Rough grassland/set-a-side.
Geology:
Cretaceous Upper Chalk (soft white chalk with many flint nodules).
Soil association:
343h – Andover 1 – shallow well drained calcareous silty soils over chalk on slopes and crests. Striped soil patterns locally.
Approximate area enclosed:
33 hectares (82 acres).
Planform:
Of roughly trapezoid form.
Form of ramparts:
A slight bank not much higher than the level of the interior but with a steep outward facing scarp fronted by a slight outer ditch on the north-east, east and south-east sections of the defences. On the north the distance from the top of the rampart to the bottom of the ditch measures up to 5m.
Entrance features:
Two entrances that can be regarded as original breach the circuit on the north-west and south-east sides of the fort. There are four other breaks in the defences (all quite close together) in the north-eastern section of the defences.

Previous finds:
Mesolithic to Roman but including an assemblage of Neolithic worked flint, a Deverel Rimbury globular urn and eight Anglo Saxon sceatta coins
Previous recorded excavation:
Crawford 1907 (schoolboy excavation)
Scheduled Ancient Monument:
Berkshire 17
County SMR No.:
01055. 01. 000
Project site code:
WHSP Site 13

Morphology and setting

Walbury (Fig 2.5) is the largest of the hillforts examined by the project with the univallate defences enclosing an area of approximately 33ha (82 acres). Set on the east–west ridge marking the edge of the north-facing escarpment of the Hampshire chalk massif, and on the highest point reached by the chalk formation in Britain, the site has extensive views in all directions, especially to the north across the Kennet Valley and onto the Berkshire Downs beyond. From the highest point of the interior, at 297m (974ft) OD, the neighbouring hillforts of Fosbury, Beacon Hill and Ladle Hill are all clearly visible. Farther afield, both Danebury and Quarley Hill are visible to the south and on the northern horizon Uffington Castle, Rams Hill and Segsbury can be made out in clear weather. The site has been classified, like Martinsell Hill in Wiltshire, as an 'Early Hill-top Enclosure' (Cunliffe 1984b), characterised by the large area enclosed, the relative slightness of the defences in relation to the area enclosed, and the general paucity of evidence for intensive activity. On the latter point the results of the geophysical survey would tend to confirm Cunliffe's observations.

Williams-Freeman (1915) stated that the site was generally considered to be 'late Celtic' on account of the huge area enclosed by the defences and the large population that would be needed to man them. However, Williams-Freeman himself considered that Walbury was 'among the earlier camps' based on the nearby concentrations of Bronze Age round barrows. Middle Bronze Age material has been found in the area more recently (*see above*). The site has never been formally excavated, although Crawford excavated two pits near the north-west entrance as a schoolboy in 1907 and recorded finds of bone, cow teeth and charcoal (Berkshire County Sites and Monuments Record entry 01055.01.400, 1988). Unfortunately nothing diagnostic of a date for occupation of the hillfort was found.

The enclosure circuit is univallate except on the north-east side where a slight outer bank cuts across a spur. On this spur, some 200m beyond the hillfort is a small earthwork enclosure of unknown date. Two entrances that can be regarded as original breach the circuit. These are on the south-east corner and north-west corner. Another breach at the north-east corner may be relatively recent, although the outer bank at this point is breached by a gap with slightly offset terminals that indicate an earlier origin. The north-west entrance (*see* Fig 2.7) displays evidence of a relatively complex sequence. Projecting from the ditch terminals are a pair of low banks forming 'barbican'-like features. This is best seen north of the entrance where later disturbance has caused less damage than on the south side. In form these relatively slight outworks are very close to other examples in Wessex, in particular the south-east entrance at Figsbury, Wiltshire (Guido and Smith 1982), the southern entrance to Beacon Hill, Hampshire (*below*, p 49; Eagles 1991) and the blocked entrance at Danebury, Hampshire (Cunliffe and Poole 1991). Beyond this, to the west, another length of bank and ditch, visible for a distance of 120m, has the appearance of a cross-ridge dyke and may pre-date the construction of the hillfort. The south-east entrance appears to be a simple, slightly offset gap through the rampart

Fig 2.5
Aerial view of the large hilltop enclosure of Walbury Hill Camp from the north-west (Copyright reserved Cambridge University Collection of Air Photographs, BWJ 019, 1976).

Fig 2.6
Aerial photograph showing
traces of field systems to the
west and south of Walbury
(NMRC; NMR 4553/53,
SU 3761/35, 1989).

although there has been severe disturbance from the passage of a modern track. Within the south-west quadrant, pits and other surface irregularities have been suggested as neolithic flint mines and casual finds of neolithic flint artefacts may lend some support to this. A Neolithic long barrow still survives as a prominent earthwork some 500m west of the western entrance.

Beyond Walbury, especially on the slopes to the west and south, there are extensive traces of prehistoric field system (Fig 2.6). This forms part of a very regular block of fields that cover an area of at least 5km sq. Earthwork and air photographic evidence also indicates that this field system has been further divided by components of a linear ditch system, although none of these can be directly related to the hillfort.

Mention has already been made of a slight enclosure 200m to the north-east of the hillfort. Approximately 700m south-east, air photographs show a pair of conjoined ditched rectangular enclosures and 500m north-west of the monument, at the foot of the escarpment, is another sub-square enclosure of 1ha.

Williams-Freeman (1915) notes that the chalk at Walbury is overlain with a considerable capping of clay and that the ground is very flinty. Throughout most of the 1980s the site is reported as being under arable

cultivation (Berkshire SMR: 01055.01.000, 1984) but this had been discontinued by the time geophysical survey took place in 1997. Several structures on concrete bases appear to have stood in the recent past at the highest point of the site in the central southern area of the hillfort possibly linked to communications, signaling or air defence. A disused access track links the site of these former structures with the main trackway that runs diagonally through the camp from east to west between the hillfort entrances. A triangulation pillar and an elderly disused circular water cistern are also present in the southern part of the fort.

Magnetometer Survey (Fig 2.7)

The purpose of the ambitious survey coverage at Walbury was to assess the internal character of one notable example of a 'hilltop enclosure' together with the similar site surveyed at Martinsell Hill (this volume) and identify any distinctive patterns of internal activity possibly associated with these large enclosures.

Magnetic anomalies within Walbury Camp are plentiful and widespread but the majority have a form only suggestive of geological features and probably reflect the natural local variability in the geology referred to by the Soil Survey of England and Wales as 'striped soil patterns' (see "soil association" in summary section above). Bands of anomalies can be seen in the southern part of the fort following a curving trend from the south-east to the west and a second pattern following a north-east to south-west trend is present in the north-east part of the fort. Similar anomalies are again present in the north-western part of the site. The site is fringed by deposits of Clay with Flints and Tertiary Debris overlying the chalk and Eocene Reading Beds (Geological Survey of Great Britain 1959) and therefore probably has a more complex geology than the geological mapping suggests. Similar striped and swirling patterns of positive magnetic anomalies that can vary in direction between different areas of the site have also been mapped at Bury Hill and Fosbury, both in north Hampshire, and at Martinsell Hill Camp in north Wiltshire. These are again likely to reflect variable drift geology.

The response from the geological features at Walbury is complex and variable and the anomalies are quite accentuated in places. Clay features within chalk that are known from excavation occur at the hillforts of Uffington Castle and Segsbury farther

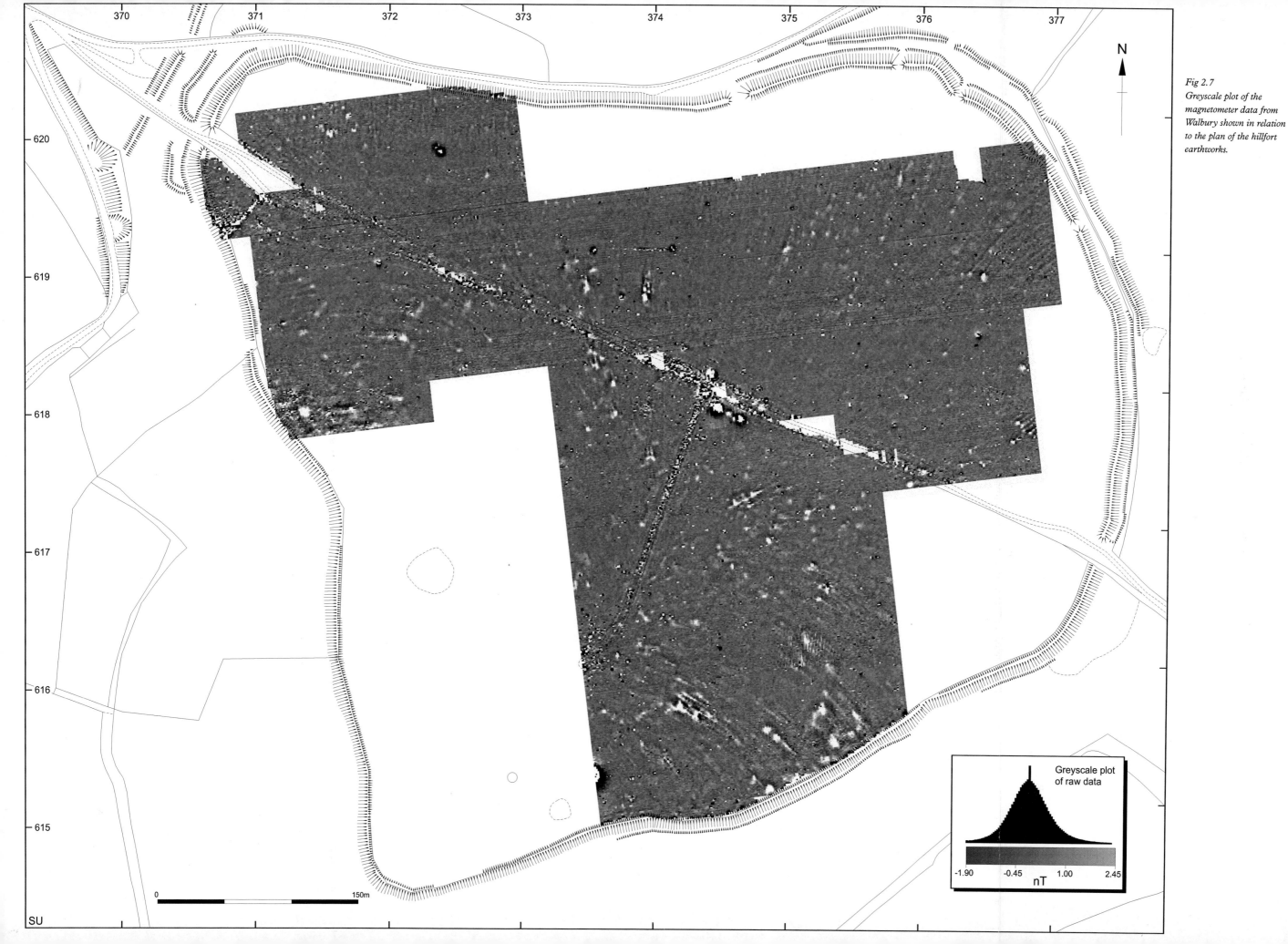

Fig 2.7
Greyscale plot of the
magnetometer data from
Walbury shown in relation
to the plan of the hillfort
earthworks.

Greyscale plot
of raw data

-1.90   -0.45   1.00   2.45
nT

orth, on the Lambourn Downs, and are nown to produce substantial magnetic nomalies. The anomalies at Walbury are he most extreme examples of this type ncountered anywhere in the project area. The only anomalies of certain human rigin at Walbury relate to modern features ncluding former standing structures of ecent date and the trackways that cross hrough the enclosure.

Discussion

A substantial sample of the interior of Walbury was surveyed by the project but he results unfortunately present major roblems for the reliable identification of rchaeological features. The difficulty lies in letecting what may well be fairly ephemeral races of minor structures against an over-iding response to variation in the natural geology. The recognition of anomalies of rchaeological significance is problematic in uch conditions where the magnetic results re so obviously strongly influenced by fea-ures of geological origin. The presence of rchaeological features at Walbury is likely nly to be determined by intrusive tech-niques that can more easily distinguish natural features from those constructed in he past by human agency. Despite the confusing response there are no obvious rchaeological features such as ring-gullies or regular groupings or clusters of pits revealed as magnetic anomalies inside the camp. On this basis it can tentatively be suggested that Walbury contains only a low evel of archaeological activity but this claim cannot be confirmed without further supporting evidence.

The results from Walbury display a mea-sure of consistency with those from the other possible example of a large hilltop enclosure investigated by the Wessex Hill-forts Survey at Martinsell Hill Camp, Wilt-shire. Both sites appear to contain magnetic anomalies mainly of superficial geological origin and few responses consistent with large numbers of archaeological features. The combined results suggest that Walbury and Martinsell may both indeed belong to a common class of early enclosures charac-terised partly by a low level of internal activ-ity. Unfortunately this conclusion can only be tentative because of the possibly that the magnetometer is failing to detect traces of small archaeological features such as post-hole structures. It is highly possible that such features may have been widespread in these earliest hillforts as suggested by the

evidence from Danebury and Balksbury (Cunliffe 2000) and Harting Beacon (Bed-win 1978). The sites in this group neverthe-less display a relative paucity of internal activity compared to later smaller and more intensively used hillforts which should be distinguishable by magnetometer survey.

Hampshire

Beacon Hill Camp: Burghclere; NGR SU 458 572

Summary
Date of survey:
2 to 9 October 1997.
Landuse at time of survey:
Grassland with some thin scrub
Geology:
Cretaceous Upper Chalk.
Soil Association:
342a – Upton 1 – shallow well drained cal-careous silty soils over chalk.
Approximate area enclosed:
3.8 hectares (9.5 acres).
Planform:
Roughly hourglass shaped.
Form of ramparts:
Ditch set between two banks with quarry features along the inward facing side of the inner rampart.
Entrance features:
Entrance at the south–south-east corner elaborated by additional outworks project-ing from the main rampart and in-turns of the rampart in the interior extending the length of the entrance corridor. A blocked entrance is present on the north-west side.
Previous finds:
Half a dozen sherds of probable pre-Roman Iron Age pottery (type not identified), several sherds of possible Neolithic pottery. Rim, body and base sherds of a type 1 Globular Urn of the Middle Bronze Age period with five other body sherds of similar date. Also a post-medieval brick fireplace, tobacco pipes, iron objects, pottery and building materials from a pit excavated by Woolley in 1912 and reused for a shelter probably associated with the use of the site for a beacon (source : Hampshire SMR entry).
Previous recorded excavation:
1912 (Sir) Leonard Woolley, with the Fifth Earl of Carnarvon, dug into four features – one hut circle and three pits (Woolley 1913). A small amount of possible Bronze Age pottery was recovered.

Scheduled Ancient Monument:
24318 (previously Hampshire 65).
County SMR No.:
SU45NE 48 A.
Project site code:
WHSP Site 18.

Morphology and setting

The univallate enclosure of Beacon Hill (Fig 2.8) is set on the highest point (260m) of a prominent tongue of the Upper Chalk projecting from the north-facing escarpment of the Hampshire downs. It is the best pre- served of the 6 hillforts forming the Nort Hampshire Escarpment Group (*below*, p 133 and is 9km east of Walbury (*above* pp 44–7 and 2km west of the unfinished hillfort o Ladle Hill (*below*, pp 62–5). The site ha extensive views across the Kennet Valley an onto the Berkshire Downs and overlook (with Ladle Hill) a deep dry valley that give easy access from the chalk massif of centra Wessex into the Kennet Valley, a natura north–south route used today by the A34 The distinctive 'hourglass' shape of th hillfort is dictated by the topography of th

Fig 2.8
Aerial view of Beacon Hill from the east showing well preserved earthwork evidence of occupation within the fort including numerous circular habitation structures (NMRC, NMR 18695/05, SU 4557/107, 2000).

hilltop with the circuit following the contours and enclosing 3.8ha (9.5 acres). A single rampart and ditch with a substantial counterscarp define the enclosure circuit. There is one entrance, on the south-east, flanked by parallel inturned banks approximately 12m in length. This entrance has hornworks forming a semicircular projection of very similar form to that at Figsbury, Wiltshire (Guido and Smith 1982) and the blocked south-west entrance at Danebury (Cunliffe and Poole 1991). In a recent, detailed earthwork survey of the site for the Royal Commission on the Historical Monuments of England, Eagles (1991) notes that the counterscarp bank is markedly reduced at the junction with the arms of the hornworks. This might indicate that the hornworks were a subsequent addition to the original circuit and entrance. On the western side of the circuit, overlooking a precipitous slope, the earthworks strongly suggest the presence of a second, now blocked, entrance. The main rampart still retains distinct signs of slight inturning, 8m apart, with a noticeably lower bank between the original terminals. The corresponding point in the counterscarp is conspicuously higher, probably as a result of infilling using material derived from a quarried-out causeway across the ditch.

The interior of the site has never been cultivated and there are extensive and well-preserved earthworks indicating circular structures, pits and a series of internal quarry scoops behind the rampart (Eagles 1991, fig 1). The density of the structures and pits is similar to that recorded at a number of other Wessex hillforts such as Hambledon Hill and Hod Hill (RCHM 1970c), although, as Eagles notes (ibid), the structures lack the annexes so evident at the latter site. The earthworks indicate a complex sequence of occupation. A number of circular structures survive as earthworks within the silted quarry scoops (*see* terrain model, Figs 2.11 and 2.12) and at other points structures are so close that contemporaneity is unlikely. In addition to the surface features, geophysical survey also recorded other anomalies of an archaeological character.

The features within the hillfort, recorded following surface observation and analytical earthwork survey by the RCHME during 1978–9, can be grouped into the following five categories:

1. Pennanular banks approximately 11m in diameter surrounded by an external ditch up to 15m in diameter, often appearing to have gaps on the east, representing east-facing entrances. There are eight or nine examples of this type 1 structure visible inside the hillfort.
2. Smaller rings approximately 9m in diameter defined by slight banks but with no clear ditch.
3. Circular or sub-circular platforms cut into the slope and partly surrounded by a bank and ditch.
4. Platforms without banks. These latter features are most well represented on the eastern slopes of the hill and in the areas of the quarry ditches on the far eastern and northern edges of the site.
5. Pits visible as surface depressions (approximately 60 occurrences of this type of feature were recorded by the RCHME).

The RCHME investigation observed that there is distinct clustering of huts of similar form in some areas of the hillfort (for example features 2.10–2.12 on the RCHME plan in Eagles, 1991). The apparent proportion of pits to buildings is very low indeed, which may mean a relatively short occupation. In all there are at least 30 clear hut sites and another 30 which could be either hut sites or working platforms. The distribution of round building foundations and stances within the fort suggests a general avoidance of the exposed valley-head southern slopes. Around the highest point of the domed interior two short lengths of bank and ditch (RCHME features 2.24E and 2.24W) give the appearance of a possible earlier sequence of enclosure.

Within the south-west corner of the hillfort is the grave of the Fifth Earl of Carnarvon, sponsor of the Tutankhamun excavation. At Beacon Hill in 1912 the Earl and (Sir) Leonard Woolley investigated one probable hut and three pits, recovering 'bronze age' pottery (Woolley 1913). One pit was found to have been reused as a shelter linked to the beacon situated on the hill in medieval and post-medieval times, and produced numerous finds of medieval date. During the earthwork survey of the site, pottery was found on the surface. This, and earlier surface finds, have been identified as ranging in date from the Neolithic, Bronze Age (including a Middle Bronze Age Type 1 Globular Urn) and Iron Age (Eagles 1991). Beyond the hillfort there are extensive, but fragmentary, traces of field-systems. These are visible both on air photographs and the ground south and west of the monument but do not approach the immediate vicinity of the hillfort. On the end of the spur beyond the north-western corner of the hill-fort there is an undated cross-ridge dyke with a round barrow beside it. North of Beacon Hill, on the middle and lower chalk, there are few traces of the prehistoric land-scape visible and much of this area is now under woodland forming part of the High-clere Castle estate. Across the valley to the east, on Great Litchfield Down and Ladle Hill, air photography reveals more blocks of fields and linear features associated with an unfinished hillfort (*below*, pp 62–5).

Beacon Hill Camp is currently managed as a public open space by Hampshire County Council. Various archaeological features within the hillfort lie on or close to footpaths worn into the grassland turf (*see* Fig 2.8) and are therefore vulnerable to erosion by the constant wear and tear of passing walkers.

Magnetometer survey (Figs 2.9, 2.10 and 2.12)

Magnetometer survey of the internal area of the fort, excluding the fenced area containing the tomb of Lord Carnarvon, was carried out in October 1997. The site was selected for survey to provide infor-mation to support the future management of the site and secondly to test the response of the magnetometer over a hillfort containing unusually well preserved evi-dence of former occupation in the form of earthwork remains.

In spite of the recognised presence of numerous archaeological features within the interior of Beacon Hill Camp surviving as slight earthworks, the magnetic response from these structures is very weak and is limited to the most substantial examples

Fig 2.9
Greyscale plot of the magnetometer data from Beacon Hill in relation to the plan of the hillfort earthworks.

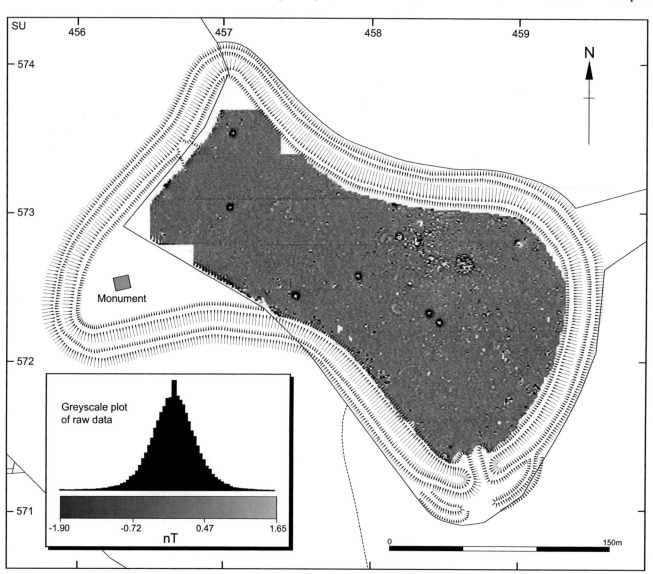

Greyscale plot of raw data

-1.90   -0.72   0.47   1.65
nT

Monument

0   150m

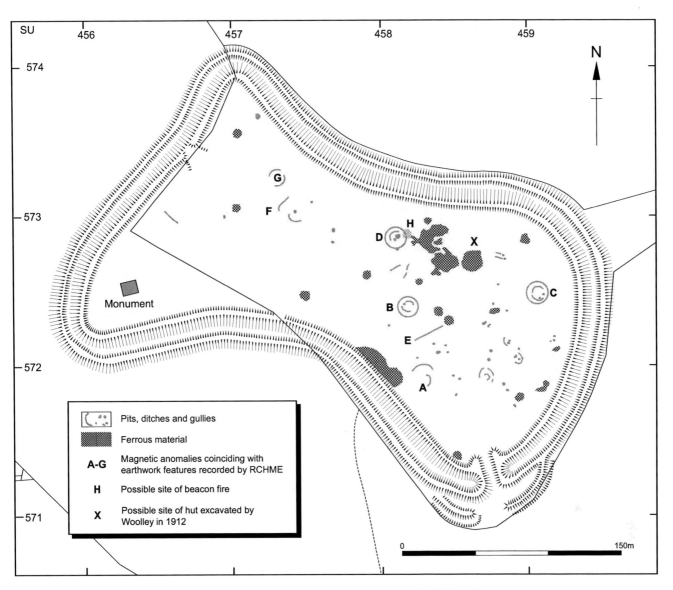

Fig 2.10
Interpretation of the magnetometer data from Beacon Hill.

(those defined by ditches such as the hut circles with a wide diameter and a surrounding ditch) and the pit-type features. The density of archaeological features in the hillfort interior therefore appears far lower in the magnetometer survey compared to the earthwork survey – which mapped a wider range of features – and the magnetic evidence gives the hillfort a much emptier appearance, which probably under represents the true density of occupation activity. The reason for this is that the magnetometer is selective in the type of feature it detects. (For features to be detectable it is usually necessary for them to contain a filling of more magnetic soil or silting, for them to be heavily burnt or made of a contrasting magnetic material from the surrounding soil.) Because many of the features survive in the form of upstanding earthworks or

surface depressions it is likely that some of the above requirements have not been met, thus explaining the marginal response of the magnetometer to the majority of the features recorded by the RCHME. The few features that have produced distinct anomalies are generally those that will have been partially in-filled with magnetically enhanced material such as pits and the slight ditches surrounding the larger house sites. Significant infilling is also less likely to have taken place in an unploughed environment and the magnetic signal from these features is still extremely weak in relation to comparable plough flattened sites (*see* Segsbury and Castle Ditches for example; this volume). Their distribution in the magnetic data is in broad agreement with the RCHME plan of the hillfort (Eagles 1991).

Fig 2.11
High resolution digital
terrain model of the interior
of Beacon Hill produced
using Leica Geosystems 530
GPS equipment with a 1m
reading density. The data is
presented from a vertical
viewpoint and also an
oblique view facing towards
the west (from EH, Centre
for Archaeology).

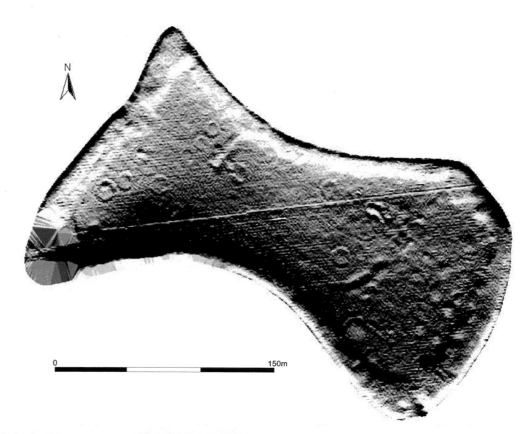

N

0   150m

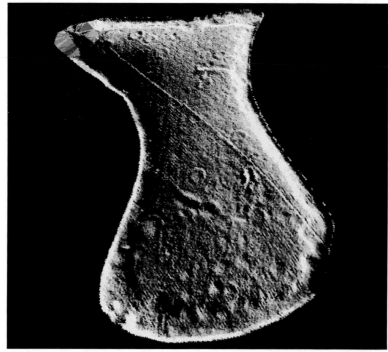

The clearest anomalies in the magnetic data – of which there are five or six examples – are annular in form and correspond to the pennanular bank and ditch features (of type 1) recorded by the RCHME in at least nine places. These are interpreted as the remains of more substantial dwellings or buildings, possibly with cob-built walls, now surviving as low banks of annular plan broken by possible entrances generally facing east. These structures occur more rarely than the simpler earthworks of types 2–4 described by the RCHME, representing smaller and less complex structures within the fort. The magnetometer survey has largely failed to respond to these more numerous but ephemeral shallow scoops and platforms terraced into the hillside. The survey has likewise failed to respond to the irregular quarry ditches running along the inside of the rampart (again these are still present as clear depressions in the topography and would therefore not necessarily be expected to produce a robust magnetic anomaly due to a lack of infilling or silting up with more magnetic sediment). In addition to the annular features the magnetometer survey has detected the presence of at least 45 individual pit-type features; a lower number than that estimated by the RCHME. The RCHME evidence suggests a very thin scatter of pits throughout the majority of the hillfort. The geophysical evidence suggests a greater concentration of pits on the east-facing slopes of the interior, north of the imposing entrance into the fort, where occupation activity is particularly dense on the basis of the number of hut sites of embanked or scooped form visible in the RCHME and topographical survey (Fig 2.11).

The concentration of pits revealed by the magnetometer in the eastern and south-eastern areas of the hillfort north of the entrance correspond to the highest incidence of the largest round gullies of type 1. This continues a trend already observed at Segsbury and at Liddington Castle (*see below*) where pit groupings appear to be closely associated with circular gullies. The Beacon Hill pits are often arranged in clusters or closely spaced pairs as found at Uffington Castle (Payne 2003a). The density of pits falls off dramatically towards the centre of the hillfort and only a thin scatter of pits is present in the western more exposed part of the fort. This lack of evidence for occupation at the centre of the site is mirrored at other hillfort sites included in the project sample including Perborough Castle and Norsebury Ring. At other sites such as St Catherine's Hill and Segsbury the opposite appears to hold true.

The discrepancy between the density and distribution of pits recorded by the two different survey methods is probably a result of several factors. Firstly it is possible that some buried pits could no longer be apparent as depressions in the topography depending on the extent to which they have been infilled or have naturally silted up in the past. Secondly the ability of the magnetometer to detect the pit type features would depend on them containing a magnetically enhanced fill which would not necessarily apply for all of the pits. A pit largely filled in with chalk rubble would be unlikely to register an appreciable magnetic contrast with the surrounding soil.

The short stretches of bank and ditch east and west of the summit recorded in the RCHME survey (features 2.24E and 2.24W; Eagles 1991) are replicated in the magnetic data, although as would be expected in the case of the magnetic evidence, the survey has only defined the ditches. There is no evidence in the magnetic data for the continuation of these ditch features beyond those known from the surviving topographical features. This brings into doubt the possibility touched upon in Eagles (1991) that they may be traces of a possible earlier causewayed enclosure of Neolithic date. Having said this, there is no reason why these features could not still be of Neolithic date even though they appear not to represent a full scale enclosure. Given

that these features are overlain and cut by later hut-site occupation and the linear quarries, a Bronze Age origin could also be a possibility.

An area of intense magnetic disturbance is present in the northern part of the hillfort near the modern triangulation pillar. This disturbance derives from a concentration of ferrous and burnt material in the soil associated with the former use of this area as the site of a beacon and ground disturbance linked to the excavations carried out in the early 20th century by Woolley in the area previously utilised for the beacon. It is possible that the roughly circular area of intense magnetic disturbance at (**X**) on the interpretation of the magnetometer survey (Fig 2.10, corresponding to 3.26 on the RCHME plan) could represent the single hut-site documented as having been dug into by Woolley in 1912.

In summary the magnetometer data from Beacon Hill, while inferior to the topographical plan of the site produced by the RCHME, has nevertheless revealed evidence of occupation consisting of circular structures representing buildings and a moderate density of pits with a higher concentration towards the eastern side of the fort. Precise dating evidence is obviously lacking for much of this occupation at the present time, and is largely reliant on the surface finds of pottery that are occasionally recovered from the site.

Discussion

Ploughing has the effect of levelling out sites and filling in pits and depressions with magnetically enhanced material derived from the topsoil. On a site in un-ploughed grassland this does not happen so that although the archaeological features are still clearly visible on the surface in the form of earthworks, they produce a much weaker response in a magnetometer survey compared to in-filled features.

The results from Beacon Hill suggest that the efficacy of magnetometer survey is more limited on sites with well preserved earthwork evidence in their interiors compared to plough levelled sites. This conclusion is borne out by surveys of similar sites such as Old Winchester Hill (*see* Chapter 1, this volume) and Cissbury Ring (Payne 2001) where again the results were not of particularly high quality. This should not normally be a problem because where these conditions exist and magnetometer survey fails to be informative, analytical earthwork or

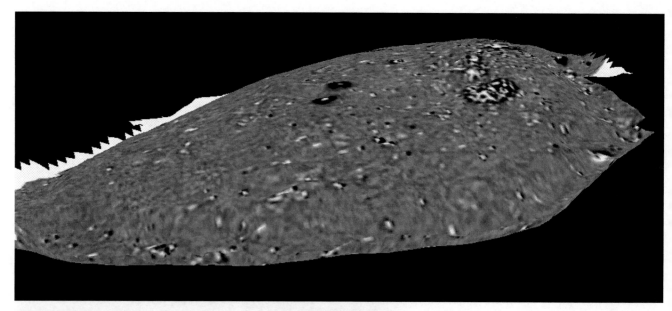

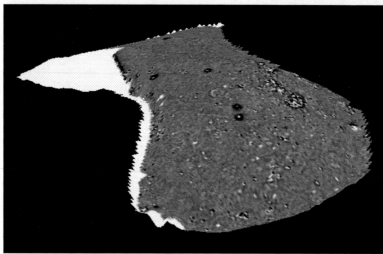

Fig 2.12

The magnetometer data from Beacon Hill draped on the surface model of the hillfort interior i) upper image – close low level view of the draped magnetometer data viewed from the eastern side of the site; ii) lower image: distant higher view of the draped magnetometer data looking from the south-east (from EH, Centre for Archaeology).

topographical survey should be by far the more effective technique and should result in the provision of a more detailed and complete picture. Magnetometer survey is of greater value on such sites where sub-surface features belonging to earlier phases of activity (for example of Neolithic or Bronze Age date) are overlain by earthwork evidence relating to more recent phases of occupation (for example of Middle Iron Age or Romano-British date).

The digital terrain model produced by the Central Archaeology Service in 1997 (Figs 2.11 and 2.12) does not add any significant new information to the earlier RCHME analytical earthwork survey (Eagles 1991) but the two forms of survey replicate each other extremely well in the level of detail of the surface topography of the hillfort interior that they provide

including evidence for the larger embanked circular dwellings faintly detected by the magnetometer and the smaller platforms recessed into the slopes of the hill. The high concentration of the platform features on the south-east side of the hillfort is particularly marked in the digital terrain model.

Bury Hill: Upper Clatford; NGR SU 346435

Summary
Date of surveys:
4 to 7 August 1997 & 19 to 24 September 1997.
Landuse at time of survey:
Grass ley.
Geology:
Cretaceous Upper Chalk.
Soil Association:
343i – Andover 2 – shallow well drained calcareous silty soils over chalk.
Approximate area enclosed:
Earlier univallate fort (Bury Hill I) enclosing 10ha (24 acres) and a second bivallate earthwork (Bury Hill II) enclosing 4.7ha (11.5 acres) superimposed on the south and east sections of the earlier defences.
Planform:
Bury Hill I – egg-shaped, Bury Hill II – approximately circular.
Form of ramparts:
Bury Hill I – single timber revetted chalk bank and external ditch surviving now only as a scarp, Bury Hill II – massive ditch flanked inside and out by a bank.
Entrance features:
Bury Hill II has an entrance on the south-east consisting of a simple break in

he ramparts. A second possible entrance may exist on the north-west. The entrances of the earlier fort are uncertain.

Previous finds:
Small amount of Mesolithic worked flint, large finds assemblage from two excavations (*see below*). Haematite coated ware was associated with the earlier enclosure and the pottery assemblage associated with the later defences was dominated by saucepan pots of 2nd to 1st century BC date (Hawkes 1940).

Previous recorded excavation:
Limited excavations by Hawkes 1939 (Hawkes 1940). Other sample excavations were carried out in both forts by the Danebury Environs Project in 1990 – fully reported in Cunliffe and Poole (2000(b)).

Scheduled Ancient Monument:
Hampshire 57.

County SMR No.:
SU34SW 20A.

Project site codes:
WHSP Sites 12 and 16.

Morphology and setting

Bury Hill (Fig 2.13) is a multi-phase hillfort of unusual form located on a gentle hill overlooking the confluence of the River Anton and the Pillhill Brook, being tributaries of the River Test. Less than 1km to the north, on the other side of the Pillhill Brook, is Balksbury, a univallate enclosure of 18ha (44 acres) constructed perhaps as early as *c* 1000 BC and occupied intermittently until the early post-Roman period (Wainwright and Davies 1995).

Bury Hill is of two principal phases, the earlier, known as Bury Hill I and dated to the Early Iron Age, is marked by a univallate enclosure of 10ha (24 acres) with a massive timber revetted rampart (Hawkes 1940; Cunliffe and Poole 2000(b)). The available excavated evidence suggests that there was little, if any, permanent settlement inside Bury Hill I. In the late 2nd or early 1st century BC a new earthwork – Bury Hill II, set within Bury Hill I, was constructed. This enclosed 4.7ha (11.5 acres) and is of unusual form in being nearly circular (although straight sections are discernible in plan) and having an outer bank that is, in many places, higher than the inner rampart (Cunliffe and Poole 2000(b), fig 2.3; p 11). This latter feature is rarely encountered in Wessex.

The only entrance now visible is that on the south-eastern side of the circuit where the ramparts of Bury Hill I and II are coincident. The configuration of the earthworks and the results of the geophysical survey (*see below*) strongly suggest that Bury Hill II originally had another entrance on the north-west, subsequently blocked (*contra* Hawkes 1940). Whether Bury Hill I also originally had a second entrance here is less certain and the earthworks at this point are too degraded to allow a confident interpretation.

The interior of Bury Hill II is densely packed with pits except for a broad zone, up to 12m wide, running between the south-east entrance and the now probable

Fig 2.13
Aerial photograph of Bury Hill Camp and its environs. The enclosure in the field adjacent to the hillfort (WHSP Site 16) is in the bottom right of the photograph (NMRC; NMR 4586/14, SU 3443/18, 1990).

55

north-west entrance. The nature of the material recovered from these pits in the recent excavations (Cunliffe and Poole 2000(b)) is remarkable for the lack of carbonised grain and human remains such as those recovered from Danebury, and the emphasis on horse harness and related trappings (Cunliffe 1996; Cunliffe and Poole 2000(b), 79–81). Furthermore the very high percentage of horse remains (48.2%), when taken with the metalwork, strongly suggests a highly specialised focus within, and probably beyond, Bury Hill II.

Air photography, supplemented by geophysical survey, has located a remarkable cluster of features some 150m beyond the eastern entrance of Bury Hill II (Fig 2.13; NMR 4586/14, SU 3443/18, 1990). Here an oval enclosure of approximately 1.6ha (4 acres) is visible. There are a number of gaps in this circuit, the largest being on the west, facing towards Bury Hill. On the east side there appears to be a pair of 'antennae' ditches leading out from the enclosure but no break in the enclosure ditch is visible, possibly suggesting a realignment of the main approach to the site. Along the south side of the enclosure is a substantial linear ditch, or perhaps a trackway, possibly partially impinged upon by the settlement. Additional ditches to the east show that activity was extensive and features beyond the enclosure suggest a number of phases and a complex sequence. The occurrence of enclosures and other possible settlement features in close proximity to hillfort entrances is discussed in greater detail below (pp 139–41). It should be noted that Hawkes encountered evidence of late 1st century BC and early 1st century AD activity around the eastern entrance to Bury Hill II (Hawkes 1940) and it is quite possible that at least some of the features mentioned here may be part of this very Late Iron Age focus. The 'antennae' ditches, however, are far more typical of developed Early to Middle Iron Age enclosures such as Gussage All Saints and Little Woodbury, and a long sequence should be assumed until proven otherwise.

Beyond the immediate environs of Bury Hill the most striking feature of the landscape is the lack of evidence for field systems or other settlement forms (Palmer 1984). The linear ditch along the south side of the extra-mural enclosure can be traced for a distance of 500m to the south-east of Bury Hill while another complex of ditches is known to the south-west (ibid). The nearest large blocks of field system, however, are nearly 3km south and south-west, in the environs of Danebury. It is tempting to compare this apparent large tract of open land to the pattern observed by Bowen in the environs of Gussage All Saints in Dorset (Bowen 1979). Evidence of Late Iron Age production of horse related equipment here led to the suggestion of a highly specialised economy and landscape based on horse rearing. If this were also the case at Bury Hill it would, on our current understanding of the date of linear ditch systems in Wessex imply a very long special use for the landscape, predating the Late Iron Age date for the metalworking at Bury Hill II by a considerable length of time. The landscape around Bury Hill is in many respects similar to that around Norsebury in that we appear to be seeing significant differences when compared to many of the other Wessex hillforts examined during this project. The evidence for date is in most cases slim, but if the Late Iron Age dates suggested here are correct we must ask just how far back these more 'specialised' landscapes can be taken.

Current understanding of the development of Bury Hill relative to the neighbouring hillforts in the region including Danebury (6km to the south) and Balksbury (1km to the north on the opposite side of the valley of the River Anna) is fully described in Chapter 1.

Magnetometer survey (Figs 2.14 and 2.15)

Sample magnetometer surveys of both enclosures were carried out in advance of limited excavations by the Danebury Environs Project in 1990 (Cunliffe and Poole 2000(b); Payne 2000c) in order to assess the internal character of the successive hillforts and reveal any significant differences between them. The subsequent excavations opened up areas within the early enclosure outside the later defences and within the later fort to assess the character of the archaeological activity present and provide evidence of the dating, structure and condition of the ramparts defining the two enclosures.

Initially fluxgate magnetometer survey was carried out over slightly under half of the main inner fort (Bury Hill II) and a more limited area of the outer camp or earlier enclosure (Bury Hill I). Further survey was undertaken by the Wessex Hillforts Survey during 1997 to complete the coverage as far as possible of the two hillfort interiors.

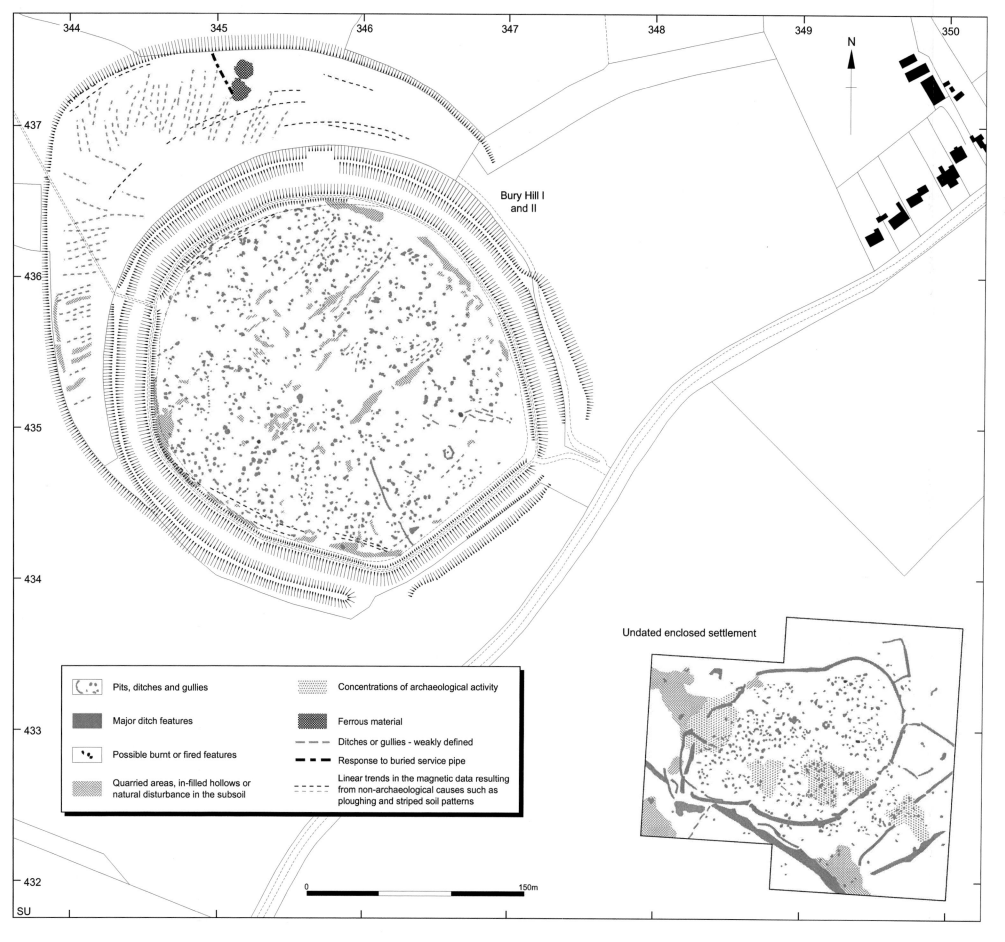

Bury Hill I and II

Fig 2.15
Interpretations of the
magnetometer surveys
at Bury Hill.

Undated enclosed settlement

Pits, ditches and gullies	Concentrations of archaeological activity
Major ditch features	Ferrous material
Possible burnt or fired features	Ditches or gullies - weakly defined
Quarried areas, in-filled hollows or natural disturbance in the subsoil	Response to buried service pipe
	Linear trends in the magnetic data resulting from non-archaeological causes such as ploughing and striped soil patterns

N

0   150m

SU

The primary aim of the surveys was to attempt to demonstrate the relative intensity of occupation in each of the forts by surveying sufficiently large areas to show contrasting or recurring patterns of activity. The clearly differing character of occupation in the two forts could be easily recognised in the first set of results obtained in 1990. These suggested that the early fort was largely devoid of significant features in sharp contrast with the later fort, which appeared to contain a high density of pits scattered evenly across the area surveyed. These initial conclusions were subsequently confirmed and reinforced by the excavation and the subsequent extended magnetometer coverage.

In the area excavated inside the earlier hillfort, the only archaeological features discovered were three small postholes. This absence of structures is entirely consistent with the results of the magnetometer survey, which suggested that the area surveyed was barren of significant soil disturbance except for bands of closely spaced weak linear positive magnetic anomalies produced by striped soil patterns of periglacial origin. These features are aligned north–south in the northernmost part of the outer enclosure changing to an east–west alignment on the western side of the outer enclosure and appear to be absent from the eastern part. They also appear to extend into the northern part of the area occupied by the later fort where they are visible as parallel bands of increased magnetic response orientated south–west to north–east. Striped soil patterns were also present within the excavated site of Balksbury located a kilometre to the north across the valley of the River Anna. Here they were described by the excavators as 'sandier deposits' (Wainwright and Davies 1995).

Excavation in the later fort showed that the general picture of regular pits presented by the magnetometer survey was largely correct. Of the features found in the excavation, the larger pits of beehive profile were the most clearly resolved in the magnetometer survey but shallow gully complexes and the concentrations of smaller features inside them in the southern part of the excavation were generally not detected by the magnetometer. One small pit (P49) in the excavated area gave rise to a pronounced positive magnetic anomaly of 13 nanotesla (nT) magnitude, accounted for by the presence of burnt daub in the pit filling. On the western side of the excavated area a narrow strip of more deeply stratified deposits in the lee of the rampart had survived the effects of cultivation, which had removed most of the archaeological levels in the majority of the hillfort interior. Significantly the magnetometer survey has clearly defined this zone of better preserved deposits around the perimeter of the later fort due to the stronger magnetic signal generated by the build-up of soil against the inner face of the rampart. The survey evidence suggests that the zone of stratified deposits is present around the majority of the defensive circuit. Future management will be able to take this variable preservation of archaeological deposits in the hillfort into account and thus avoid damage to the sensitive areas bordering the ramparts.

It was not until the full coverage of the interior of Bury Hill II was completed in 1997 that a wide road corridor became apparent – indicated by a linear zone largely free of magnetic anomalies – running through the centre of the interior between the opposed entrances on the south-east and north-west sides of the fort. The presence of this roadway suggests that both gaps in the perimeter earthworks are original features contemporary with the main occupation of the fort. This evidence conflicts with the earlier view of Hawkes (1940) that originally there was only a single entrance into the main fort on the south-east side. It is possible that the entrance on the north-west was blocked and the causeway across the ditch removed at a later stage once the roadway had become an established feature, influencing the layout and distribution of settlement within the hillfort but no longer used as a route for passing through the enclosure. Several other features of potential interest are indicated by the magnetometer in the later fort. These include:

i) A narrow, slightly curving length of ditch indicated by a positive linear magnetic anomaly in the southern part of Bury Hill II running approximately north-north-west to south-south-east. It seems to run straight into the main rampart and therefore may represent an earlier pre-rampart boundary feature. The ditch may be related to the external enclosed settlement identified to the south-east of the hillfort and may even represent an extension of the major linear feature that runs along the southern side of this complex on a south-east to north-west heading towards the south-east boundary of the hillfort.

ii) A series of weakly defined linear anomalies on the line of the eastern entrance extending into the hillfort on the northern side of the possible roadway. These may represent foundation slots for supporting a timber-lined entrance passage.

iii) On the south side of the possible road, set back a little into the fort from the eastern entrance, an anomaly suggestive of a sub-circular gully 8.0m long and 6.0m wide with a possible central internal feature is present. This may tentatively be interpreted as a structure such as a look out or guard-post.

The external settlement

After the completion of the survey coverage inside the hillforts in 1997, the opportunity was taken to conduct an additional magnetometer survey over the site of an apparent ditched enclosure partially visible from the air in the arable field immediately to the south-east of the fort at NGR SU 349433. The settlement is only 200m south-east of the south-east entrance of Bury Hill on an easterly continuation of the same area of level high ground occupied by the hillfort. At least one possible entrance of the enclosure appears to be aligned towards the fort.

The results of the magnetometer survey revealed an enclosure of irregular plan defined by ditches interrupted by several possible entrances and with several ditches radiating out from the main enclosure ditch. Antenna-like ditches project outwards from the main boundary of the Bury Hill enclosure on the eastern side and on the south side there is an entrance formed by the ditches of the southern boundary curving in towards one another. A possible wider entrance with flanking ditches may be present on the north-west side facing the hillfort, parallel with the wide linear that runs immediately south of the enclosure on a heading towards the hillfort. Within the enclosure there are signs of intensive occupation in the form of large numbers of pits most of which appear to respect the boundary of the enclosure. The pits appear less substantial in form compared with those in the neighbouring hillfort. Broader and weaker anomalies within and around the enclosure are likely to represent quarrying activity. The core settlement extends over an area of some 2–3ha and appears to be situated alongside a linear ditch or trackway (visible as a broad linear positive magnetic anomaly) possibly linking it to the nearby hillfort.

The possible phasing of this newly planned enclosed settlement in relation to the nearby hillfort is considered in more detail in the preceding section.

Danebury: Nether Wallop; NGR SU 324 377

Summary
Date of survey:
28 July to 1 August 1997.
Landuse at time of survey:
Managed open woodland with clearings.
Geology:
Cretaceous Upper Chalk.
Soil Association:
343h – Andover 1 – shallow well drained calcareous silty soils over chalk on slopes and crests. Striped soil patterns locally.
Approximate area enclosed:
5 hectares (12 acres) enclosed by innermost defensive earthwork.
Planform:
Approximately oval.
Form of ramparts:
Main inner earthwork constructed in several phases initially timber-framed but consisting in its later phases of a dump constructed rampart the front face of which continued downward into a deep ditch of V-profile with an external counterscarp bank (correctly a bank formed from periodic clearing-out of the ditch). Middle earthwork consisting of a smaller dump-constructed rampart fronted by a V-shaped ditch defining an elongated enclosure between the earthworks of the two entrances. Outer earthwork consisting of a shallow ditch with a slight external bank running around the contour of the hill outside the main hillfort earthworks (known as the Outer Enclosure) and continuing as a linear earthwork (the Danebury Linear) to the south-east. The defences are not multivallate in the normal use of the term (closely set multiple ramparts present at sites such as Maiden Castle, Hambledon Hill, Battlesbury etc).
Entrance features:
Two elaborate entrances on the east and south-west sides of the fort. The south-west entrance was blocked in the 4th century BC. The main eastern entrance, continuously remodelled and reconstructed in seven main phases, started as a simple gate in a gap in the inner rampart but in its developed form (in Period 5) was augmented by the addition of a hornwork projecting from the inner rampart and two more projecting outworks that meet to form an outer entrance creating

long winding corridor approach commanded by the inner hornwork.

Previous finds:

See Cunliffe and Poole 1991: *Danebury. An Iron Age Hillfort in Hampshire. Vol.5, The Excavations 1979-1988: The finds* (CBA Res. Rep. 73: London).

Previous recorded excavation:

The hillfort of Danebury was the subject of an extended campaign of excavation spanning 20 field-work seasons from 1969–1988. 57% of the main enclosed area was excavated and the defences and gates examined (Cunliffe 1984a, 1995; Cunliffe and Poole 1991).

Scheduled Ancient Monument:

Hampshire 53.

County SMR No.:

SU33NW 93 A.

Project site code:

WHSP Site 11.

Danebury (Fig 2.16) is so well known from the literature arising from the excavations, 1969–1988, and subsequent aerial survey and detailed study of the surrounding landscape that no further description of the morphology or setting is necessary here (Cunliffe 1984a, 1995; Cunliffe and Poole 1991; Cunliffe 2000; Palmer 1984). Discussion is here focussed on the new geophysical evidence.

Magnetometer survey (Figs 2.17, 2.18).

In 1997 a limited magnetometer survey was carried out retrospectively at Danebury nearly ten years after excavation ceased. The purpose of the survey was to collect a magnetometer data-set that could be evaluated against the actual evidence beneath the ground at Danebury so well known from many years of excavation on the site (Cunliffe 1984a, 1995; Cunliffe and Poole 1991). It was hoped that a magnetometer data-set from a chalkland hillfort such as Danebury, with well understood archaeological deposits in the interior, would serve as a control method for enabling the likely effectiveness and possible limitations of magnetic survey on other unexplored Wessex hillforts to be more reliably judged.

The control data was collected from three sample areas set out within the hillfort on an approximation to the original site grid employed during excavation (Fig 2.17). The location of these areas was influenced largely by the distribution of trees and ground vegetation in the fort in the summer of 1997. Practical considerations dictate that areas too overgrown with vegetation or obstructed by trees are not suitable for magnetometer survey, especially when the purpose is to gain a control sample as part of a wider study.

The largest area of survey (MG1) was in the north-east half of the fort, west of the eastern entrance. A more limited second area (MG2) was set out south-east of the centre of the fort and the third area (MG3) was set back by a distance of about 30m from the blocked entrance on the southwest. An attempt was made to lay out the survey areas approximately on the line of the original site grid so that it would be possible to relate the magnetometer surveys to areas that had previously been excavated (Cunliffe 1995, fig 1) and also cover areas previously untouched by excavation. Area MG1 coincides with an area of the site (N4; Cunliffe 1995, figs 7 and 8) left largely undisturbed, flanked by roadways 1 and 5 to the south and north. The lines of Road 1 and Road 4 (which branches off the former) should pass through the lower half of the magnetometer survey at MG1. Large numbers of storage pits (primarily dating from the early period of Danebury) were present in the excavated areas immediately to the east and west of the sample magnetometer survey MG1 and were expected to extend into the survey area (Cunliffe 1995, figs 8 and 9). Area MG2 was positioned to explore an unexcavated part of the site designated S3 (Cunliffe 1995, fig 7). This area should have a lower density of pits but also contains remains of square timber (four-post) structures. Finally area MG3 should contain the continuation of Road 1 running towards the blocked western entrance of Danebury and a combination of pits and four-post structures.

Fig 2.16
Aerial photograph of Danebury hillfort showing the complex earthworks at the eastern entrance visible in the middle foreground (NMRC; NMR 15740/25, SU 3237/95, 1997).

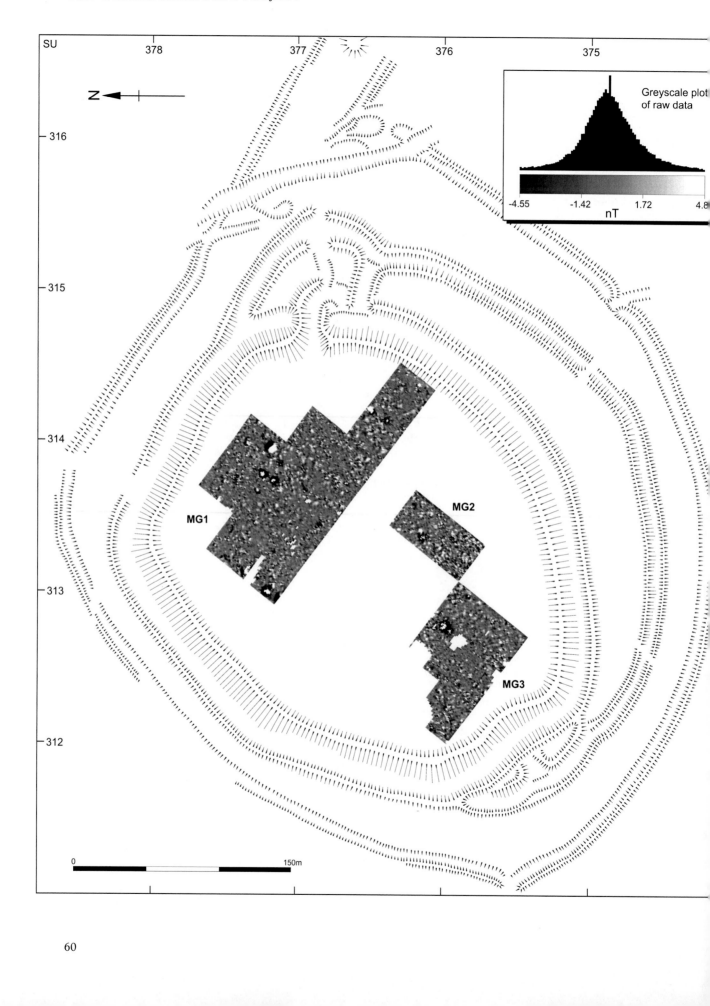

SU

N

378   377   376   375

316

315

314

313

312

MG1

MG2

MG3

Greyscale plot
of raw data

-4.55   -1.42   1.72   4.8
nT

0   150m

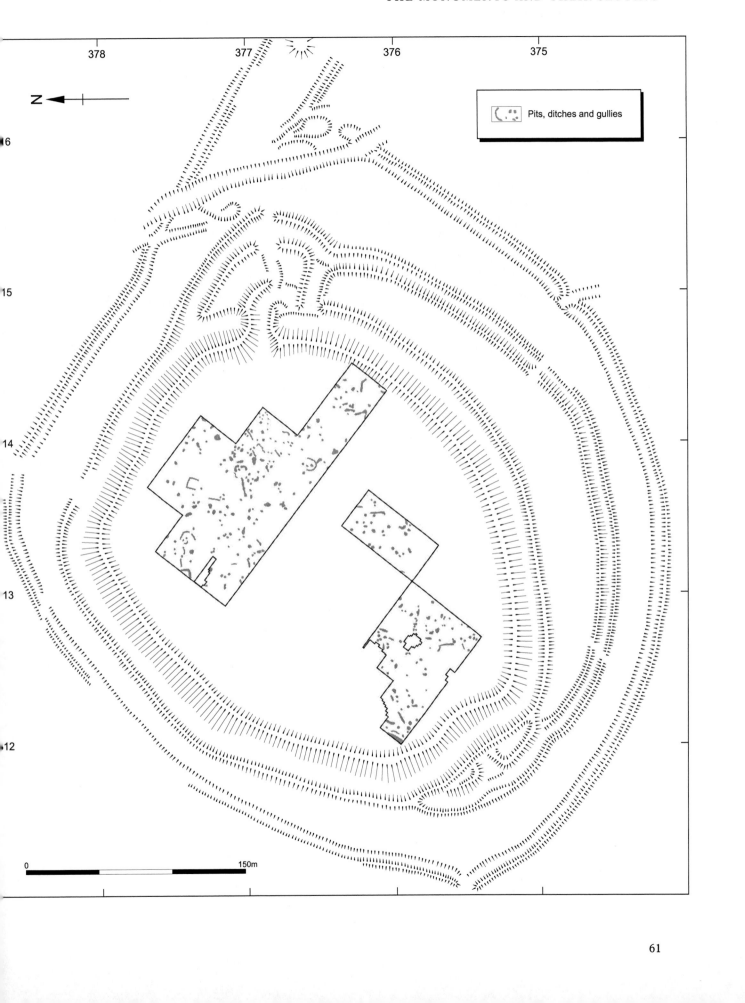

The survey results

The areas surveyed inside Danebury generally display a very disturbed magnetic response within which it is difficult to isolate responses to individual features. At other excavated sites, such as Alfred's Castle (Lock and Gosden 1999) and Maiden Castle (Sharples 1991; Payne 1996), this has been shown to be indicative of a great profusion of archaeological features so densely distributed that their individual magnetic signals blend together into an almost continuous sea of anomalies. The interpretation of the magnetometer data in Fig 2.18 only shows the most obvious discrete anomalies that stand out visibly from the general 'noisy' magnetic response across the site. This has the slightly misleading effect of under-representing the true density of anomalous activity inside Danebury. The results from Danebury, despite being difficult to interpret, are therefore totally in keeping with the known density, character and form of archaeological features at the site. The widespread anomalous activity is probably indicative of large numbers of closely packed pits and other inter-cutting features and is comparable with the magnetic activity newly mapped inside Barbury Castle, Wiltshire (this volume).

The data from Danebury demonstrates that fluxgate magnetometry can only provide a coarse picture of the form and layout of archaeological features at a hillfort site with dense internal occupation, compared to what can be obtained by excavation. This has to be expected, but the technique is nevertheless sufficient to show the general character of the site. Although lacking fine detail, the magnetometer survey of Danebury can be regarded as a truthful reflection of the intensive occupation known to have taken place on the site.

The widespread occurrence of anomalies produced by ferrous material in the Danebury data reflects recent activity on the site (including excavation, tree-felling, bonfires and visitor activity). This has contributed considerably to the already disturbed magnetic response. The reactions to modern, near-surface ferrous material have obscured the response to deeper archaeological features in many parts of the hillfort, resulting in an incomplete map of the sub-surface archaeology. Notwithstanding this problem, the majority of the remaining anomalous activity at Danebury is likely to be archaeological in origin based on the relative weakness of the magnetic signals.

Lines of roadways are faintly visible in the data as areas of reduced magnetic activity similar to the roadways previously located at Bury Hill, Segsbury and Maiden Castle. The roads at Danebury are clearest in area MG3 near the western entrance.

Ladle Hill: Great Litchfield Down, Litchfield and Woodcott; NGR SU 479 568

Summary
Date of survey:
16 to 25 July 1997.
Landuse at time of survey:
Rough grassland.
Geology:
Cretaceous Upper Chalk.
Soil Association:
343h – Andover 1 – shallow well drained calcareous silty soils over chalk on slopes and crests. Striped soil patterns locally.
Approximate area enclosed:
3.5 hectares (8.6 acres).
Planform:
Oval.
Form of ramparts:
Irregular and incomplete, but the earthworks suggest univallate defences in the process of construction but left unfinished.
Entrance features:
Two probable entrances to the east and west.
Previous finds:
None documented.
Previous recorded excavation:
None, analysis of surface evidence by Piggott (1931).
Scheduled Ancient Monument:
25616 (previously Hampshire 64).
County SMR No.:
SU45NE 15.
Project site code:
WHSP Site 10.

Morphology and setting

The incomplete circuit on Ladle Hill (Fig 2.19) is the best known of all the unfinished hillforts in Britain (Feacham 1971). First correctly identified as an unfinished hillfort and described in detail by Piggott (1931), the site is situated 2km east of Beacon Hill (this volume) at a height of 234m. The unfinished works give a clue to the methods employed in the creation of a univallate enclosure, presumably of earlier Iron Age date. The circuit was intended to enclose an area of approximately 3.5ha (8.6 acres) and was marked by a slight ditch (or possibly an earlier palisaded

Fig 2.19
Aerial photograph of the unfinished hillfort on Ladle Hill looking north. Note the adjacent linear earthworks and narrow "setting-out" ditch on the north-east side of the partially constructed defensive circuit (NMRC, NMR 15453/28, SU 4756/74, 1996).

nclosure). The description given by Piggott (ibid) is still valid and will not be repeated here. Of interest, however, is the unit length discernible in the unfinished stretches of rampart, discussed in greater detail below (pp 136–8). Apart from the dumps of material associated with the abandoned construction works, the interior has very few other earthworks of intelligible character.

The immediate environs of the monument contain a number of features of considerable interest. The north-western arc of the unfinished perimeter partially overlies a linear ditch that runs along the crest of the west-facing escarpment of Great Litchfield Down and Ladle Hill. This can still be traced intermittently for at least 2km, apparently terminating on a slight spur overlooking the valley floor barrow cemetery of Seven Barrows. For the kilometre or so of its known southern course, this linear forms the western boundary of an extensive field system on Great Litchfield Down (Fig 2.20). This field system does not extend northwards as far as Ladle Hill, its northern limit being approximately 850m south of the unfinished enclosure. Immediately east of the unfinished enclosure is another linear ditch. This is not overlain by the enclosure circuit and runs for a distance of at least 700m towards the head of a coombe below Hare Warren Down. To the east of this linear ditch is another extensive field system, visible both as areas of earthworks and as soilmarks and cropmarks on air photographs.

370m to the south-west of Ladle Hill two sub-square enclosures, each of approximately 0.3ha (0.7 acre), survive as earthworks. Both are undated, but Cunliffe (1991, 386) has noted the similarity

Fig 2.20
Aerial photograph of the extensive field system on Great Litchfield Down near Ladle Hill Camp (NMRC, NMR SU 4755/1, 1967).

between such enclosures, linear ditches and areas of probable grazing during the Late Bronze Age/Early Iron Age transition. More recently similar patterns have been observed and commented upon on the eastern side of Salisbury Plain (Bradley *et al* 1994) and between Fosbury and Walbury hillforts (Massey 1998). It is noteworthy that both the examples discussed here are well beyond the northern limit of the known field system on Great Litchfield Down and west of the fields on Hare Warren Down and Nuthanger Down. Thus the unfinished hillfort appears to be in one of the 'classic' Wessex locations, close to major linear components of the landscape and in an area whose immediate environs are devoid of field system. Elsewhere in the region site such as Quarley Hill (Palmer 1984), Sid bury (McOmish *et al* 2002) and Yarnbu (Bowden 1999) display similar patterns.

Some 30m north of Ladle Hill lies a we preserved disc barrow and beyond this, the apex of the spur, Piggott (193 reported traces of platforms that may repre sent traces of an unenclosed settlemen This complex has never been surveyed detail and while an open settlement is a po sibility, other causes, such as localised su face quarrying, must also be considered.

Magnetometer survey (Fig 2.21)

Ladle Hill is a highly significant site an one of considerable rarity, as it appear

Fig 2.21
Greyscale plot of the
magnetometer data from
Ladle Hill Camp in relation
to the plan of the incomplete
hillfort earthworks.

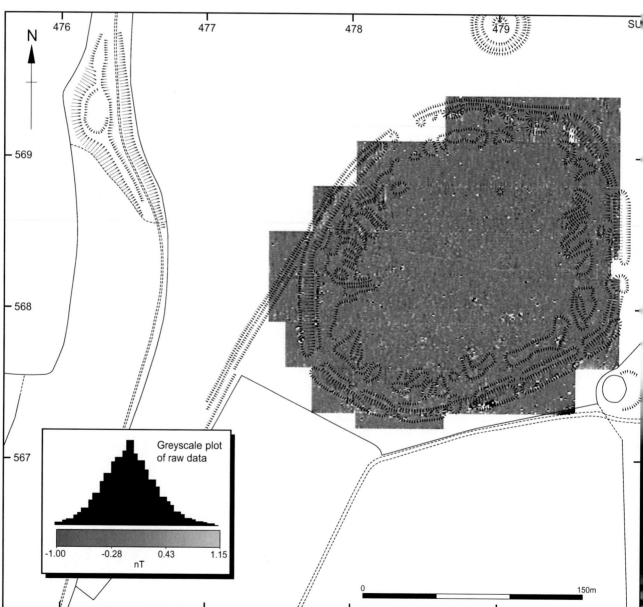

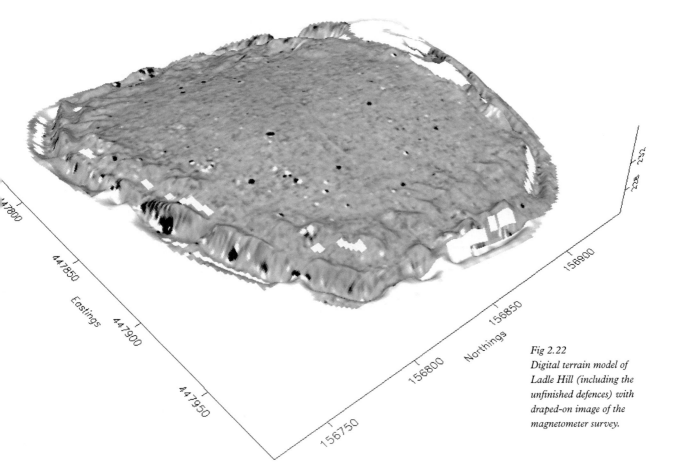

Fig 2.22
*Digital terrain model of
Ladle Hill (including the
unfinished defences) with
draped-on image of the
magnetometer survey.*

to represent the remains of a hillfort abandoned part of the way through the process of construction. The partially constructed state of the site reveals features that would be concealed in a completed example (including a possible setting-out ditch and piles of chalky soil initially quarried from the ditch and deposited in the interior for finishing the rampart). Ladle Hill therefore provides an insight into the methods employed in the construction of the defensive architecture of a hillfort on chalk geology.

It has long been suspected that the area demarcated by the unfinished earthworks never contained a settlement, although there is a possibility that the hillfort had been constructed over an earlier unenclosed settlement. The main purpose of the magnetometer survey at Ladle Hill Camp was to verify the suspected absence of a settlement focus in the area occupied by the partially-constructed earthwork complex, compatible with the unfinished status of the hillfort.

As predicted the magnetic signal from the site is exceptionally subdued and shows none of the variation normally associated with former occupation sites on chalk geology. This would seem to confirm that a set-tlement with typical Iron Age characteristics (such as storage pits) was never established within the boundary of the earthwork, in accord with the apparent early abandonment of the site before the earthworks were even completed.

The topographical model of the site produced by the Central Archaeology Service in 1996 (Fig 2.22) provides a valuable three-dimensional view of the unfinished earthworks of the hillfort defences that may serve as a useful management tool, but does not provide any significant new archaeological information.

A small, low mound, approximately 3m in diameter, thought to be a disc barrow, in the northern half of the camp did not produce any trace of a surrounding ditch in the magnetometer survey. The mound, if it still survives as a raised feature, was also unresolved in the topographical model on account of the relatively coarse 2–3m measurement-interval employed. Early aerial photographs of the site (for example SU 4756/47, CCC 8960/02160, 1929) indicate that the mound was better preserved at the time of Piggott's investigations in the first half of the 20th century.

Norsebury: Micheldever; NGR SU 490 400

Summary

Date of survey:
25 September to 1 October 1997.
Landuse at time of survey:
Arable, planted with a young crop.
Geology:
Cretaceous Upper Chalk.
Soil Association:
343h – Andover 1 – shallow well drained calcareous silty soils over chalk on slopes and crests. Striped soil patterns locally.
Approximate area enclosed:
3.5 hectares (8.6 acres).
Planform:
Oval.
Form of ramparts:
Univallate defences badly damaged by ploughing and now only partially preserved on the north and west sides of the defensive circuit. The inner bank has almost gone and is now only apparent as a scarp sloping down from the interior (even this is missing on the eastern side and therefore the eastern extent of the enclosed area is unclear). The ditch survives on the north and west sides and an outer bank survives (to 1.5m) only on the north side.
Entrance features:
No longer apparent on the ground owing to the poor preservation of the enclosing earthworks.
Previous finds:
Sherds of middle and late Bronze Age pottery and Bronze Age flints were found during fieldwalking by the M3 Archaeological Committee. Roman building materials (including box-flue tile) and pottery have also been recovered in the near vicinity of the fort.
Previous recorded excavation:
None documented. Field Survey and pla[n] by Williams-Freeman (1915).
Scheduled Ancient Monument:
Hampshire 109.
County SMR No.:
SU44SE 4.
Project Site Code:
WHSP Site 17

Morphology and setting

Norsebury (Fig 2.23) is a univallate enclosure of approximately 3.5ha (8.6 acres) site[d] below the crest of a low hill with a south-an[d] west-facing aspect overlooking the Rive[r] Dever, a tributary of the Test. The locatio[n] is to the east of the main Hampshire hillfor[t] concentration and its situation, even befor[e] the results of the geophysical survey wer[e] known, suggested that this was a rather dif[-] ferent form of Iron Age enclosure. Much o[f] the circuit and all of the interior have bee[n] heavily degraded by ploughing. The south[-] ern and eastern sections of the defences hav[e] been ploughed out to such a degree that th[e] area enclosed by the hillfort is no longe[r] clearly visible above ground, leading t[o] uncertainty over its exact plan and extent[.] The defences on the east were already muc[h] reduced when J P Williams-Freeman pro[-] duced a plan of the site in the early years o[f] the 20th century, indicating that most of th[e] damage had already taken place by this tim[e] (Williams-Freeman 1915). Although the sit[e] continues to be ploughed, the appearanc[e] and condition of the Norsebury earthwor[k] seems to have altered little in the intervenin[g] period up to the present day. Only on the[e] north and west can the ditch be seen as [a] clear earthwork, with a counterscarp up t[o] 1.5m high also intact. The surviving earth[-] work stretches of the monument do no[t] appear to have been breached by an entranc[e] and the original entrances could only b[e] identified with confidence after the geophys[-] ical survey had been undertaken (*see below*).

The site has no record of any excavation[,] although late Bronze Age pottery an[d] Bronze Age flint was recovered from field[-] walking by the M3 Archaeological Commit[-] tee (source: Hampshire SMR).

The environs of the site are of some inter[-] est as Norsebury Ring is located in an area o[f] the Hampshire chalk where there are signifi[-] cant clusters of 'banjo' and other later Iro[n] Age enclosure types. These appear to form [a] focus on the upper reaches of the Dever Val[-] ley and the gentle rolling chalkland north o[f] the River Itchen (Barrett *et al* 1991, fig 6.6[)]

Fig 2.23
Aerial view of the partially ploughed-out remains of Norsebury Ring looking south. The hillfort ramparts survive as substantial earthworks in the wooded belt around the northern side of the large arable field containing the fort, but the east and south sections of the defences have been almost completely ploughed away. Note the absence in the aerial photograph of evidence for any occupation in the interior in contrast with the magnetometer survey results (NMRC, NMR 15705/34, SU 4940/36, 1997).

Fasham 1987; Perry 1970, 1986). One banjo, on Hunton Down, is less than 1km north of Norsebury, with its entrance funnel facing directly towards the hillfort. Approximately 1.5km to the north-west a cropmark (NMR 2161/027) near Upper Cranbourne Farm (itself another cluster of banjo enclosures) appears to show a possible square barrow, a Late Iron Age form when encountered in Wessex (*see* Corney 1989). Approximately 500m south-east of the south-eastern entrance of Norsebury Ring air photographs show pit clusters and part of an enclosure of probable Iron Age date.

The general character of the activity in the environs of Norsebury points to a major Late Iron Age focus in the region and, as is so often the case in this part of Hampshire, there is strong evidence for continuity into the Roman period. A number of proven or probable villas are known in the vicinity, many overlying or adjacent to banjos and other later Iron Age settlement types (Fasham 1987; Perry 1970, 1986).

Fragmentary traces of field system are seen on the air cover over much of the area around Norsebury Ring, but the effects of modern ploughing now makes detailed mapping and analysis difficult. Earlier activity is also evident on the air cover with a ring-ditch complex immediately south of the River Dever only 600m from Norsebury Ring (NMR 4680/24).

Magnetometer survey (Figs 2.24–2.26)

Prior to the magnetometer survey in 1997 very little archaeological information on the site was available except for the short description and plan in Williams-Freeman (1915) and the previous limited fieldwalking by the M3 Archaeological Committee (*see above*). The site was selected for inclusion in the Wessex Hillforts Survey as it was important to assess the survival of archaeological features potentially vulnerable to erosion by ploughing in the interior, and also to assess the differences in results obtained by magnetic survey from substantially plough-levelled hillfort interiors, such as Norsebury, and well preserved hillfort interiors in unploughed grassland, such as Beacon Hill. A further site-management-related aim was to define the exact plan and full extent of the monument on the side where the defences have been levelled to help ensure that in the future the scheduled area is of the correct size to afford full protection to the monument. Norsebury was also surveyed in pursuit of one of the original goals of the

project concerned with the identification of contrasting or recurrent patterns of activity in medium-sized hillforts of univallate form. These are arguably the most well-represented hillfort type in the study region.

The magnetometer survey of Norsebury proved particularly effective and the results provided a considerable amount of new information about the site. The following features were detected by the magnetometer survey:

i) The circuit of the defensive ditch where it no longer survives as a recognisable feature above ground on the degraded west, south, south-east and east sides of the enclosure. The edges of the southern section of ploughed-out ditch are very irregular and it is possible that the ditch was widened in this area by quarrying of the sides. This practice has previously been observed in the Late Iron Age phases of the Nettlebank Copse banjo settlement excavated by the Danebury Environs Project in 1993 (Cunliffe and Poole 2000d, 134). An alternative is that the main hillfort ditch cuts through an area containing earlier quarry features. Excavation would be required to determine the actual sequence.

ii) Two entrances – one on the south-west corner flanked by a deep 90° in-turn of the western hillfort ditch on the north side of the entrance passage and the other in the centre of the eastern arc of the hillfort ditch, possibly augmented by outworks consisting of symmetrical smaller ditches projecting out from the main ditch on both sides of the entrance.

iii) A series of positive linear magnetic anomalies representing narrow ditches extend into the interior of the hillfort from the newly-identified south-west entrance. The linear anomalies branch around a large oval ditched enclosure located just east of the centre of the hillfort and with a single south-east-facing entrance orientated towards the eastern entrance to the hillfort. The long axis of the oval enclosure is approximately 34m and the shorter (south-west–north-east) axis is approximately 30m. A dipolar magnetic response to a large ferrous object overrides the anomaly to the ditch on the south side of the enclosure. This might represent a ferrous object stratified in the fill of the ditch but could equally be a modern near-surface piece of iron, such as a stray plough blade. At least five large pits are present within the boundary of

Fig 2.24
*Greyscale plot of the
magnetometer data from
Norsebury Ring in relation
to the plan of the surviving
hillfort earthworks.*

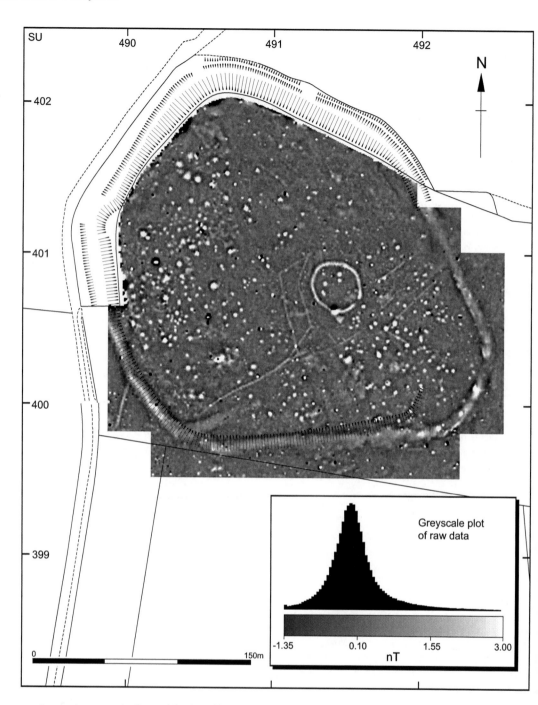

the enclosure – indicated by localised positive magnetic anomalies – but these need not necessarily be contemporary with the enclosure ditch and may simply represent a continuation of the larger spread of pits in the main hillfort interior outside the enclosure to the east, which could be of earlier or later date.

iv) The eastern portion of the hillfort is very densely occupied by the above distribution of pits, ranging from one or two metres in diameter up to five metres. The pits seem to exhibit a zoned distrib-

ution with the density of pits falling off considerably towards the centre of the site in the areas immediately west and north of the oval enclosure and increasing again along the western side of the hillfort to a similar or even greater density than that on the east. Within the zones of pit disturbance a number of other larger, more amorphous areas of magnetic disturbance are visible that may represent areas of quarrying, aggregates of closely intercutting pits or 'working hollows'. Also within the zones

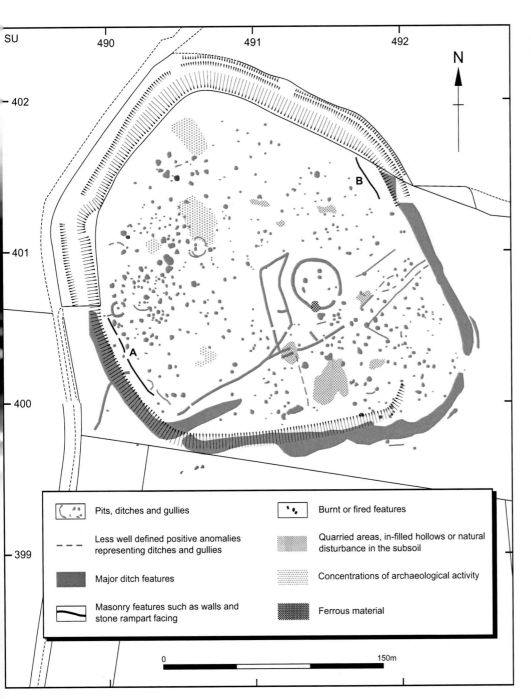

Fig 2.25
Interpretation of the
magnetometer data from
Norsebury.

of pitting are a number of weakly-defined narrow annular or arcing positive anomalies that may be indicative of circular gully structures or dwellings. A few strongly positive localised anomalies (again within the main pit distribution), may represent fired or industrial features such as hearths, furnaces or ovens.

v) A single linear ditch in the form of a positive linear magnetic anomaly can be seen running up to the hillfort defences on the south, but this does not seem to continue far under the defences into the

enclosed area. This probably represents an earlier pre-hillfort boundary feature. No continuation of this feature was noted on the available air cover.

vi) Emptier areas immediately inside the line of the hillfort ditch where it is ploughed-out may represent the former rampart. Unlike some of the hillfort ramparts covered by the Wessex Hillforts Survey there is no evidence of burning of this structure. The presence of a possible internal masonry (or chalk rubble) rampart revetment is suggested by narrow negative linear anomalies visible at two points along the ploughed-out defensive circuit (A and B on Fig 2.25).

Magnetic susceptibility survey

Magnetic susceptibility data (Fig 2.26) collected on a 5m grid at Norsebury in 1998 (Bartlett 1999 and Chapter 1 this volume) shows a clear relationship between areas of high susceptibility readings and increases in the concentration of silted pits (and therefore areas of occupation) mapped by the magnetometer survey. At both Norsebury and Castle Ditches (*see below*) surveyed using the same method, the susceptibility values also diminish in areas containing few magnetic anomalies.

Discussion

The newly identified entrances on the south-east and south-west corners are an unusual configuration in Wessex hillforts. That on the south-east appears as a simple gap approximately 10m wide with hints of slight outworks. On the south-west a more

elaborate and unusual plan is evident wit the ditch on the west side making a 90° tur into the interior for almost 60m and form ing a long internal projection. The characte of the ramparts at each entrance unknown, these having long succumbed t the effects of ploughing. The internal fea tures of the site are also of interest with cle evidence of zoning represented by dens clusters of pits, notably in the western ha and south-eastern corner, and a number linear features. The prominent oval ditche enclosure just east of the centre of the hil fort is without parallel in central Wessex hil forts. The entrance of this inner enclosur faces directly towards the south-easter entrance of the fort suggesting a layou planned deliberately in accordance with th access and viewpoint through the main hil fort rampart.

The results from Norsebury suggest densely occupied hillfort but with a cohe ent internal layout possibly indicative of on major phase of occupation within which wide range of activities were carried ou

Fig 2.26
Magnetic susceptibility
survey results from
Norsebury (from Bartlett-
Clark Consultancy).

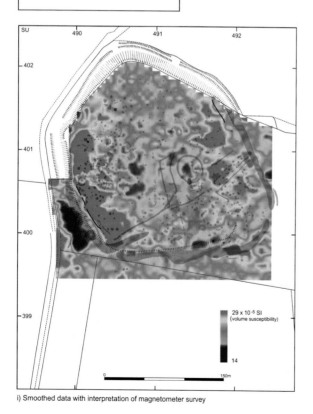

i) Smoothed data with interpretation of magnetometer survey

(ii) Median filtered data

iii) Data as for plot (ii)

Surveyed by Bartlett - Clark Consultancy for Wessex Hillforts Projec

The elaboration of the entrance features is typical of a later date range in the Iron Age – possibly indicative of a relatively late hillfort development such as Bury Hill 2 or an earlier hillfort that continued in occupation for a lengthier time than some of the neighbouring sites in Hampshire. Although the resemblance may be superficial, in terms of entrance configuration and internal layout, Norsebury also shares several features in common with ditched enclosures recently investigated in the Danebury area of Hampshire, such as the site at Rowbury Farm (Cunliffe 2003; Payne 2003b). The latter site was established in the Early Iron Age but was subsequently reoccupied in the Late Iron Age and continued into the Roman period, when a series of smaller internal enclosures and linear sub-divisions were established within the bounds of the original larger ditched enclosure.

The extent of the monument is greater than originally anticipated on the basis of the Ordnance Survey evidence. The new geophysical evidence shows that it is considerably more elongated to the east.

St Catherine's Hill: Winchester; NGR SU 484 276

Summary
Date of survey:
13 to 17 October 1997.
Landuse at time of survey:
Grassland with some trees and scrub.
Geology:
Cretaceous Upper Chalk.
Soil Association:
343h – Andover 1 – shallow well drained calcareous silty soils over chalk.
Approximate area enclosed:
7.6 hectares (18.8 acres).
Planform:
Oval.
Form of ramparts:
Univallate defences encircling St Catherine's Hill, consisting of a rampart and outer ditch and a non-continuous counterscarp bank.
Entrance features:
Original clearly defined in-turned entrance at the north-east excavated in 1927–8.
Previous finds:
Finds assemblage from excavation (*see below*) spanning the Early Iron Age to Medieval periods.
Previous recorded excavation:
The site was partially excavated in 1927–8 by Hawkes, Myres and Stevens (Hawkes

et al 1930, Hawkes 1976).
Scheduled Ancient Monument:
Hampshire 28.
County SMR No.:
SU42NE 5 A.
Project site code:
WHSP Site 19.

Morphology and setting

The hillfort on St Catherine's Hill (Fig 2.27) is situated on a spur of chalk overlooking the valley of the River Itchen on the west and a narrow dry valley cutting through Twyford Down to the south and east. The site is now more isolated from the surrounding chalk downland by the deep cutting through Twyford Down containing the modern extension of the M3 motorway. The A33T road, which the new motorway replaced, formerly ran immediately below the line of the western defences (Fig 2.27). Despite the proximity of the new motorway and the busy centre of Winchester, the site remains a tranquil island and forms part of a nature reserve managed by the Hampshire Wildlife Trust. Visitor erosion to the ramparts and rabbit disturbance are problems. Scrub clearing helps to deter rabbits and in 1996 paths were cut through the grass inside to disperse visitors and reduce erosion.

The land enclosed by the hillfort consists of a flattish summit area beyond which the ground slopes down towards the ramparts, particularly steeply on the western side overlooking the Itchen Valley. The defences consist of a main rampart of simple dump (or *glacis*) type construction fronted by an external ditch and a counterscarp bank is present along the northern and western sections of the defences where the natural slope is least severe. The rampart seems to have been built from the start as a dump (as is also the case at Woolbury and Quarley Hill) and was apparently not preceded by a timber constructed box rampart as at some Wessex hillforts (Hawkes 1976; Cunliffe 1991, Chapter 14, 322). Heightening and thorough rebuilding of the rampart, and simultaneous re-modelling of the entrance, took place during the earlier part of the Middle Iron Age around 400–300 BC, associated with saucepan forms of pottery of the St Catherine's Hill group. The site appears to have been abandoned relatively soon after this (Hawkes 1976).

The north-eastern arc of the defences is broken by a single entrance of inturned type, facing the most moderate gradients leading up to the hillfort and therefore the

Fig 2.27
Aerial photograph of St
Catherine's Hill near Winchester and the A33T (now
grassed over), before construction of the M3 (on opposite
side of hill). (Note placement
of ramparts well down-slope
from crown of hill and beech
clump shrouding remains of
late Norman chapel)
(NMRC, NMR 3184/25,
SU 4827/51, 1987).

most accessible approach to the site. The
side containing the entrance is further augmented by the counterscarp banks already
mentioned, presumably to strengthen the
most vulnerable section of the defences.

The layout of the defences conforms
to the brow of the hill, so as to command
the steeper slopes beneath them, and the
hillfort interior therefore includes some
steeply-sloping areas unsuitable for occupation without prior levelling or terracing –
primarily the western side of the enclosed
area. The downslope siting of the ramparts

in this fashion is repeated at numerous
other hillforts in the south of England,
including Old Winchester Hill (Hampshire);
Sinodun Hill Camp (Oxfordshire);
Chalbury (Dorset) and The Caburn (East
Sussex) (see Figs 1.8 and 1.17). This would
have allowed the interiors of the sites to
be clearly viewed from afar. Hamilton and
Manley (1997) have commented on the
possible symbolic or territorial aspects of
this form of rampart construction in relation
to the hillforts on the Sussex Downs (see
Chapter 1).

A late Norman style chapel (cruciform with a central tower, destroyed circa 1538–40) was erected in the fort before the mid-12th century. A large mound, shrouded in a grove of beech trees in the centre-north of the fort, is all that now remains of this building. A dwelling was present at the east end of the chapel and boundary ditches to the west, probably enclosing a cemetery. Medieval chalk pits and rubbish pits associated with the chapel were excavated by Hawkes, Myres and Stevens in the 1920s (see below). A 15th-century boundary ditch forms a wide arc 80ft (24m) west of the chapel and between the chapel site and the original entrance to the hillfort is a maze consisting of a narrow channel cut in the turf at ground level. The maze is believed to have first been cut between 1647 and 1710 and was recut in the period 1830–40 (English Heritage documentation).

The 1927–8 excavations

St Catherine's Hill was the first of a series of Hampshire hillforts (the others being Buckland Rings, Bury Hill and Quarley Hill) excavated on a small scale by C F C Hawkes in the late 1920s and 1930s (see Chapter 1, Introduction). St Catherine's was excavated over the course of two seasons by the team of C F C Hawkes, J N L Myres and C G Stevens during 1927 and 1928 (Hawkes et al 1930) following two previous seasons of excavation on the site of the medieval chapel described above. As was common archaeological practice at the time (see Chapter 1), Hawkes and his team undertook only very limited excavation inside the hillfort, preferring to place more emphasis on the careful excavation of the original entrance on the north-east side of the hillfort and sections through the defences in two places. The main objective was to arrive at an understanding of the chronological development of the hillfort through identification of the main structural phases of the defences and entrance. Hawkes recognised that the original entrance to a hillfort is so often the area where the number of phases of activity associated with the use of a hillfort site can be best understood, because it is the area most sensitive to modification and reconstruction over time. Our present understanding of the chronological development of the hillfort is still largely based on these important excavations, which were reassessed in the light of more recent fieldwork at sites such as Danebury, in a paper published by Hawkes in 1976.

Extensive stripping of internal areas was largely unknown at the time Hawkes was excavating, and with the exception of the area containing the remains of the medieval chapel, the 1928–9 excavations were limited to small key-hole test areas, opened up to examine individual pit-type features suspected on the basis of small depressions in the ground surface. The scale and quantity of these trenches was inadequate to give a clear idea of the overall density and layout of features inside the hillfort, but did shed important light on the history of occupation of the hilltop.

In total 13 pits were excavated, spanning the whole range of occupation of the site from the end of the Bronze Age to the medieval period. Finds included Iron Age pottery of Early to Middle Iron Age date (the earlier material being more abundant), worked stone, a saddle quern stone, worked bone, bronze and iron objects, two whetstones, clay spindle whorls, burnt flint, faunal remains of Celtic shorthorn ox, sheep or goat, pig, horse, red-deer and dog and charcoal remains of ash and oak. Finds of Roman date included 1st–3rd century AD pottery types, a bronze fibula (late 1st century AD) and a bronze coin of Carausius (AD 286–93). Finds of stratified pottery essentially of a final Bronze Age type and date (coarsely gritted haematite coated wares belonging to the All Cannings Cross tradition), obtained from the base of one of the pits (Pit A) in the south-eastern part of the fort, indicated an earlier pre-hillfort phase of occupation on the site in the Early Iron Age, possibly beginning around 600 BC.

South of St Catherine's Hill itself, in an area now largely destroyed by the building of the M3, was an extensive area of field systems and a small Late Iron Age/Romano-British settlement centred at Arethusa's Clump, excavated by J D M Stuart and J M Birkbeck in 1933–4 (Stuart and Birkbeck 1936). Leading east along the ridge was a major multiple linear earthwork, combining a trackway with elements of field and possible territorial boundaries. This led to a second block of regular sub-rectangular fields approximately 1km east, similar in size and shape to those around Arethusa's Clump. Situated approximately midway between these two blocks of fields, in an area occupied by the Hockley Golf Course, is an earthwork enclosure similar in size and shape to Late Iron Age enclosures, but recorded as a Romano-British farmstead due to the presence of Roman pottery and

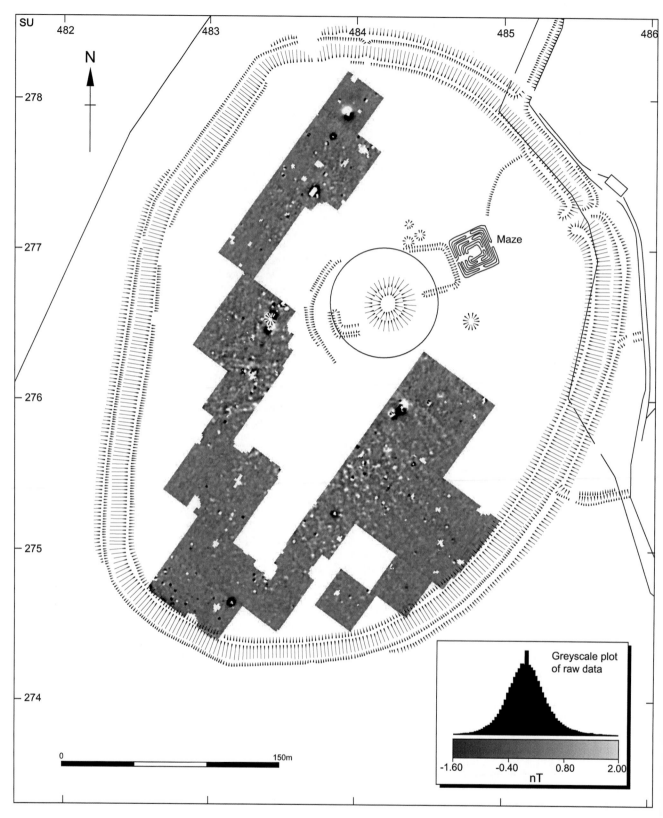

Fig 2.28
Greyscale plot of the magnetometer survey of a sample of the interior of St Catherine's Hill Camp in relation to the plan of the hillfort.

tile found in an excavation by Winchester College Archaeological Society. This is an important area in terms of British archaeology with the presence of a hillfort and associated farmstead settlements and field systems, which may suggest a successive process of settlement from the hillfort to the farmsteads to the Roman city at Winchester.

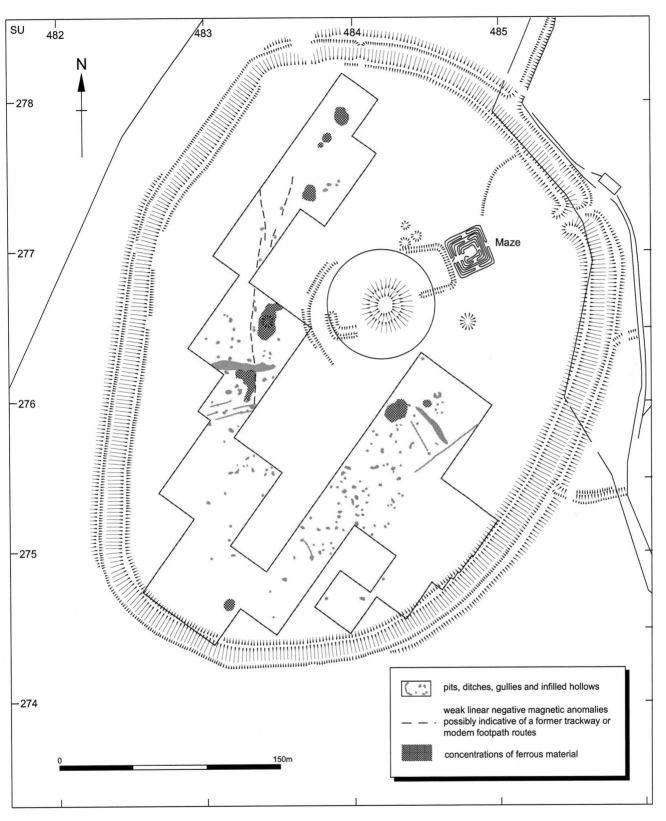

SU

Maze

pits, ditches, gullies and infilled hollows

weak linear negative magnetic anomalies
possibly indicative of a former trackway or
modern footpath routes

concentrations of ferrous material

0   150m

Magnetometer Survey (Figs 2.28 and 2.29)
St Catherine's Hill was included in the sample of sites investigated by the Wessex Hillforts Project on management and academic

grounds. The popularity of the site as a recreational area close to the city of Winchester means that it is at risk from erosion on visitor route-ways but at the same time

Fig 2.29
Interpretation of the magnetometer data from St Catherine's Hill Camp.

considerable scope exists for raising public awareness and understanding of the archaeological importance of the monument. Because the site is managed primarily as a nature reserve, it is important to understand the archaeology it contains in order to prevent any management conflicts between conserving wild-life habitats and preservation of the archaeology. Although the chronology of the site is reasonably well understood as a result of the limited excavations described above, the overall character of the internal utilisation of the site is less well understood because of the small-scale nature of the excavations in the interior.

Magnetometer survey was only possible over a sample of the hillfort interior in areas where vegetation cover was sufficiently open to allow unobstructed survey. The central area of the site had to be excluded from the survey owing to the dense tree cover around the site of the medieval chapel, which extends to the south-west along the crown of the hill. The western part of the site was omitted because of the steep gradient of the slope, as was the north-west sector, because this was trial trenched by Hawkes in the 1920s and was therefore a low priority for survey. It was hoped that the survey coverage over the remaining areas of the site would be sufficient to be able to recognise the general pattern and character of occupation across the fort interior. Slightly less than 50% of the interior (comprising 37m × 30m grid squares – 3.3ha in total) was covered by the survey.

The survey results reveal a high concentration of archaeological activity immediately south and south-west of the chapel site, situated on the highest ground. The middle of this zone of activity is unfortunately obscured by the tree cover. The activity appears to decrease down-slope towards the ramparts forming the south-east, south and south-west sides of the hillfort. The anomalies mapped by the survey are indicative of a moderately high distribution of pits and several ditches. A possible trackway may be present on the western flank of the hill running towards a break in the ramparts on the northern perimeter of the fort. On the evidence of Hawkes' limited excavations, the magnetic anomalies probably reflect a combination of Early Iron Age and medieval activity but this cannot be determined with certainty without excavation. Pits and ditches belonging to both periods were shown by Hawkes to be present on the hilltop and there is no reliable way of differentiating between the two in a magnetometer survey.

If the majority of pits are in fact Early Iron Age, St Catherine's Hill would be comparable in its layout to Danebury hillfort in its earlier phases in the 5th–4th centuries BC.

Woolbury: Little Somborne/ Stockbridge; NGR SU 381 353

Summary
Date of survey:
1 to 5 September 1997.
Landuse at time of survey:
Arable.
Geology:
Cretaceous Upper Chalk capped in parts by clay-with-flints plateau drift.
Soil Association:
343h – Andover 1 – shallow well drained calcareous silty soils over chalk on slopes and crests. Striped soil patterns locally.
Approximate area enclosed:
7 hectares (17 acres).
Planform:
Roughly pear-shaped (decreasing in width from west to east).
Form of ramparts:
A simple dump-constructed rampart reaching a maximum height above the interior of 2.7m sloping down to a ditch. An external counterscarp bank is present along the north and south-west sections of the circumference. The north-east and eastern sections of the defences have been entirely levelled by ploughing but the course followed by the missing section of the defences was recovered by excavation in 1989.
Entrance features:
A simple gap through the rampart and ditch is present on the south-west side of the hillfort providing access to Stockbridge Down along the line of the ridge on which the fort is situated. A second entrance was probably present on the opposite (east) side of the hillfort in the now ploughed-out section of the defensive circuit.
Previous finds:
Flint scatters (including Mesolithic material). Beaker burials and collared urn cremations and associated bronze objects on nearby Stockbridge Down (Stone and Hill 1940, Stone 1948).
Previous recorded excavation:
Sample area excavation was undertaken by the Danebury Environs Project in the north-east area of the hillfort in 1989 (Cunliffe and Poole 2000a). As well as sampling the deposits in the hillfort interior, the excavation extended across the plough levelled section of the hillfort defences.

Scheduled Ancient Monument:
HA 52
County SMR number:
SU33NE 24
Project site code:
WHSP Site 14

Morphology and setting

Woolbury (Fig 2.30), a univallate enclosure with an internal area of 7ha (17 acres), is located on Stockbridge Down 2km east of the valley of the River Test and 6km east south-east of Danebury. The location is remarkable for the Hampshire chalk, in that much of the area south of the hillfort remains undisturbed downland with extensive earthwork remains of field system, linear ditches and barrow groups (Crawford and Keiller 1928; Eagles 1989). The hillfort itself, though, has suffered severe damage from cultivation, with the whole interior under plough and the easternmost part of the defences having been completely levelled. Where best preserved, largely on the north and west, the defences display good evidence of 'unit length' construction with stretches averaging 35m in length visible. A simple break in the rampart and ditch at the south-west corner is most likely an original entrance and another might have existed on the north-east corner, now plough-levelled.

Recent excavation by the Danebury Environs Programme has established a mid 1st-millennium BC date for the construction of the hillfort, although evidence of intensive use was sparse (Cunliffe and Poole 2000a). In the Late Iron Age a small enclosed settlement developed in the eastern side of the fort, later extending beyond the defences, and continuing to be occupied into the late Roman period (ibid).

Ground survey, supplemented by air photography, has shown that Woolbury developed at a junction of pre-existing linear ditches associated with an extensive field system (Cunliffe and Poole 2000a; Eagles 1989; Palmer 1984) to the north and south-east. It is highly likely that the southern side of the defences are actually constructed over an existing linear ditch that is set back from, but ran parallel to, the edge of the north-west-facing escarpment. This feature can be seen on air photographs as a double ditch to the north-east of the hillfort and still survives as an earthwork by the south-west corner, from where it continues as a single scarp for at least 700m across Stockbridge Down (Eagles 1989, fig 2). Close by the south-west corner of the hillfort is a junction with another linear ditch that can be traced in a south-easterly direction for at least 600m. This ditch marks the western limit of a block of fields that covers at least 1 sq km and may link to other fragmentary remains

Fig 2.30
Aerial photograph of Woolbury hillfort on Stockbridge Down, Hampshire showing the ploughed interior and adjacent plough-levelled field system (Copyright reserved Cambridge University Collection of Air Photographs, ANE 77, 1966).

visible on air photographs farther to the east. North of Woolbury, at the foot of the escarpment and beyond, another block of fields can be traced almost to the banks of the River Test (Palmer 1984).

On Stockbridge Down, beyond the areas of prehistoric cultivation bounded by the linear ditches, earlier activity is represented by 14 mounds, most of which are likely to be barrows of Early to Middle Bronze Age date (Eagles 1989). The Down has also produced an isolated Beaker burial and stray finds of Middle Bronze Age pottery and flints; settlement of the latter date in the immediate vicinity seems probable (ibid).

Other settlements of the 1st millennium BC in the immediate vicinity are relatively few in number. Across the River Test, some 2km west, is the Early to Middle Iron Age enclosed settlement on Meon Hill (Liddell 1933) and, 1km north of this, the Iron Age settlement and Roman villa at Houghton Down (Cunliffe and Poole 2000e). Some 3km to the south, Neal (1980) investigated a Middle to Late Iron Age settlement at Little Somborne and on Steepleton Hill, 1.5km west-south-west, a

Fig 2.31
Greyscale plot of the magnetometer data from Woolbury in relation to the plan of the partially removed hillfort earthworks.

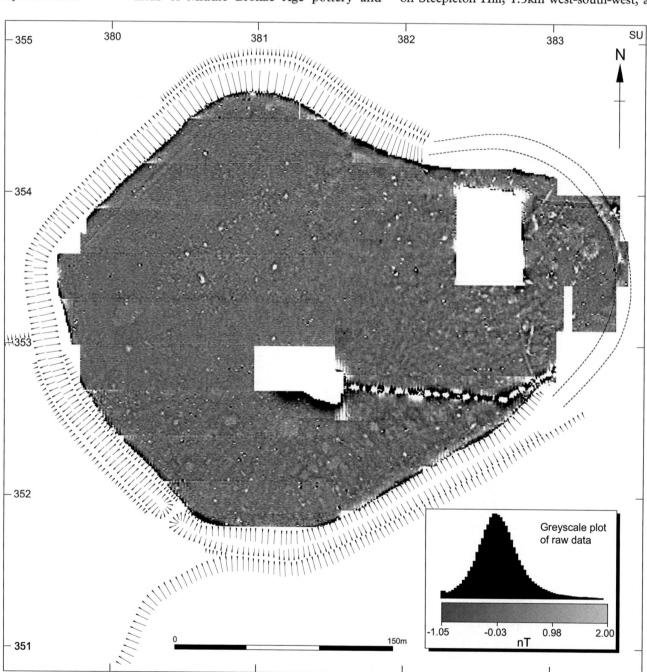

78

large, bivallate, enclosure of Suddern Farm type is known from parchmarks, but is as yet undated (Cunliffe 2000, 23–4).

Magnetometer survey (Figs 2.31–2.32)

Magnetometer survey was first employed at Woolbury in support of the excavations carried out by the Danebury Environs Project in the eastern half of the hillfort in 1989

(Cunliffe and Poole 2000a). The initial coverage concentrated on exploring this zone of the hillfort in order to provide advance information on the distribution of archaeological features in the area selected for excavation and the location of the ploughed-out eastern section of the hillfort rampart. At this stage resources were not available to extend the survey across the whole of the

Fig 2.32
Interpretation of the magnetometer data from Woolbury.

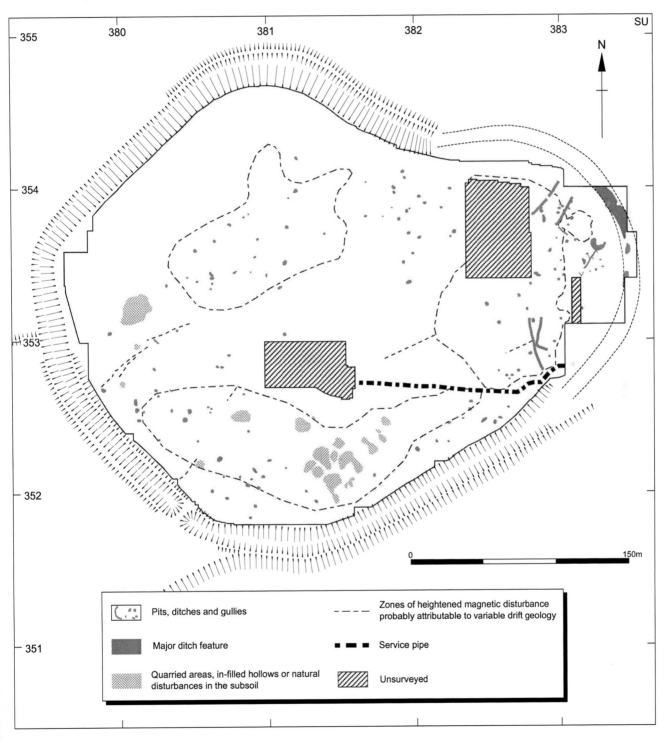

Pits, ditches and gullies

Major ditch feature

Quarried areas, in-filled hollows or natural disturbances in the subsoil

Zones of heightened magnetic disturbance probably attributable to variable drift geology

Service pipe

Unsurveyed

0   150m

hillfort interior, but the initial results from the eastern half provided a sufficient sample of the internal area to enable the overall character of the archaeological activity within the hillfort to be reliably predicted (Payne 2000b). After a six-year gap the magnetometer survey of the hillfort was finally completed in 1997 by the Wessex Hillforts Survey.

Observation of the completed survey shows that the excavated area at the eastern extremity of the fort contains a greater complexity of archaeological activity than the remainder of the enclosed area and is untypical of the general low level of internal activity at Woolbury. Throughout the majority of the survey the only anomalies present are occasional positive anomalies indicative of isolated pits. Some clustering of pits occurs in the middle of the northern half of the fort repeating a trend seen at other hillforts with a relatively low level of internal activity such as Uffington Castle (Oxfordshire), Perborough Castle (Berkshire) and Beacon Hill (Hampshire), where greater concentrations of pits occur in discrete areas.

On the evidence of excavation, the pits at Woolbury are probably of Early to Middle Iron Age date. Four out of a total of five Middle Iron Age pits uncovered in the 1989 excavation were previously detected in the magnetometer survey and as the discrete anomalies in the rest of the fort are similar to the anomalies from the excavated pits, there is a high probability that they represent other occurrences of this type of feature. The very low density of pit-type anomalies mapped across the interior of Woolbury confirms the impression gained from the more limited sample excavation that contemporary use of the hillfort was only sporadic or of limited duration or intensity.

There is a considerably higher density of archaeological activity in the eastern sector of the hillfort than in other areas, as evidenced by several linear-positive magnetic anomalies indicative of ditches. These appear to be absent elsewhere in the hillfort and it is now known from excavation that they correspond to a phase of Late Iron Age and Roman re-use of the site after the hillfort had fallen in to disrepair, when a settlement was established in the eastern part of the old hillfort extending for an undefined distance outside the hillfort ditch. Excavation by the Danebury Environs Programme in 1989, although limited in extent, has shown that the settlement area was divided by small ditches into a number of enclosures or paddocks (Cunliffe and Poole 2000a). More linear features, which probably belong to this same phase of occupation, are visible in the magnetometer survey, indicating that activity in this period spread south of the excavated area but was concentrated in a relatively confined area in the eastern end of the site. The Late Iron Age–Roman activity does not appear to extend to the western parts of the hillfort, which might have been preserved for agricultural use by this time (Cunliffe and Poole 2000a). In addition to the ditched enclosures, other features belonging to the later phase detected by the magnetometer survey (as positive anomalies) included a Roman period pit (F10) and a quarry hollow (F13) within one of the enclosures.

The line of the missing eastern section of the hillfort defences was mapped by the magnetometer survey as a broad shallow positive anomaly. There is a gap in this anomaly at the extreme eastern limit of the magnetometer coverage suggesting the presence of an entrance but the survey coverage is insufficient to be certain of the continuation of the ploughed out ditch to the south. The rampart seems to have been obliterated and the ditch filled in during the phase of secondary reoccupation of the site in the Roman period.

Some of the weaker large and irregular positive anomalies that occur in the western, south-western and southern areas of the hillfort are best interpreted as geological variations or perhaps evidence of quarrying of unknown date. Some of these anomalies also show as patches of darker soil on aerial photographs (Fig 2.30). A series of trial trenches excavated across the hilltop in 1989 demonstrated that the site is only partially covered by deposits of clay-with-flints and that the composition of this is very varied. This could easily account for some of the more irregular anomalous areas in the survey.

Conclusions

The magnetometer survey results fully support the conclusions of the Danebury Environs Project that Woolbury probably never became a major settlement focus and only underwent a low level of use in comparison to Danebury following its construction in the 5th century BC. The chronology and development of the site in relation to Danebury is discussed fully in Chapter 1 (pp 10–14).

Oxfordshire

Alfred's Castle: Ashbury; NGR SU 277 822

Summary

Date of survey:
12 to 13 August 1996.
Landuse at time of survey:
Rough grassland (mown prior to survey).
Geology:
Coombe Deposits (Pleistocene chalky drift) over Cretaceous Middle Chalk.
Soil Association:
511f – Coombe 1 – well drained calcareous fine silty soils, deep in valley bottoms, shallow to chalk on valley sides in places.
Approximate area enclosed:
Interior area of 1.2 hectares (c 2.75 acres).
Planform:
A small earthwork enclosure of approximately hexagonal shape situated at the southern end of a much larger, now plough-flattened, elongated ditched enclosure.
Form of ramparts:
A single internal bank formed of six relatively straight sections fronted by a ditch (3m deep with a V-shaped profile and narrow flat-bottom where excavated) clearly visible on the south, east and west, but less distinct on the north. The ramparts were constructed from blocks of the local sarsen stone augmented by chalk, probably in several phases.
Entrance features:
There are three breaks through the defences, two are opposed to one another on the south-east and north-west sides of the earthwork and another gap is present in the centre of the north-east section of the defences.
Previous finds:
Surface pottery collected from within the enclosure includes fabrics of Iron Age and Romano-British date. The larger ploughed-out enclosure is associated with later Iron Age pottery (source : Oxfordshire SMR).
Previous recorded excavation:
Excavations were carried out at Alfred's Castle by the Hillforts of The Ridgeway Project between 1998 and 2000. These were aimed at determining the form and development of the earthwork defences defining the fort, the dating of the entrances relative to the construction of the defences and the character and chronology of any internal occupation.
Scheduled Ancient Monument:
English Heritage scheduled monument number 28163, formerly Berkshire 89 and Oxfordshire 203.
County SMR No.:
733.
Project site code:
WHSP Site 3.

Morphology and setting

Alfred's Castle (Fig 2.33) differs from the other enclosures in the so-called 'Ridgeway grouping' of hillforts not only in terms of size but also because of its position in the landscape. The majority of the other hillforts in the Lambourn and Marlborough Downs area occupy sites on the edge of the chalk escarpment (or in the case of Hardwell Camp on the side of the escarpment) facing north across the lower lying Vale of the White Horse and the Thames Valley (Fig 1.17, sites 2–8). Alfred's Castle is situated some way to the south in a more central downland position and, unlike its neighbours on the Ridgeway to the north, does not occupy a readily defensible hilltop or scarp edge location. The site sits in a well-defined block of downland forming a shallow bowl bordered by higher ground east and south and the main chalk escarpment slope farther north. Alfred's Castle is an anomaly in the regional distribution of hillforts not just because of its topographical situation. The visible earthwork defences, although of hillfort proportions, enclose a relatively insignificant area of approximately 1.2ha, particularly when compared with the larger neighbouring sites of Segsbury (enclosing 12ha) and, Uffington on a slightly smaller scale, (enclosing 3.3ha). Furthermore, cropmark evidence shows Alfred's Castle located within a wider landscape, and given this apparent complexity, the term hillfort seems not an entirely adequate description for this site.

Fig 2.33
Aerial view of the small fort of Alfred's Castle from the west with the National Trust property of Ashdown House visible in the background (NMRC, NMR 15073/32, SU 2782/17, 1993).

The earthwork enclosure and ramparts that form Alfred's Castle date from the Early Iron Age, but excavations within the enclosure have revealed a longer history of settlement on the site. The earliest features date to the Late Bronze Age, then the main enclosure was constructed in the Early Iron Age, with evidence of later occupation in the form of a small late 1st to late 3rd century AD villa building. This marked the end of occupation on the site.

Evidence from aerial photographs indicates that Alfred's Castle is located on the edge of a more complex archaeological landscape than the earthwork evidence implies. Alfred's Castle itself is situated within the southern end of an earlier elongated ditched enclosure visible only as a cropmark. This enclosure lies on the eastern edge and forms part of a system of large single ditched enclosures or fields that occupy the natural bowl described above. The cropmark remains of at least nine of these irregular ditched enclosures were traced over an area of approximately 3 sq km centred on SU 2650 8280.

These enclosure ditches have their origins in the Late Bronze Age with two of the ditches appearing to be aligned on existing Early Bronze Age round barrows, one respecting the barrow and the other cutting through. There is evidence that these ditches were being used well into the Late Iron Age–Romano-British period, allowed to partly silt up and then recut along the same course at a later date in the Iron Age. In their final phase they were incorporated into part of a system of villa estates identified in this area.

These villa estates have large field systems associated with them, and where the ground rises sharply to the east of Alfred's Castle there are extensive remains of small embanked co-axial field systems. These differ from the large ditch defined fields described earlier and post-date the 'hillfort' phase of Alfred's Castle.

Alfred's Castle, therefore, appears to occupy a focal point in a landscape already divided up by linear boundaries and earlier field systems, and these features seem to have influenced the location of the site more than topographical or defensive considerations. Nearby Weathercock Hill and Tower Hill have both previously produced evidence of Late Bronze Age settlement (Bowden *et al* 1993, Miles *et al* 2003) and there may be a link between this activity and the location of Alfred's Castle.

Survey and excavation (Figs 2.34–2.36)

Background

Alfred's Castle was selected for inclusion in the Wessex Hillforts Survey Project on three major grounds. Firstly, although the defensive earthwork at Alfred's Castle is of hillfort sized proportions, the area enclosed is only ~1.2ha (2.75 acres). The site was included in the overall sample in order to help achieve a balanced sample of different recognised hillfort types and inclusion of examples of smaller hillforts where available was important for meeting this objective. Secondly, Alfred's Castle provided a suitable example of a hillfort interior under stable grassland containing the possiblity of well preserved archaeological features undisturbed by ploughing.

The topography of the interior of Alfred's Castle suggests that it has never been ploughed in historical times, the whole of the site being covered with humps and hollows suggesting the presence of largely undisturbed buried structural features (Fig 2.36). The site was therefore also included in the project to balance the number of surveyed hillfort sites with surviving earthwork remains in the interior with less well preserved sites under arable cultivation. Thirdly, Alfred's Castle is part of wider grouping of hillfort sites distributed across the North Berkshire Downs often termed the 'Ridgeway Hillforts', which are the subject of wider study (Miles *et al* 2003; Lock and Gosden 1997a, 1997b, 1998, 2000; Gosden and Lock 1999, 2001, and 2003). The majority of the hillforts in this well defined group (*see* Fig 1.17) were included in the sample studied by the Wessex Hillfort Survey in order to satisfy the aim of investigating identifiable groupings of hillforts.

The Ridgeway forts form the most obvious group on the overall distribution map of sites investigated by the project for undertaking such a study. Because of the considerable variation in size and form exhibited by the Ridgeway hillforts it was important to explore the relative differences or similarities between the internal characteristics of the sites as a group. It was hoped that by revealing the nature of the internal activity at each hillfort the magnetometer surveys would allow the project to study relationships between the varying surface characteristics of the individual hillforts and possible differences of function or occupation histories. Questions that might be answered by the availability of such data include:

- Do hillforts with more elaborate defences and entrances exhibit greater internal complexity indicative of a lengthy sequence or several episodes of occupation?
- Does the size of the enclosed area bear any relation to the nature of the internal activity?

Survey and excavation (1996 and 1998–2000)

Magnetometer and topographical surveys of the internal area of Alfred's Castle were carried out for the Wessex Hillforts Survey in 1996. These were followed, between 1998 and 2000, by a campaign of targeted excavation forming part of the Hillforts of the Ridgeway Project, undertaken by Oxford University (Gosden and Lock 1999; Lock and Gosden 2000). Although limited in scale by the conditions of Scheduled Monument Consent (SMC) these excavations attempted to determine the form and developmental sequence of the rampart and ditch enclosing Alfred's Castle and the character and chronology of any internal occupation of the site. Additional excavations were carried out in the immediate environs of the castle earth-

work to investigate other possible associated earthwork features including linear ditches and the larger plough-flattened elongated ditched enclosure extending to the north.

The magnetometer survey of Alfred's Castle took place two years in advance of the excavations and because of the complexity of the archaeological deposits – now known to be present – the magnetometer data was initially difficult to interpret in any detail other than to say that it suggested intense activity. The data is similar to that obtained from Barbury Castle and Danebury in this respect (*see below*). The availability of the excavation record subsequently enabled the geophysical data to be considerably better understood and a more refined level of interpretation can now be advanced than was initially possible. This process demonstrates the value of following up initial geophysical exploration of the internal area of hillforts with more limited excavation of selective areas (for other examples *see* Payne 2000a). Initial geophysical survey lessens the danger of opening up unproductive trenches particularly when time, resources and permission for

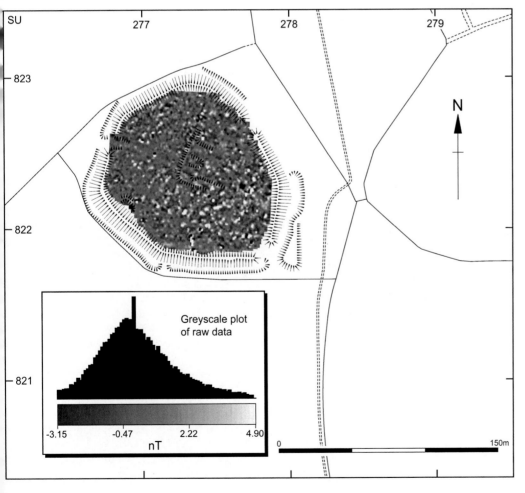

Fig 2.34
Greyscale plot of the magnetometer data from Alfred's Castle shown in relation to the plan of the hillfort earthworks.

Fig 2.35
Interpretation of the
magnetometer data from
Alfred's Castle.

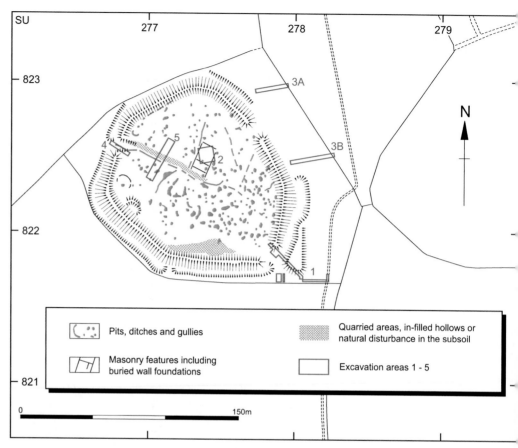

Pits, ditches and gullies

Masonry features including
buried wall foundations

Quarried areas, in-filled hollows or
natural disturbance in the subsoil

Excavation areas 1 - 5

0   150m

excavation are limited. Where only limited trenches are allowed, in order to minimise disturbance to a protected site, their contents are interpretable in a wider context with the aid of geophysical evidence. Geophysical survey can also help predict the complexity of the archaeological evidence that is likely to be encountered in different areas of the site, enabling appropriate sampling strategies to be devised and adequate resources to be allocated to the excavation process. In turn the excavation refines and extends the limited interpretation that is possible based on the geophysical data alone. The mutual effectiveness of such a combined approach cannot be over-emphasised.

Analytical earthwork survey would also have been a worthwhile approach prior to excavation in the case of Alfred's Castle given the well-preserved topographical detail in the interior. This would probably have provided a greater understanding of the internal earthworks than was subsequently provided using the simple height mapping methods of contour survey and digital terrain modelling.

The results of the 1996 magnetometer survey were different in character to those from many of the other hillforts examined

during the Wessex Hillforts Survey but were difficult to interpret with confidence and required testing by excavation. The Hillforts of the Ridgeway Project excavations described below fortunately provided the opportunity for this to take place.

The interior of Alfred's Castle is characterised by a generally disturbed magnetic response, suggesting intensive activity and widespread ground disturbance in the past but with little coherent pattern. Following excavation, this is now understood to be a reflection of the well preserved deep stratigraphy and succession of features belonging to several phases of occupation from the Bronze Age to the Roman period. Evidence of plentiful pits uncovered during excavation is fully supported by the magnetometer data which suggests that these are densely and widely distributed throughout the interior of the enclosure. Anomalous activity is most pronounced towards the south-eastern side of the site indicating that the late prehistoric occupation was particularly concentrated within this area (again this is compatible with excavation evidence from Trench 1; *see below* and Fig 2.35).

Linear anomalies running into the enclosure from what is now known to be an original entrance on the north-west towards the site of the Roman building, are interpreted as a roadway worn into the surface of the chalk from prolonged use and subsequently silted following abandonment of the site. This feature remains uncorroborated by excavation but is clearly visible as a topographical feature – a linear depression – in the digital terrain model (Fig 2.36). Other smaller linear and circular magnetic anomalies are probably indicative of gully features that might have surrounded former timber structures.

The rectangular Roman masonry building, now known from excavation, is vaguely visible as a series of extremely weakly resolved parallel negative magnetic anomalies (located immediately north of the centre of the enclosed area). The geophysical evidence suggests overall dimensions of approximately 12m wide by 25m long, an estimate that accords reasonably well with the actual recorded dimensions of the building (12.6m × 22.5m) after it was fully revealed by the third season of excavation in 2000. The poor definition of this major Roman masonry structure in the magnetometer data is understandable owing to the amount of ferrous metal and collapsed building material on the site.

Discussion

The results of the magnetometer survey at Alfred's Castle contrast with those obtained from the other small hillfort included in the study at Oliver's Camp (*see* pp 128–130). With the exception of pronounced anomalies derived from modern structures, the remainder of Oliver's Camp appears devoid of internal occupation contemporary with the hillfort defences. The magnetic response found at Oliver's Castle is replaced at Alfred's Castle by a much more disturbed response arising from the numerous archaeological features of Early Iron Age and Roman origin that are now known from excavation to be present. These results indicate that, other than sharing a probable Late Bronze Age or very Early Iron Age origin, the two sites seem to have undergone very different subsequent occupation histories, highlighting the danger of placing such sites into neat categories through the use of terminology such as 'small hillforts'. A closer parallel to Alfred's Castle might be the small hillfort at Lidbury Camp located near the north-east edge of Salisbury Plain where evidence was uncovered of a high density of storage pits in a limited area excavation (Cunnington and Cunnington 1917).

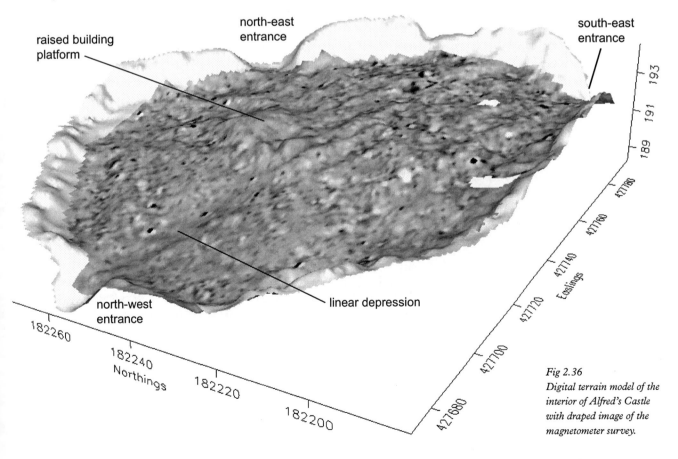

Fig 2.36
Digital terrain model of the interior of Alfred's Castle with draped image of the magnetometer survey.

The high density of anomalous magnetic activity recorded at Alfred's Castle is paralleled by the magnetic results obtained from some larger and more complex chalkland hillforts such as Barbury Castle, Danebury and Maiden Castle. This trend would seem to indicate that there is a distinctly identifiable, or even diagnostic, geophysical signature associated with chalkland hillforts containing a high density of internal occupation activity and a rich artefact assemblage. Because of the richness of the archaeological deposits these sites contain, they stand out as having high potential for socio-economic reconstruction as proved by the wide range of archaeological materials recovered from Alfred's Castle. The ability of magnetometer survey to predict effectively the presence of such important archaeological deposits is truly a valuable aid for ensuring the future safe-guarding of such sites, but also raises questions of how to proceed with researching the more numerous emptier hillforts.

Excavations in 1998–9 – comprising Trenches 1 and 4 (Fig 2.35) – were positioned to investigate possible entrances cut through the south-eastern and north-western sides of the earthwork in an attempt to determine if these were part of the original design of the fort. (This section is based on interim reports and information kindly supplied by Dr Gary Lock.)

Trench 2 (a 10m × 10m square) was positioned to examine a prominent raised platform (clearly visible as a rectilinear topographical feature in the digital terrain model; see Fig 2.36) suggestive of a probable buried building situated towards the middle of the fort interior. The raised area also coincided with a series of weakly defined low magnetic gradient anomalies that suggested the presence of a rectangular pattern of buried masonry walls of flint or chalk construction and therefore reduced magnetic susceptibility to the surrounding soil matrix. Trench 2 was subsequently extended in 2000 by a series of limited exploratory trenches (11–19) to trace the full extent of the building verified by the initial season of excavation.

Another trench (Trench 5) was opened to provide a sample of the archaeological deposits in the north-western sector of the fort interior. The magnetometer and topographical surveys show a linear feature in this area running from the north-western break in the defences to the southern edge of the building mound investigated in Trench 2. This feature is interpreted as a possible long-lived roadway or hollow-way providing access via the original north-west entrance into the fort.

Trenches 3, 6 and 8 were positioned to investigate the large outer ditched enclosure immediately north of the smaller upstanding earthwork of Alfred's Castle. This feature, which was identified by aerial photography, was not included in the magnetometer survey carried out in 1996.

Other trenches (10, 20, 21 and 23) were opened in 2000 to examine earlier ditch systems in the area around Alfred's Castle in order to determine their relationship to the hillfort.

The results of these excavations can be summarised as follows:

i) The defences and entrances: The 1999 season of excavations revealed that the eastern rampart of Alfred's Castle is composed of large sarsen blocks laid in four or five approximate rows parallel with the ditch to give a width of approximately 1.5m. Only the lowest one or two courses remain and behind these is an area of compacted chalk with a possible rear revetting slot and internal structural postholes. These latter features might comprise a second phase during which the rampart was widened. It is immediately noticeable that the rampart is very different in character to nearby Uffington (a 'classic' sequence of box rampart replaced by a dump rampart (Miles and Palmer 1995; Miles et al 2003)), Liddington (similarly, Hirst and Rahtz 1996), and Segsbury (a complex sequence of palisades with ultimate dump rampart (Lock and Gosden 1998)). The picture that has emerged from these combined excavations highlights the diversity within a relatively localised group of sites of rampart construction techniques and development of hillfort defences instead of a common regional style or sequence.

The main hillfort ditch at Alfred's Castle was cut into bedrock chalk, to a depth of 3m with a V-shaped profile and a narrow flat bottom. The stratigraphy in Trench 1 is complex, indicating a sequence of natural and artificial fill events. Sarsen stone is present in the bottom of the ditch and throughout the lower half of the fill and presumably represents material fallen from the rampart above, either as a product of natural decay or intentional destruction. It appears that the destruction of the rampart began when the ditch was empty and continued slowly over a long period of time (perhaps suggesting an initial act of deliberate slighting followed by a long period of gradual decay). A concentration of sarsen in the upper fill of the ditch in Trench 1, associated with Romano-British material, is linked to the filling of the ditch in this area to create a new entrance through the south-west section of the Iron Age defensive circuit in the Roman period (*see below*). A late 1st to early 2nd century AD date is suggested for this episode.

A second ditch section in Trench 3b (60m north of the Trench 1 section) produced a ditch similar in profile but with a quite different infill. This emphasises the dangers of relying on a single section through the defences for understanding the overall sequence.

Several pieces of evidence point to the south-eastern entrance not being an original prehistoric entrance, but a break through the rampart established during Romano-British times and probably associated with the stone building in the centre of the enclosure. The building does in fact seem to be oriented south-east so that this entrance would form the main access to it. Evidence from a small test pit (Trench 1B) indicated that the main pre-Roman enclosure ditch was originally continuous around the south-eastern corner of the enclosure and the south-eastern entrance was a later adaptation. A possible Late Bronze Age (naturally silted) ditch was encountered in Trench 1 underlying the hillfort defences inside the south-east entrance

Trench 4 examined the north-west entrance of Alfred's Castle and uncovered evidence for the presence here of an original prehistoric entrance contemporary with the construction of the hillfort earthworks. It was found that the main enclosure ditch does not continue across the break in the rampart and the presence of an original entrance is further supported by the ramparts terminating in rounded ends and the presence of well defined ditch terminals. An additional point of interest was that the structure of the rampart in Trench 4 varied considerably from the structure revealed in a comparable section through the defences in Trench 1 on the opposite side of the enclosure. In Trench 4 the sequence of the rampart was similarly of two phases, the initial sarsen boulder faced rampart was enlarged by the addition of a substantial chalk bank at the front and revetting posts at the rear unlike the rampart on the east which was widened by the addition of chalk at the back. This means that the rampart as a whole has a complex development, with different sections showing distinct variation in construction style. This unconformity suggests the main rampart of Alfred's Castle as it exists today was not constructed as a single unit and although it has only one major phase of construction it shows evidence of several alterations over time.

ii) The interior: The main excavation in the interior (Trench 2 measuring 10m × 10m) was sited over the location of what turned out to be a Romano-British building surviving as a prominent surface feature near the centre of the site (Fig 2.36). The building was underlain by prehistoric layers, dating to the Iron Age. There were some 15 pits or large post-holes dating to the Early to Middle Iron Age in a band running from the north-west corner through the centre of the site. The pit assemblages included ashy deposits with carbonised material, pottery, bone (including human remains), bone tools, bronze items, loom weights and spindle whorls.

The Romano-British building (*see* Gosden and Lock 2003) overlying these features is of rectilinear plan with masonry walls running diagonally through the excavated area south-west to north-east and south-east to north-west as hinted at by the weak linear low magnetic gradient anomalies recorded in the magnetometer survey. The most northern and western of the walls revealed (2003 and 2018) were of similar thickness and represent the outer walls of the building. They are composed of chalk blocks bonded with mortar and placed on two courses of sarsens as foundations. The outer west wall (2003) survives to a maximum height of 1m. Other internal walls running off 2003 at right angles define a number of internal divisions or rooms and show evidence of being constructed in several phases.

Because the walls are composed of chalk blocks and sarsen they would be unlikely to show much geophysical contrast. Nevertheless, very faint signs of their presence in the form of extremely weak low magnetic gradient anomalies are recognisable in the magnetometer data. Large numbers of nails and roof-tiles in the destruction layers from the collapse of the building no doubt contributed to the poor definition of the anomalies from the buried walls. Coins in the destruction layers were late 3rd century AD and there was a rich array of Roman finds in the lower destruction levels/floor deposits (including glass, coins, and fine pottery of the 2nd–late 3rd/4th centuries AD).

A curvilinear feature (2006), uncovered during excavation in 1999 west of the Roman building, is thought to be a section of a round-house gully (otherwise destroyed) or a drain connected with the Romano-British building. This links with magnetic evidence from elsewhere on the site for possible curvilinear gullies.

Trench 5 was located to sample the deposits in an area of the enclosure where the surface topography suggested that masonry building remains were absent. It contained a spread of Iron Age pits similar in morphology and fill to those in Trench 2. The presence of intercutting pits in Trench 5 is consistent with the high density of anomalous magnetic activity recorded throughout the hillfort interior by the magnetometer. Remnants of poorly preserved sarsen walling revealed at the northern end of the trench may represent the remains of out-buildings at the rear of the main Romano-British building to the east. At the southern end of the trench part of the circuit of a double stake-wall round house was excavated. It was approximately 10m in diameter and the wall line was cut by at least one later pit. Ephemeral features such as this are unlikely to be detectable by geophysical means.

iii) The overall sequence: The main elements of the site recorded by the excavations consist of a substantial masonry constructed Romano-British building occupying the central northern part of the enclosure. This structure is underlain by prehistoric features dating to the Early to Middle Iron Ages including pits, postholes and a curvilinear gully, for some of which there are good indications in the magnetometer data. The excavated pits were exceptionally rich in finds. The Iron Age features indicate that the site was one of considerable richness in terms of artefacts, many of which entered the pits as placed deposits.

The overall sequence of development has five major divisions (Gosden and Lock 2003):

1. Pre-dating the enclosure are two flat-bottomed linear ditches probably of Late Bronze Age origin.
2. The hillfort type defences of Alfred's Castle were probably constructed in the Early Iron Age, utilising the two earlier linear ditches where they joined.
3. The larger, now plough-flattened, outer enclosure is part of a pre-hillfort system of enclosures, its western ditch re-cutting one of the Late Bronze Age linears. The purpose and internal character of this enclosure is as yet unknown but it possibly represents one of several field enclosures.
4. In the late 1st or early 2nd century AD, the substantial stone building was erected inside the defences of Alfred's Castle facing a newly created entrance through the earlier ramparts to the south-east.
5. The building was destroyed in the late 3rd century AD and there is no evidence for further occupation or activity at the site.

Preliminary interpretation of the site, based on an initial assessment of the excavation findings, sees it developing from a Late Bronze Age landscape (Weathercock Hill, Tower Hill and linears (Bowden et al 1993; Miles et al 2003) slightly earlier than the hillfort sites that developed at Liddington to the west and Uffington to the east. The range and richness of the finds from Alfred's Castle distinguish it from the other excavated sites of a similar period in the area suggesting it was a site of significant importance in both the Early–Middle Iron Age and Roman periods. Dense magnetic activity recorded during the magnetometer survey in 1996 can now be seen as a pointer to this.

Note on the topographical survey

The surface evidence for the existence of well preserved archaeological features in the interior of Alfred's Castle led to the decision to conduct a topographical survey in addition to the magnetometer survey to produce a terrain model of the interior to complement the geophysical data (Fig 2.36). Both surveys were carried out in 1996 two years before the commencement of excavation.

The resulting digital terrain model (DTM) has clearly defined the building platform in the northern half of the site and the hollow-way running from the original Iron Age entrance on the north-west to the platform providing good correspondence with the geophysical results. Also indicated by the survey are a series of depressions immediately inside the rampart. These probably represent quarries used to obtain chalk to widen and heighten the original rampart structure as demonstrated by excavation. The uneven ground surface indicated by the terrain model in the eastern part of the site reflects the high density of Iron Age occupation features known to be present in this area.

Segsbury Camp or Letcombe Castle: Letcombe Regis; NGR SU 385 844.

Summary
Date of surveys:
5 to 9 August 1996 (earlier surveys 1-5/11/93 and 25-29/4/94).
Landuse at time of survey:
Sheep pasture/set-aside.
Geology:
Cretaceous Upper Chalk.
Soil Association:
343h – Andover 1 – shallow well drained calcareous silty soils over chalk on slopes and crests. Striped soil patterns locally.
Approximate area enclosed:
12 hectares (30 acres).
Planform:
Approximately oval composed of several straight lengths of rampart on the south and west but following a more rounded alignment on the north side reflecting the contours of the escarpment edge.
Form of ramparts:
Main internal bank fronted by a wide deep ditch around the whole circuit of the enclosure. A counterscarp bank or second outer rampart is present on the south possibly continuing around the west side but removed by ploughing and resuming again on the north-west side. The internal bank is out-turned at the point where it meets the eastern entrance gap.

Entrance features:
The original entrance on the east is flanked by out-turns of the rampart, that on the north now plough-flattened. There are gaps in the inner bank on the north and south sides, where it has been cut through by the modern surfaced road. It is possible that the southern gap was an original entrance. Another gap on the north-west, opposite the partially preserved counterscarp bank, does not appear to be original.
Previous finds:
Sherds referred to in the sources as 'Southern Second A' and 'Southern Second B' have been picked up on the site. Roman coins of Tetricus and Maximian are also recorded.
Previous recorded excavation:
Excavation in 1871 (by Dr T Phené for the Newbury Field Club) revealed a cist in the southern section of the hillfort rampart below a sarsen slab on the hillfort bank, known as the Altar Stone (depicted on some earlier OS maps). The cist was floored with flat stone slabs, walled with flints and contained fragments of human bone, flint scrapers, the remains of a possible shield-boss and part of an urn or drinking cup. The deposits were interpreted by Grinsell as a possible secondary Saxon burial. Modern small-scale excavations were carried out in the hillfort interior and through a section of the hillfort ramparts between 1996 and 1997 by Dr Gary Lock and Dr Chris Gosden of Oxford University (Lock and Gosden 1997(b), 1998).
Scheduled Ancient Monument:
Oxfordshire 209 (formerly Berkshire 30).
County SMR No.:
7200.
Project site code:
WHSP Site 2.

Morphology and setting

Segsbury (Fig 2.37) is a large, univallate enclosure sited on the edge of the north-facing escarpment of the Berkshire Downs at 210m OD enclosing 12ha (30 acres). The location gives extensive views across the Vale of the White Horse although to the east and west visibility is restricted to little more than 1.5km. Immediately south of the monument is the Ridgeway, a track whose antiquity is the subject of ongoing debate (Fowler 2000).
The circuit at Segsbury comprises an inner rampart, a ditch and a relatively substantial counterscarp that now only survives along the south side and for a short length around

89

the north-west arc. Both the interior and th
immediate environs of the site have suffere
from extensive ploughing in recent times.

The rampart is breached at four points o
the circuit. Of these, only that on the east ca
be considered to be of undoubted Iron Ag
date and has been tested by excavation (Loc
and Gosden 1998, 62; Lock *et al* 2005). Th
entrance also has a short, out-curving ditc
flanking the northern side of the approach,
feature first revealed by the magnetomete
survey. A breach on the north-west of the cir
cuit is clearly later in date and the counter
scarp at this point is continuous. Th
remaining two breaches carry a north–south
track that gives access to the foot of th

Fig 2.37
Aerial photograph of
Segsbury Camp (or
Letcombe Castle) looking
north showing excavation
by the Hillforts of the
Ridgeway Project in
Progress during 1996
(NMRC, NMR 15519/29,
SU 3884/49, 1996).

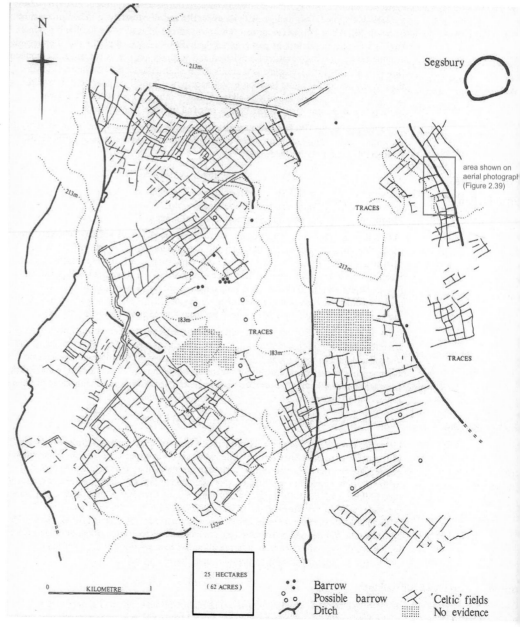

Fig 2.38
Plan of the extensive field
systems and linear boundary
works in the area south of
Segsbury hillfort (from
Richards 1978).

scarpment and the Vale of the White Horse rom The Ridgeway. Recent excavation of the outhern entrance has led to the suggestion hat it may be of Iron Age origin and the ack Roman. However the evidence is not onclusive (Lock and Gosden 1998, 60–2) nd clearly requires more work.

At a point on the west side of the circuit he earthwork evidence suggests the presnce of a blocked entrance. This is narked by a characteristic inward kink in he rampart and ditch of the type noted elsehere (cf Liddington Castle, Uffington Castle and Beacon Hill). It may be significant that outside the hillfort at this point here are cropmarks and geophysical anomalies possibly indicating settlement. In addition the magnetometer survey of the interior (*see below*) suggests a clear strip between this putative blocked entrance and the known east entrance.

Segsbury is approximately 2km west of the western known limit of the Grim's Ditch, a major linear feature that can be traced for a distance of approximately 17km along the top of the Berkshire Downs escarpment (Bradley and Richards 1978; Richards 1978; Ford 1982). South and south-west of Segsbury air photography has revealed a complex pattern of field systems and linear ditches. This covers at least 10 sq km and has been analysed in detail by a

Fig 2.39
Aerial photograph of part of the field system near Segsbury Camp (NMRC, NMR 2107/1170, SU 3783/3, 1982).

number of fieldworkers (Bradley and Richards 1978, fig 7.2; Fowler 1983). The pattern displays a complex series of relationships between fields, tracks and linear ditches (Figs 2.38 and 2.39). The plots show a series of roughly north–south aligned linear ditches, some respecting field boundaries, others apparently cutting across the field axes. None of the linears known to date can be seen to approach the hillfort circuit, the nearest example passing some 600m to the south-east. The entire system is bounded on the west by a 'terminal' linear feature, beyond which there are few if any convincing traces of fields. There are at least two ditched enclosures attached to the east side of this linear ditch, the northernmost being sited at a point where the main linear ditch bifurcates. Within the field blocks are a number of smaller rectilinear units that may be settlements, some appearing integral with the field system, with others clearly overlying it. In addition, recent aerial photography carried out by the National Mapping Programme (Bewley 2001; 2003, 133) has revealed 'banjos' apparently underlying elements of the field system.

Survey and excavation (Figs 2.40 and 2.41)

Magnetometer coverage of the interior of Segsbury Camp began in 1993 when the former Ancient Monuments Laboratory (AML) of English Heritage surveyed a 120m-wide trial transect running east–west through the centre of the interior (Payne 1993b). The original purpose of the geophysical investigation was to support the future management of the site following its conversion from arable to grass under a Countryside Stewardship management scheme. The decision to undertake an initial trial survey was influenced by the large area enclosed by the hillfort. With an internal area of 12ha, Segsbury is by far the largest of the hillforts in the Ridgeway grouping. The initial survey revealed that numerous archaeological features were present within the hillfort, including ring-gullies, pits and possible hearths. Although the overall density of features was not particularly high, several discrete areas of the fort showed a much higher concentration of pits and ring-gullies separated by areas with a lower density of archaeological features.

After further magnetometer survey was carried out at Segsbury by the AML in 1995, completion of the coverage of the site fell to the Wessex Hillforts Survey in 1996.

As well as filling in the remaining un-surveyed area of the interior, additional survey was undertaken to explore an external area adjacent to the main eastern entrance of the hillfort and a possible enclosure feature revealed as a soilmark on aerial photographs in the field immediately west of the site (NGR coordinates SU 382843). The reasons for continuing the previous non-intrusive survey work at Segsbury as part of the Wessex Hillforts Survey were:

- the group importance of the site,
- the linkage of the survey with a programme of sample excavation by the Hillforts of the Ridgeway Project (Lock and Gosden 1997b, 1998) and
- the continuing need to feed the results into improved management and presentation of the site.

Magnetometer Survey 1993–6

i) The hillfort interior. The completed magnetometer coverage inside the hillfort (Figs 2.40, 2.41) shows the greatest density of archaeological anomalies in the area just east of the centre of the enclosed area. Here there are up to six circular gullies and a high concentration of pits and other occupation features north of a wide linear zone of decreased magnetic activity, suggesting the presence of a roadway aligned on the east entrance. A considerable amount of activity is also present between this tentative road line and the southern rampart, with a particularly dense cluster of activity (two round gullies and a zone of up to 40 pits) in the main area later investigated by excavation (Trench 1; see below and Fig 2.41). Many more circular gully structures were partially resolved by the magnetometer survey and yet more were so weakly resolved as to be at the margins of visibility. In general they appear to be associated with pit clusters and are set well back into the hillfort interior – few if any occupy peripheral locations near the enclosing earthworks. Evidence of occupation activity appears to decrease considerably towards the northern and western sides of the hillfort. In these areas pits are less frequent and scattered rather than concentrated in clusters. Circular gullies are also absent.

The circular gully structures at Segsbury average around 12m in diameter but in the south-east sector of the camp there is a slightly more irregular example

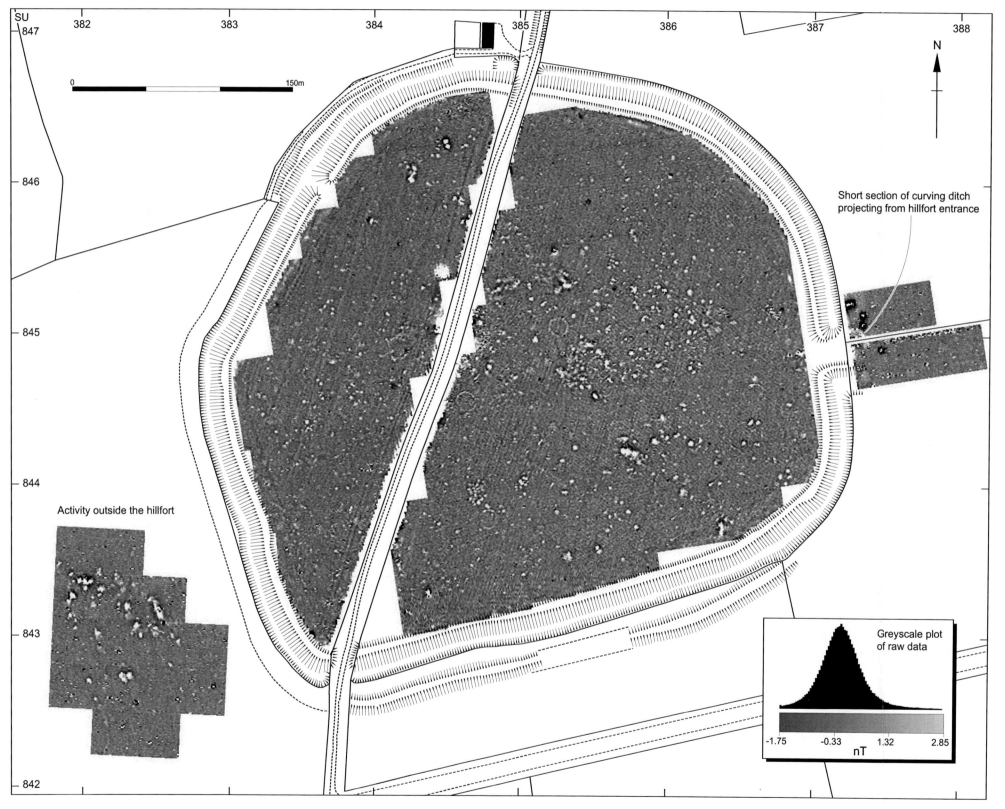

SU
847

382   383   384   385   386   387   388

846

0 ⟶ 150m

845

844

843

842

Activity outside the hillfort

Short section of curving ditch
projecting from hillfort entrance

Fig 2.40
*Greyscale plot of the
magnetometer data from
Segsbury Camp (Letcombe
Castle) in relation to the
plan of the hillfort earthworks.*

N

Greyscale plot
of raw data

-1.75   -0.33   1.32   2.85
nT

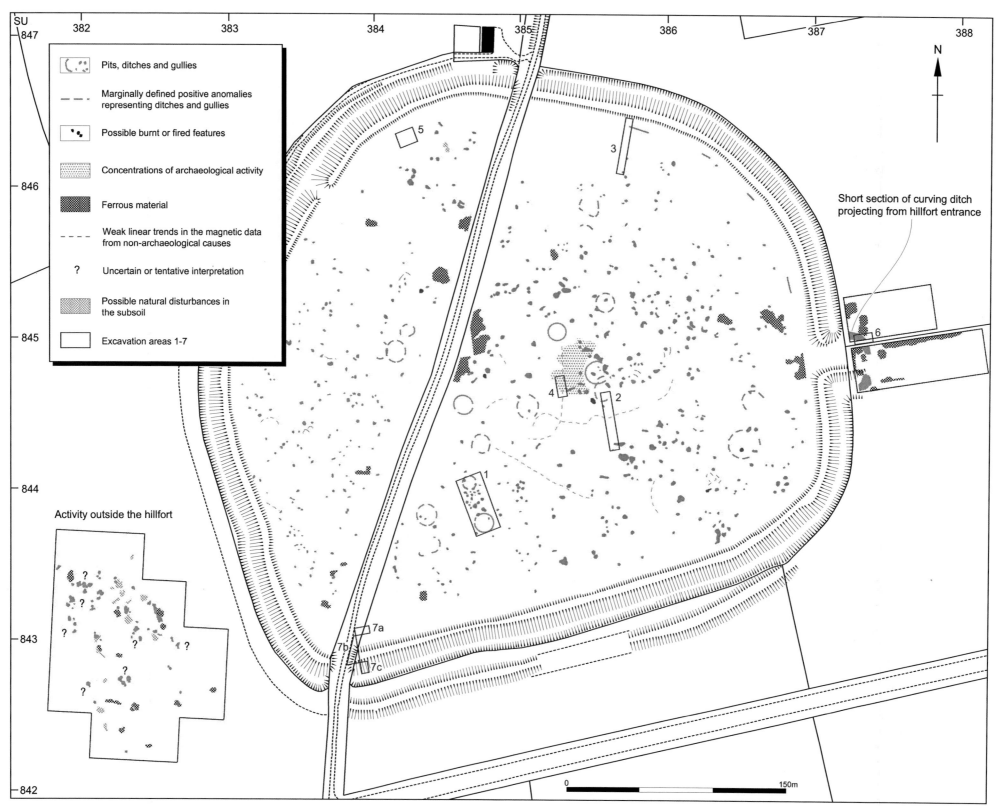

SU
847

382   383   384   385   386   387   388

N

846

Pits, ditches and gullies

Marginally defined positive anomalies
representing ditches and gullies

Possible burnt or fired features

Concentrations of archaeological activity

Ferrous material

845

Weak linear trends in the magnetic data
from non-archaeological causes

? Uncertain or tentative interpretation

Possible natural disturbances in
the subsoil

Excavation areas 1-7

Short section of curving ditch
projecting from hillfort entrance

844

Activity outside the hillfort

843

842

0   150m

Fig 2.41
Interpretation of the
magnetometer data from
Segsbury.

of 20m diameter. The latter might be more suitably interpreted as a small enclosure rather than as a gully demarcating a standing structure. By comparison the largest ring gullies at Beacon Hill are in the order of 14m in diameter, 13–16m in diameter at Oldbury and the single distinct example located within Liddington is 18m in diameter. A few possible, but poorly-defined examples at Norsebury range from 10–13m in diameter. Several anomalies; possibly representing burnt or fired features such as hearths or ovens, occur in the vicinity of the large 20m diameter ring in the south-east part of the hillfort and may be associated with this feature.

At Segsbury pits are most concentrated in the highest central area of the fort, comparable to the early period layout of Danebury (Cunliffe 1995) and the distribution of pits mapped by magnetometry at St Catherine's Hill. The circular structures at Segsbury tend to avoid the peripheral zone of the enclosure, unlike the situation at Danebury. At Segsbury the highest pit densities are clearly associated with the distribution of round structures while intervening areas lacking round structures, have a much lower density of pits. Similar patterns are apparent at the hillforts of Beacon Hill, Liddington Castle and Oldbury Castle discussed elsewhere in this chapter.

A broken curvilinear feature or series of short linear features was mapped around the northern and eastern sides of the fort interior immediately inside the line of, and concentric with, the bank of the main inner rampart. A trench was excavated over one section of the anomaly just inside the rampart and at the base of the slope in the northern part of the hillfort (Trench 3; *see* section on excavation below). This revealed a ditch sealed by a layer of tumbled chalk blocks from the later rampart above. The fill of the ditch included a dark organic layer with high concentrations of bone and pottery. This material had probably accumulated in the ditch as a result of down-slope movement of soil from the interior of the hillfort. The ditch terminated in the middle of the excavated area indicating a possible entrance gap or that the ditch is discontinuous, as suggested by the magnetic survey data. Pottery from the ditch suggests a Late Bronze Age or earliest Iron Age date.

The relationship of the excavated ditch in Trench 3 (and the more extensive related magnetic anomalies) to the main hillfort rampart remains to be fully understood. Several of the hillforts in the Ridgeway grouping are preceded by earlier enclosures of Late Bronze Age or earliest Iron Age date (for example Rams Hill and Liddington Castle). Although the ditch feature underlying the later hillfort rampart in Trench 3 at Segsbury could possibly represent a similar earlier phase of enclosure of the site, a comparable anomaly does not appear to be present around the southern half of the defensive circuit. It is possible that it could be concealed beneath the main hillfort rampart in these areas, except that no evidence was found for it in Trench 7a (*see below*). It may also have been removed by the subsequent construction of the enlarged (Phase 3) hillfort ditch in these areas (*see* p 96). Rather than being an earlier enclosure feature it could be a boundary feature such as a linear ditch partially built over by the hillfort rampart but not sharing the same layout as the whole defensive circuit. This might also explain the failure of the magnetometer survey to trace the feature around the full circuit of the hillfort.

ii) Anomalies at the eastern entrance. The additional magnetometer coverage undertaken outside the eastern entrance to the hillfort in 1996 revealed a broad but very weakly defined positive magnetic anomaly extending in a curve from the terminal of the hillfort ditch on the north side of the entrance to the south for a short distance before terminating. The anomaly represents the ditch of a now plough-flattened outwork screening the entrance to create an extended approach into the fort in a similar manner to the eastern entrance at Danebury. The magnetic response to the out-curving ditch is obscured, in part by ferrous anomalies caused by modern barbed wire fencing, but the presence of a wide, shallow, flat bottomed ditch extending outwards from the hillfort was confirmed at the location indicated by the magnetometer by excavation in 1997 (Trench 6). A slight eastward projection of the main hillfort ditch has also been detected by the magnetometer survey on the southern side of the entrance marking the southern side of the extended corridor approach into the hillfort.

iii) Anomalies of natural origin. During the excavation of Trench 3 near the northern side of the fort, a natural clay-filled pipe in the chalk, 3.5m in diameter was uncovered. This had previously produced a magnetic anomaly similar to those produced by Iron Age pits. The presence of such natural features in chalkland hillforts that geophysically can easily be confused with archaeological features has implications for the reliable interpretation of magnetometer data from Iron Age hillfort sites on chalk and needs to be borne in mind for future surveys. A more extreme response to such clay pockets was encountered in the case of a pair of pronounced positive magnetic anomalies in the northwest part of the hillfort observed after topsoil stripping but not investigated further by excavation. The presence of these geological anomalies has implications for the interpretation of the complex of magnetic anomalies mapped in the field west of Segsbury at NGR SU 382 843, previously interpreted on the basis of aerial photographic evidence as a possible pit alignment forming a rounded cornered enclosure (Oxfordshire SMR reference PRN 11027). The site was covered by an additional magnetometer survey in 1996 in order to test this interpretation further. Although the survey clearly mapped a complex of magnetic anomalies in the same location as the aerial photography, their form and magnitude is suggestive of a geological origin at least in part, in keeping with similar anomalies of recognised geological origin in the north-west sector of the hillfort. On this basis, the presence of an additional archaeological site west of the hillfort must be open to some uncertainty, but neither should it be dismissed without more investigation.

Excavation 1996–7

(This section is based on interim reports and information kindly supplied by Dr Gary Lock.)

Shortly after the completion of the geophysical survey in 1996, Oxford University initiated a follow-up programme of limited excavation at Segsbury as part of the Hillforts of the Ridgeway Project (Lock *et al* 2005: Fig 1.2). The newly available geophysical results were used to target the areas of excavation on a range of features of

potential archaeological interest identifie[d] within the hillfort. The aims of the excava[-] tions were to establish the character an[d] dating of the construction and occupation o[f] the hillfort and to verify and amplify th[e] interpretation of the magnetometer surve[y] results from the hillfort interior.

Trench 1, excavated from 1996–7, wa[s] the largest of the areas investigated inside th[e] hillfort with dimensions of 40m × 20m (Fi[g] 2.41). It contained the ring gully of a roun[d] structure 12m in diameter and a group o[f] some 40 pits immediately north of it. Thes[e] had initially been located by magnetomete[r] survey and subsequently defined in greate[r] detail by higher resolution magnetic surve[ys] including detailed fluxgate and caesium su[r]veys immediately prior to excavation (Payn[e] 2005). The interruption in the western sid[e] of the ring gully was clearly visible in th[e] higher resolution magnetometer surveys, a[s] was the ring gully of a second roundhous[e] subsequently uncovered at the very norther[n] end of Trench 1 and explored thoroughly i[n] 1997. This area was very badly damaged b[y] ploughing and erosion, resulting in seriousl[y] truncated features that were difficult t[o] resolve. This is probably also the reason wh[y] the smaller ring-gully did not show u[p] clearly in the standard magnetometer surve[y] and has obvious implications for estimatin[g] occupation densities from such data alone.

The larger circular gully was recut a[t] some stage either to produce a vestibule are[a] to the west or to reconstruct the wester[n] side of the structure. The recut terminal o[f] the reconstructed gully to the west con[-] tained what might have been a deliberat[e] deposit of red deer bones. A number of pit[s] were present in and around the circula[r] structure, two of which produced possibl[e] evidence of metal working. These wer[e] clearly resolved in the magnetometer surve[y]. Numerous small post holes and stake hole[s] inside the gully structure, undetected unti[l] excavation, may indicate a possible buildin[g] but do not form a coherent pattern. Thre[e] large post holes (*c* 500mm in diameter) nea[r] to this possible house contained part[s] of human skeletons and may represen[t] deposits in some way connected to the occu[-] pation. The large complex of pits to th[e] north, although much inter-cut, is likely t[o] be broadly contemporary with the circula[r] structure. Most were less than a metre dee[p] with near vertical sides and generally con[-] tained small amounts of pottery and bon[e] with occasional pieces of metal. A smalle[r] number had evidence of possible deliber[ate] ately placed deposits of animal bone and some larger pot sherds. A possible special deposit was discovered in one of the excavated pits [1312] consisting of a broken but almost complete decorated pot with an iron perforated disk. The design of the pottery has parallels in Wessex dated to the Middle Iron Age (the 3rd to 1st century BC). In common with most of the other excavated areas at Segsbury, Trench 1 also contained numerous natural features, including possible tree-throw holes of unknown age.

Trench 2 was located south of the main central zone of occupation in the eastern portion of the hillfort, perpendicular with the line of the possible road from the eastern entrance suggested by a linear zone containing few magnetic anomalies. The area produced partial evidence of another circular structure (not resolved by the magnetometer survey), a natural clay solution pipe and a scatter of stake holes, post pits and pits. The density of archaeological features in this area was nowhere near as great as in Trench 1.

Trench 3, opened in 1996, ran into the northern part of the hillfort interior from the inner edge of the northern hillfort rampart. The trench indicated that there had been a build-up of deposits behind the rampart on the north transported from the interior of the hillfort by down-slope soil movement (by a combination of ploughing and rain-wash). The soil depth in the trench varied from relatively shallow at the southern up-slope end (approximately 500mm deep) to a depth of 1.5m at the bottom of the slope against the foot of the rampart. The main feature of interest found in Trench 3 was the ditch described above. Trench 3 also contained a small number of pits and postholes of probable middle Iron Age date and the circular clay-filled natural solution pipe in the chalk previously mentioned.

Trench 4 was positioned to investigate a very tentative, weak, curvilinear positive magnetic anomaly appearing to define the highest area of the hilltop. Excavation revealed several pits and post holes in this area but nothing corresponding to the possible linear feature. Similar weak linear trends occur elsewhere in the magnetometer data from Segsbury and other hillforts investigated by the Wessex Hillforts Survey. Many have been shown to have no substance when investigated further by excavation, and they probably result from variability in topsoil thickness, agricultural effects, natural soil variation or even spurious artefacts of data processing.

Trench 5, measuring 10m × 10m, targeted a pair of very distinctive (strongly positive) circular anomalies in the north-west part of the hillfort identified by the Ancient Monuments Laboratory as being different to those created by storage pits. It was initially thought that these anomalies might represent hearths, but excavation revealed two solution pipes in the chalk bedrock filled with clay-with-flints, similar to those found in previous years at White Horse Hill and in Trenches 2 and 3 at Segsbury. The relative lack of other archaeological features within Trench 5 compared to the density of features found in Trenches 1, 4 and 2 could indicate zoning within the hillfort and suggest that the differences shown within the geophysics are real rather than being a product of overlying deposits masking features in the northern third of the interior.

Trench 6, opened in 1997 and measuring 10m × 5m, was positioned immediately outside the east entrance to investigate the possible curving earthwork feature extending out from the north side of the entrance, initially suggested by aerial photography and further supported by magnetometer survey. Excavation revealed the rounded terminus of a flat bottomed, steep sided ditch [6002], which appeared to be an outwork extending from the main ditch, precisely in the location expected from the geophysical survey.

Trenches 7a–c, opened in 1997, consisted of a section across the inner rampart and ditch on the southern side of the hillfort, adjacent to where the rampart is broken by the present roadway that cuts through the site. The trench was divided into three sub-areas: 7a – inside the rampart to the north, 7b – a section through the rampart and 7c – a section through the outer main ditch, together providing a continuous north–south section through the hillfort defences.

Trench 7a established that there was no pre-rampart ditch positioned inside the line of the rampart on the south side of the hillfort that corresponded with the feature on the inside of the northern rampart initially recorded by the magnetometer survey and confirmed by excavation in 1996 (Trench 3).

The stratigraphy within the rampart investigated by Trench 7b has yet to be fully resolved, but provisionally at least three phases of rampart construction are represented. The upper central area of the rampart section had been disturbed by probable 18th-century and earlier activity linked to removal of sarsen stones from the ramparts for building material. Preliminary phasing of the rampart sequence is as follows:

Phase 1 – a probable timber revetted rampart represented by a row of post holes that formed the front face of the rampart backed by a chalk bank. Timber revetted ramparts are typical of the Early Iron Age and are also known at Liddington Castle, Uffington Castle, Danebury, Bury Hill 1 and Winklebury.

Phase 2 – was a larger version of the Phase 1 rampart with a rear revetment of posts. An internal structure within the rampart was probably associated with this phase, consisting of two or three courses of crude dry-stone walling creating a two-phase cell-like structure (a later wall overlying an earlier one). This was partly destroyed by a modern robber trench.

Phase 3 – the two phases of timber revetted rampart were succeeded by a massively enlarged dump rampart retained by a sarsen wall at the rear. The external ditch was greatly enlarged to provide material for the dump rampart, cutting through and largely obliterating the Phase 1 ditch. The ditch stratigraphy suggests a combination of intentional filling in the lower half (except for an initial layer of primary chalk shatter) with slower accumulation of mainly natural fills towards the top. A group of sarsen stones within the ditch could represent tumbled material from the destruction of the rampart. Romano-British pottery occurs beneath this context and a 1st–2nd-century Samian sherd above it suggests that partial rampart demolition took place early within the Roman period.

Dates for the construction sequence of the ramparts are not available as yet, but an initial analysis of the ceramic forms and fabrics from the excavation suggests a chronological span for the occupation of the hillfort ranging from early Iron Age to late middle Iron Age with activity beginning in the 7th to 6th century BC (slightly later than at neighbouring Uffington).

The rampart sequence at Segsbury is far from simple and the excavators state that 'There isn't an obvious simple solution based on the accepted sequence of early box ramparts replaced by later dump ramparts and the complexity of the evidence needs to be confronted' (Lock and Gosden 1998, 62). Broadly speaking, however, the evidence does conform to the widely accepted pattern in Wessex (see Chapter 4).

Conclusion

The pattern of occupation revealed inside Segsbury by the magnetometry, combined with evidence for multiple phases of rampart construction culminating in a massively enlarged dump rampart replacing earlier forms, and pottery of Early Iron Age to Middle Iron Age date, all suggest that Segsbury represents a developed form of hillfort. Occupation may not have been continuous or as long-lived as at Danebury, but Segsbury certainly appears to have many of the attributes that we would attach to hillforts of so called developed status. Evidence recovered by the geophysics and subsequent excavation for the lengthening of the approach into the hillfort at the eastern entrance by the addition of an outward projecting hornwork and the possibility of later blocking is a further indication that the site continued to be occupied into the Middle Iron Age. The majority of the occupation at Segsbury seems to date from the Middle Iron Age although there are signs that the origins of the hillfort were much earlier. What differentiates Segsbury from the neighbouring hillfort sites in the area at Uffington and Liddington is the intensity of occupation in the interior, the range of activities represented and a longer sequence of occupation.

Uffington Castle: Uffington, NGR SU 299 863

Summary
Date of survey:
Surveyed prior to Wessex Hillforts Project during the 26-28 April 1989 and 17–19 July 1995.
Landuse at time of survey:
Stable managed grassland.
Geology:
Cretaceous Middle Chalk.
Soil Association:
343h – Andover 1 – shallow well drained calcareous silty soils over chalk on slopes and crests. Striped soil patterns locally.
Approximate area enclosed:
3.3 hectares (8.25 acres).

Planform:
Approximately a five-sided polygon composed of several straight sections of rampart.

Form of ramparts:
Main inner bank constructed in two major phases initially a timber revetted box rampart then enlarged into a dump-constructed rampart. External to the rampart is an outer ditch recut to a wider and deeper profile in the second phase and a secondary outer bank (or counterscarp).

Entrance features:
A well preserved entrance is present on the western side of the fort formed by the rampart terminals on either side of the entrance gap being out-turned to form a 16m long entrance passage. The out-turned banks of the entrance passage then turn again to connect with the line of the counterscarp. A blocked entrance, indicated by a conspicuous kink in the rampart, is present on the opposite eastern side of the fort.

Previous finds:
Saxon and Roman objects and burials and an "ancient urn" excavated from nearby barrows on White Horse Hill by Atkins in 1857. Late Bronze Age and Middle Iron Age pottery from the hillfort.

Previous recorded excavation:
19th century excavations by Martin Atkins. Modern excavations by Oxford Archaeological Unit (White Horse Hill Project) 1989–90 and Hillforts of the Ridgeway Project 1994–5 (Miles *et al* 2003).

Scheduled Ancient Monument:
21778.

County SMR No.:
7304

Project site code:
Not applicable.

Although not strictly included in the Wessex Hillforts Survey, having been surveyed some years previously in 1989, Uffington Castle is included here because it is one of a well-defined group of hillforts on the northern escarpment of the Berkshire and Marlborough Downs, linked by the route of the Ridgeway, and therefore one of the group termed the Ridgeway Hillforts. The majority of these sites were investigated by the Wessex Hillforts Survey in 1996 but the geophysical results from Uffington are published in detail elsewhere (Miles *et al* 2003; see also pp 24–6).

Uffington Castle, (Fig 1.15), like Segsbury 8km to the east, is set on the edge of the north-facing escarpment of the Berkshire Downs. It is one of three large enclosures that cluster at the point where the escarpment makes a sharp turn to the south-west. Hardwell Camp (an enigmatic site of which very little is known) and Rams Hill, a hillfort with a long and complex sequence beginning early in the 1st millennium BC and continuing into the Roman period (Bradley and Ellison 1975; Piggott and Piggott 1940), is 1.5km to the east.

Uffington Castle is a univallate enclosure of 3.3ha (8.25 acres). Excavation of the hillfort and its immediate environs over the past decade has made this the most informative of all The Ridgeway group of sites (Miles *et al* 2003; Lock and Gosden 1997(a)). There were originally two entrances of Iron Age date. That on the west is a simple gap with the out-turned rampart terminals forming a deep passageway before turning onto the line of the counterscarp. To the east, the earthwork evidence – a characteristic slightly in-turned kink in the ditch and rampart – strongly suggested the presence of a blocked entrance, now confirmed by excavation (Lock and Gosden 1997(a)). Two other breaches, on the north-east and south-east are later, and have been suggested as possibly Roman in date (ibid).

The origins of the hillfort appear to lie in the later Bronze Age–earliest Iron Age and to be contemporary with a linear ditch approaching the site from the south, neighbouring Ram's Hill and the settlement on Tower Hill, some 2km to the south-west (ibid). Uffington castle has produced evidence of both Middle Iron Age and intensive Romano-British activity. The nature of the Romano-British material has led the excavators to suggest a possible ritual focus either within the hillfort or centred on a rectilinear enclosure 50m beyond its southwest corner (ibid).

South of Uffington Castle air photography has revealed an extensive area of field system associated with the linear ditch referred to above. This system covers at least 5 sq km and is separated from the major block of fields around Segsbury Camp (*above*, p 91) by the upper reaches of the Lambourn Valley, where a large Bronze Age barrow cemetery (the Lambourn Seven Barrows) might represent an area of reserved ground that was effectively a boundary (Bradley and Richards 1978). The field system is of regular form with a north-east–south-west axis and has a number of rectangular enclosures integrated into its layout (ibid, fig 7.6).

Wiltshire

Barbury Castle: Ogbourne St Andrew; NGR SU 149 763

Summary

Date of survey:
14 to 21 August 1996.
Landuse at time of survey:
Stable managed grassland.
Geology:
Primarily Upper Chalk, overlain by clay-with-flints towards the eastern end of the site.
Soil Association:
341 – Icknield – shallow, mostly humose, well drained calcareous soils over chalk on steep slopes and hill tops.
Approximate area enclosed:
5 hectares (12.3 acres).
Planform:
Approximately oval/eliptical.
Form of ramparts:
The fort is defined by a double line of ramparts with an external counterscarp around most of the circuit. The defences appear to have developed in several phases.
Entrance features:
Opposed entrances are present on the east and west sides of the hillfort. The original form of both entrances is now difficult to reconstruct due to widening in relatively recent times. A forework is present outside the eastern entrance.
Previous finds:
Early and Middle Iron Age pottery, a hoard of ironwork dated to the 2nd or 1st centur[y] BC, Roman pottery and a brooch and spoo[n] of late 1st to early 2nd century AD date, [a] 6th or 7th century Saxon scramasax, kniv[es] and a spearhead (found 1934) and possibl[y] Saxon inhumations discovered in the ram[parts] (Meaney 1964, Cunnington, M[?] 1934, 174; Meyrick 1947; MacGregor an[d] Simpson 1963; Bonney 1966.
Previous recorded excavation:
Military digging in 1939-45 exposed pi[ts] containing Early and Middle Iron Age po[t]tery (Meyrick 1947, 260; Bonney 1966, 28[?] Officers' Reports 1971), 198). Analytica[l] earthwork survey was carried out by th[e] RCHME in 1998 (Bowden 1998).
Scheduled Ancient Monument:
WI 4.
County SMR No.:
SU17NW200.
Project site code:
WHSP Site 4.

Morphology and setting

Barbury Castle (Fig 2.42) is a multiphase bi-vallate hillfort on the north-facing escarp[ment] of the Marlborough Downs. At 265m OD, the location gives extensive views in al[l] directions and the neighbouring hillforts o[f] Liddington Castle and Martinsell Hill ar[e] visible from here. On the northern side o[f] the circuit there are traces of a third an[d] outer circuit (Bowden 1998). The characte[r] of this is uncertain and it may be part of a[n] earlier circuit or of an unfinished additio[n]

Fig 2.42
Aerial photograph of Barbury Castle taken from the north-west. Note the pock-marked appearance of the interior, the impressive double line of ramparts with a slighter outer earthwork, truncated outer ramparts at the western entrance and quarry disturbance on the north side (NMRC, NMR 15074, SU 1476/51, 1983).

Flint quarrying has damaged the ramparts on the northern side of the hillfort and sections of the outer rampart have been removed outside the western entrance (partly as a result of military activity on the site in the Second World War). Evidence of secondary heightening of the rampart was photographed by Keiller during one episode of demolition.

The site has two entrances, on the east and west. There is some indication of in-turning of the inner rampart terminals at the west entrance, but the original form of both entrances is now difficult to reconstruct owing to widening in relatively recent times when the ends of the ramparts were truncated and the ditch terminals partially infilled. A curvilinear forework is present outside the eastern entrance, well preserved to the south but seriously reduced by ploughing to the north. A similar feature is present at the south-east entrance to Chiselbury hillfort, overlooking Fovant, in southern Wiltshire (Crawford and Keiller 1928, 74, plate VII). The northern part of the Barbury forework is cut by the outer ditch of the main hillfort and it would therefore appear to be a feature earlier than the ultimate hillfort defences (Bowden 1998).

The earthworks of the defences indicate that Barbury should be viewed as a 'classic' developed hillfort. Within the interior are extensive earthwork remains of pits and circular structures, many of which are probably prehistoric in origin and reinforce this view of a developed and densely occupied hillfort. This surface evidence is corroborated by the dense pattern of anomalies recorded during the magnetometer survey and the uneven, cratered appearance of the terrain model (*see below*).

There has been no formal excavation within Barbury Castle, but military activity between 1939–45 exposed pits and other features associated with Early and Middle Iron Age pottery (Meyrick 1947). A hoard of iron work including tools, weapons and vehicle fittings can be dated to the 2nd or 1st century BC (MacGregor and Simpson 1963). The area just outside the north-west ramparts has produced considerable quantities of Roman pottery associated with a small mound and consisting mainly of Savernake Ware (a typical domestic assemblage of the late 1st century to early 2nd century AD). Limited finds of Roman material from within the hilfort include a later 1st- or early 2nd-century brooch, a silvered bronze spoon and the lower part of a rotary quern.

Post Roman activity is represented by a 6th- or 7th-century Saxon scramasax, knives and a spearhead (Swanton M J 1973), and possible Anglo-Saxon burials were recovered from the ramparts in 1939–45 (Cunnington, M E 1934; Meyrick 1947; Macgregor and Simpson 1963; Bonney 1966).

The immediate environs of Barbury Castle are rich in monuments of prehistoric date. A major linear ditch passes immediately by the eastern side of the monument and can be traced as a substantial earthwork down the scarp slope north of the hillfort before disappearing in modern arable ground. Below the western side of the fort is a disc barrow and a small cemetery of bowl barrows (Grinsell 1957). Extensive tracts of field system are known to the east and south-east of the hillfort, most notably on Burderop Down (this being an exceptionally well-preserved block) and Smeathe's Ridge, the latter also having evidence of extensive Bronze Age and Iron Age settlement. To the north, at the foot of the escarpment adjacent to Wroughton Copse, is a large settlement of Romano-British date. The settlement is partially overlain by a post-medieval penning earthwork that in the past was misidentified as a Roman military earthwork. Half a kilometer south of the hillfort, adjacent to Barbury Castle Farm and occupying the end of a deep coombe, are the extensive earthworks of a shrunken medieval settlement (Crawford and Keiller 1928, plate XLVI) that has also produced a small amount of Romano-British pottery. An earthwork survey of Barbury Castle was carried out by the Royal Commission on the Historical Monuments of England in 1998 (Bowden 1998).

Magnetometer survey (Figs 2.43–2.45)

i) Objectives. Located within the Barbury Castle Country Park owned by Swindon Borough Council, Barbury Castle was included in the Wessex Hillforts Survey programme primarily to assist the interpretation of the monument to the public and inform the future management of the archaeological component of the country park. Prior to the 1996 geophysical and 1998 earthwork surveys the site was poorly understood due to minimal previous serious archaeological investigation. Barbury is a clear example of a hillfort defined by multiple earthwork defences and such sites are relatively rare in Wessex compared to simpler univallate forms of hillfort. This was another reason for inclusion as it was an important

Fig 2.43
Greyscale plot of the
magnetometer data from
Barbury Castle shown in
relation to the plan of the
hillfort earthworks.

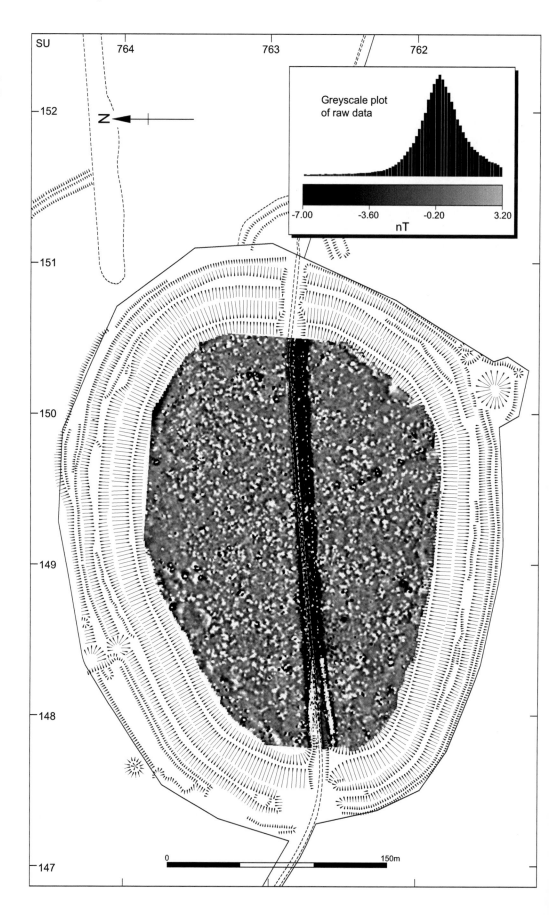

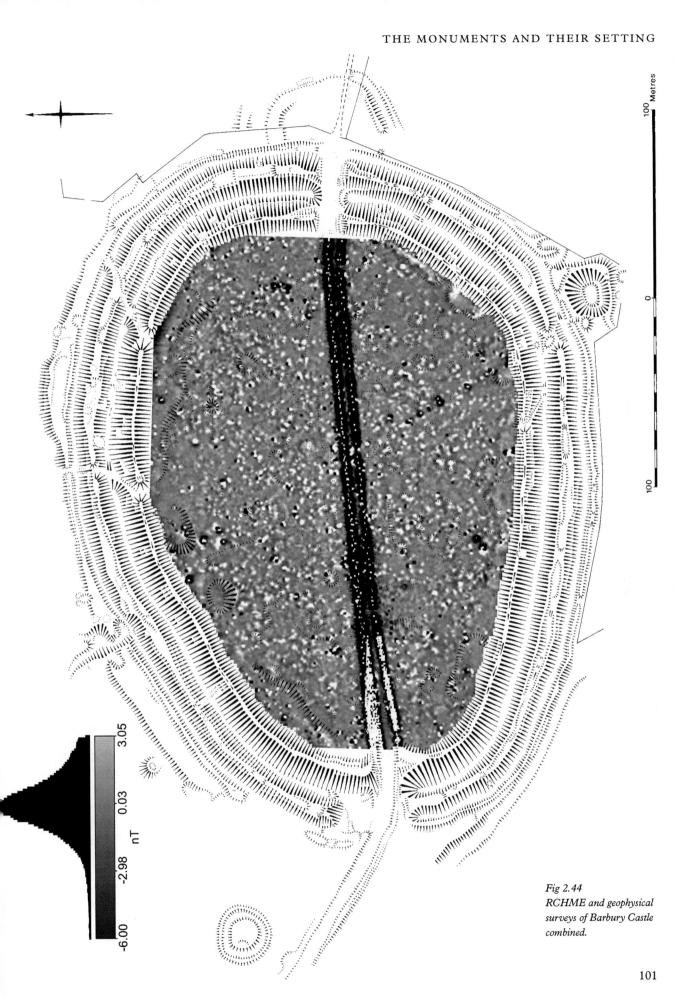

Fig 2.44
RCHME and geophysical
surveys of Barbury Castle
combined.

aim of the project to examine examples of these rarer bivallate and multivallate sites where they occur. Barbury is also one of a well-defined group of hillforts occupying the top of the northern escarpment of the Berkshire, Lambourn and Marlborough Downs. There were strong academic reasons for investigating this group as a whole rather than carrying out individual site specific work. Finally, Barbury was included in the survey programme as an example of a site under stable grassland management.

ii) Results. The magnetometer survey carried out over the full 5ha of the fort interior in 1996 indicates that it contains a high density of anomalous activity comparable to results obtained in the 1980s at Maiden Castle (Sharples 1991). This evidence is probably indicative of a great many pits (almost too many to distinguish separately) suggesting intense or prolonged occupation of the site in agreement with the suggested phased development of the hillfort defences. Some of the magnetic anomalies mapped in the interior are probably due to recent activity, but the likelihood is that most relate to the prehistoric occupation of the site. A band of intense

magnetic disturbance, running between the hillfort entrances, results from the remnants of the metal fences that formerly lined both sides of a trackway passing through the centre of the hillfort. The position of another former fence may be indicated by another alignment of intense magnetic anomalies running approximately north–south in the south-east quadrant of the interior.

Consideration of the combined earthwork and geophysical evidence (Fig 2.44)

The interior of the fort is full of slight earthwork features and in suitable natural lighting conditions the ground surface has a very pock-marked appearance when viewed from the air (NMR 14873/04, 1997, NMR 15862/15, 1997). This is suggestive of considerable ground disturbance in the past as would be caused by pit digging over an extended period of time. Surface observations by the RCHME (Bowden 1998) suggest the presence of remains of hut circles in the form of hollows and terraces with crescentic backscarps, between 35 and 40 in number, and showing a particular concentration in the eastern part of the fort. There is no obvious relationship between this distribution of surface features and the

Fig 2.45
Digital terrain model of the internal area of Barbury Castle with draped image of the magnetometer survey results.

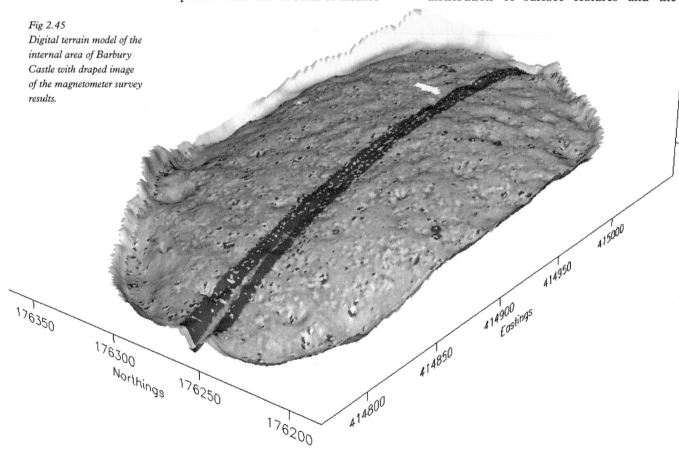

evidence from the magnetometer survey, which suggests that the fort interior is uniformly covered with sub-surface disturbance. Many of the hollows mapped by the RCHME survey – particularly those in the south-eastern part of the fort interior – have discrete positive anomalies (probable pits) associated with them, lending weight to their interpretation as possible house sites – but this is not exclusively so and, given the great density of pit-type anomalies mapped by the magnetometer at Barbury, could be coincidental. In the north-western half of the hillfort, the arcs of several possible circular gully structures are just visible amid (and partly obscured by) the widespread responses to pit type features that dominate the magnetic results (*see* Fig 2.43). There are no accompanying signs on the ground of these tentative features (Fig 2.44). Deeper, sharper defined earthwork features within the hillfort are interpreted by the RCHME (Anderton 1998) as the product of Second World War gun positions, trenches and bomb craters. These are probably linked to the use of the hillfort during the Second World War for anti-aircraft defences covering the approaches to Wroughton airfield and Swindon.

Quarry scoops up to 1.6m deep are present behind the ramparts around most of the circuit of the enclosure and are clearly visible in the terrain model of the hillfort interior produced by the Central Archaeology Service in 1996 (Fig 2.45). The larger and deeper quarry scoops are also clearly resolved in the magnetometer survey as areas of raised positive magnetic response. These anomalies are particularly clear south of the eastern entrance. The possible presence of earlier round barrows within the area later occupied by the hillfort (Bowden 1998, 6–7) was not confirmed by the magnetometer. A large pond lies immediately adjacent to the counterscarp on the south-east side of the fort and a second similar feature visible as a rounded depression (and a broad weakly positive magnetic anomaly) may be present adjacent to the inner rampart on the northern side of the fort interior.

Conclusion

The density of activity within Barbury contrasts strongly with the other 'Ridgeway' hillforts of Liddington and Uffington to the east of Barbury where occupation is less dense and largely confined to the late Bronze Age and Early Iron Age.

Barbury can now be recognised as a hill-fort of developed status, containing a much higher density of occupation features than the neighbouring hillforts in the district. The multiple lines of ramparts and the density of features in the interior revealed by magnetometry indicate that Barbury was a substantial defended settlement probably occupied for several centuries in the mid-1st millennium BC and perhaps combining domestic, agricultural, military and sacred functions. The position of the hillfort in the landscape would have allowed it to dominate and exploit the resources of the surrounding downs and the vale to the north. The ultimate hillfort defences at Barbury were possibly preceded by a slighter hill-top enclosure as known at other hillforts on the Marlborough and North Berkshire Downs including Rams Hill, Liddington Castle and possibly Segsbury (*see above*). No pottery identified as Late Iron Age has been recovered from the enclosed area but abandonment of the hillfort in the 1st century BC would be consistent with the evidence from other developed hillforts in the region.

Castle Ditches Camp: Tisbury; NGR ST 963 283

Summary
Date of survey:
8–18 September 1997.
Landuse at time of survey:
Arable (immediately after crop harvesting).
Geology:
Cretaceous Upper Greensand (sand and cherty sandstone).
Soil Association:
541B – Bearsted 2 – deep well drained coarse loamy soils, locally very stony.
Approximate area enclosed:
9.7 hectares (24 acres).
Planform:
Approximately an equilateral triangle with rounded corners.
Form of ramparts:
On the edge of the natural escarpment to the west the fort is defined by a triple tier of ramparts with two intervening ditches now heavily wooded. Across the neck of the promontory on the more easily approachable south-east side of the fort three massive banks and external ditches were constructed, measuring 75m wide overall. Two additional outer banks and ditches of smaller size reinforce and protect the winding eastern entrance into the hillfort north of the entry point of the modern farm-track into the site.

Entrance features:

There are two major entrances and possibly another two simpler ones. The eastern entrance takes the form of a hollow-way between the middle and outer rampart which serves as a hornwork and has an additional outer bank and ditch. The middle and inner ramparts were crossed through simple staggered gaps. The west entrance takes the form of a track 180m long and up to 6m deep incised into the side of the hill leading up to the fort through the ramparts at an oblique angle. Below the ramparts, the approach is protected on the lower (west) side by an additional bank. On the north-east and south sides of the fort interruptions in the ramparts suggest additional entrances of more simple form.

Previous finds:

Haematite pottery (source : Wiltshire SMR).

Previous recorded excavation:

Repair work by Wessex Archaeology in 1989 recorded a partial section of the inner ditch and part of the outer bank (Fielden 1991).

Scheduled Ancient Monument:

WI 11.

County SMR No.:

ST92NE200.

Project Site Code:

WHSP 15.

Morphology and setting

Castle Ditches Camp is a large multivallate hillfort, roughly triangular, enclosing an area of 9.7ha (24 acres) with an overall area, including the defences of 17.5ha (43 acres). The site occupies the western end of a greensand promontory at 191m OD and dominates the central area of the Vale of Wardour and the valley of the River Nadder. Around the escarpment edge Castle Ditches is defined by three ramparts separated by two ditches. Now covered in mature, and in places very dense, woodland the defences are of massive proportions, measuring an average of 45m in width with ditches still up to 6m deep. On the south-eastern approach, across the neck of the promontory, the defences comprise three massive banks, each with an external ditch, with an overall width of 75–85m. Overall Castle Ditches bears a striking similarity to the developed hillfort at South Cadbury, some 30km to the west (Barrett *et al* 2000).

In 1997 when fieldwork was conducted, the interior of the hillfort was under intensive cultivation, contrasting sharply with the predominant present day pastoral economy of the Vale of Wardour. In the early 19th century Sir Richard Colt Hoare recorded that 'the entire area of this camp is under tillage, and the greater part of the ramparts are so concealed by thick copse wood that no adequate idea of their strength and boldness can possibly be formed' (Colt Hoare 1812). It is evident from this that the condition of the site has changed little down the centuries and it is encouraging how much archaeological evidence still survives in the interior, based on the magnetometer survey, (*see below*) despite so many years of gradual degradation by ploughing.

There has been no major excavation of the site, although Sumner recorded 'haematite' coated pottery and the author (M Corney) has noted Middle to Late Iron Age and Romano-British pottery in the ploughed interior. A hoard of late 2nd-century AD *sestertii* was found on the hilltop in the 1980s (Dr P Robinson pers comm) and emergency work by Wessex Archaeology in 1989 recorded a partial section of the southern defences following a landslip (Fielden 1991). No suitable aerial photograph of the site was available because the dense woodland covering the ramparts effectively obscures the view of the site from the air.

The circuit is breached at four points, two of which, on the east and west, are undoubtedly original. The principle entrance is that on the east side, giving access from the greensand promontory. This is a complex structure 140m in length and, although now damaged by a modern farm track and a small reservoir on the inner rampart, its original form can still be discerned (Fig 2.46). The outermost rampart forms a substantial hornwork from which the original hollow-way turns sharply west across the line of the middle rampart. To reach the innermost rampart and entrance proper, the track turns south-west and then west to give passage into the interior. At this point, modern damage coupled with the ongoing cultivation of the interior has removed any surface evidence of an inturned entrance, although the line of the approach track can be seen to continue as an east–west route across the hillfort on the magnetometry survey (Fig 2.46). This route can be traced to the other major original entrance located on the western side of the hill. As at the east entrance, part of the outer rampart deviates from the line of the defences to create a hornwork flanking a very deep (up to 6m in depth) and well-defined hollow-way. The hollow-way cuts diagonally across the defences for a total distance of 180m, and then enters the hillfort by way of a very deep and well-worn cut with a steep gradient, that extends into the interior for a distance of 25m. As with the eastern entrance, ongoing cultivation has seriously degraded the inner rampart and the original form of the entrance is now obscured.

There are two more breaches in the circuit on the north and south respectively. The latter, despite some modern damage and a very dense cover of vegetation, has certain characteristics suggestive of some considerable antiquity. The ramparts either side of the gap are markedly offset, a feature observed on many earlier Iron Age hillfort entrances. There is also some evidence on the geophysical plots of a possible track or road heading towards this gap from the possible blocked entrance on the northern side of the hillfort (below). It is possible that the southern break in the defences is also an earlier entrance, subsequently blocked. The long-term cultivation of the interior has seriously degraded the inner rampart in the areas discussed and surface observation and remote sensing alone cannot provide the crucial evidence of proof.

On the northern side of the hillfort the earthworks of the middle and outer ramparts suggest the presence of a second blocked entrance. This is especially clear on the outer rampart where the terminals either side of the break are markedly offset. Evidence of blocking on the inner rampart is now difficult to discern due to dense vegetation, the cultivation of the interior and the accumulation of plough-soil behind the bank. As with the suggested southern entrance, it is likely that excavation would be required to confirm the field observations.

Sumner (1913, 1988) considered Castle Ditches to be one of the finest camps in the Cranborne Chase area (covering north-west Hampshire, south-west Wiltshire and north-east Dorset) regarding it as a 'British tribal centre' on the strength of the earthworks and the sizable area enclosed. The scale of the surviving earthworks coupled with the complexity of internal features recorded by magnetometry (below) clearly demonstrates that Castle Ditches is a developed hillfort with a long sequence of occupation. The morphology of the internal features shows at least two major phases, one associated with numerous circular structures and a second with a large number of sub-angular enclosures. Pits and other features are also widely distributed across the interior suggesting intensive activity. If the postulated earlier entrances on the northern and southern sides should prove to be correct it also implies that the axis of the site may have been changed at some point. Hillforts in Wessex with more than two entrances are extremely rare. Equally rare are hillforts with north- and south-facing entrances (see Hill 1996, 110). Generally two are the norm, often with one subsequently being blocked, such as those recorded at Danebury (Cunliffe 1984a) or Beacon Hill (Eagles 1991). It may be that Castle Ditches has undergone at least one period of abandonment or reduced use and on renewal of activity the axis of the site was re-aligned between the more developed east and west entrances.

The presence of Romano-British material from the hillfort is of some interest. One possibility is that a shrine or temple was constructed within the site, although there is no evidence for such a structure on the geophysical survey. A phase of late and post-Roman reoccupation could be an alternative possibility. The Vale of Wardour is an area where a significant number of British place-names and river names have survived (Eagles 1994 and in litt). The site should be regarded as having high potential as a post-Roman centre.

Contemporary features in the immediate environs of Castle Ditches are few. Just beyond the outermost rampart at the north-west corner there is a short (40m) length of bank with a ditch on the south side. This feature is undated, covered by very dense vegetation, and may be part of a more extensive group of earthworks observed but not recorded in detail in Haredene Wood, a large and well-established block of woodland covering an area of some 500ha immediately north of Castle Ditches.

Owing to the nature of the Greensand sub-soil and predominance of a pastoral economy in the Tisbury area, aerial photography has been of little value in identifying new sites. However in 1994, a series of air photographs of a low knoll situated 500m west of the western entrance into Castle Ditches recorded the faint earthwork remains of a univallate enclosure of approximately 3ha (NMR15161/23-28). This is oval in shape and although undated does have the appearance of a prehistoric feature. The occurrence of smaller enclosures in close proximity to hillfort entrances is a phenomenon noted at many sites in Wessex and is discussed in greater detail below (pp 139–41).

Magnetometer survey (Figs 2.46–2.48)

Castle Ditches was selected as a priority for survey because it represents a large hillfort, defended by impressive multivallate defences with complex entrances, suggestive of late occupation. In complexity it is comparable to other hillforts farther west in Dorset and West Wiltshire such as Battlesbury Camp, Badbury Rings, Hod Hill and Hambledon Hill. Hillforts defined by multivallate ramparts are relatively rare in the core study area of the Wessex Hillforts Survey in central Hampshire and north Wiltshire and where they do appear in this region they generally seem to represent a relatively late development in hillfort design or augmentation (for example at Bury Hill). Multivallate defences become increasingly common towards the western edge of the survey region towards Dorset and Somerset where hillfort occupation persisted for longer and celebrated examples of these strongly developed hillforts appear including Hambledon Hill, Hod Hill, Maiden Castle and South Cadbury Castle. The interior of Castle Ditches has been under the plough for many years (with obvious implications for the long-term preservation of any archaeological features contained within it), a factor that further reinforced the need for geophysical investigation.

The magnetic results from Castle Ditches are among the most striking produced by the Wessex Hillforts Survey and reveal a complex and interesting pattern of archaeological features. The features mapped within the fort by the magnetometer are clearly of several phases, as indicated by overlapping anomalies. At least two distinct phases of activity appear to be represented. One phase is characterised by circular anomalies indicative of hut emplacements. These vary in diameter from 10m to 15m and number no fewer than 20, although as many as 50 may be present. They appear to concentrate in the northern half of the hillfort and are often arranged in lines (A and B on Fig 2.47) similar to the layout of such structures around the periphery of Danebury in its Late period (Cunliffe 1995, fig 9, 24). Some of the circular features appear to overlap indicating periodic replacement of some structures and several phases of building. Though the circular structures cannot all be contemporary, their overall number suggests that a sizeable community probably inhabited the hillfort over a period of time.

The second series of features mapped by the survey consists of a system of irregularly shaped ditched enclosures laid out along the axes of, and divided by, the north–south and east–west roadways running between the two sets of probable entrances (see above). In several places the enclosure ditches cut unconformably across the circular features (or vice-versa depending upon phasing) suggesting they each represent separate phases of activity. The circular features also seem to occupy the lines of the trackways defined by the enclosures suggesting that the roadways had fallen out of use or had yet to be established at the time when the circles were constructed. The extensive network of enclosures is associated with a zone of elevated magnetic susceptibility readings (15–20×10^{-5} SI volume susceptibility; Fig 2.48) extending across the interior to the north-west from the ramparts on the south-east side of the hillfort (Bartlett 1999 and see pp 35–6). In contrast the eastern, northern, and western periphery of the enclosed area is characterised by much lower MS readings (below 10×10^{-5} SI). The susceptibility values are particularly low in the south-west area of the site where there is a corresponding reduction in magnetic anomalies.

A sparse scatter of pits is evident throughout much of the hillfort tending to occur in loose clusters (as at numerous other hillforts). Greater concentrations of pits occur towards the northern periphery of the site and among the enclosure features in the southern half of the fort. One concentrated group of strong positive magnetic anomalies between two open ended enclosures (75m west of the east entrance) occupies the centre of an area of particularly high MS suggestive of some type of high temperature industrial activity. The cross-roads at the intersection of the two possible trackways running through the hillfort is also associated with a peak in the magnetic susceptibility but, other than suggesting intense occupation, the exact cause of these high readings is not known.

A series of broad linear zones of magnetic disturbance behind the internal face of the inner rampart revealed by the magnetometer survey suggests the presence of quarries dug to provide material for heightening and extending the hillfort ramparts. Quarry hollows such as these are generally indicative of numerous phases of rampart development and continual augmentation characteristic of the Middle to Late Iron Age examples of devel-

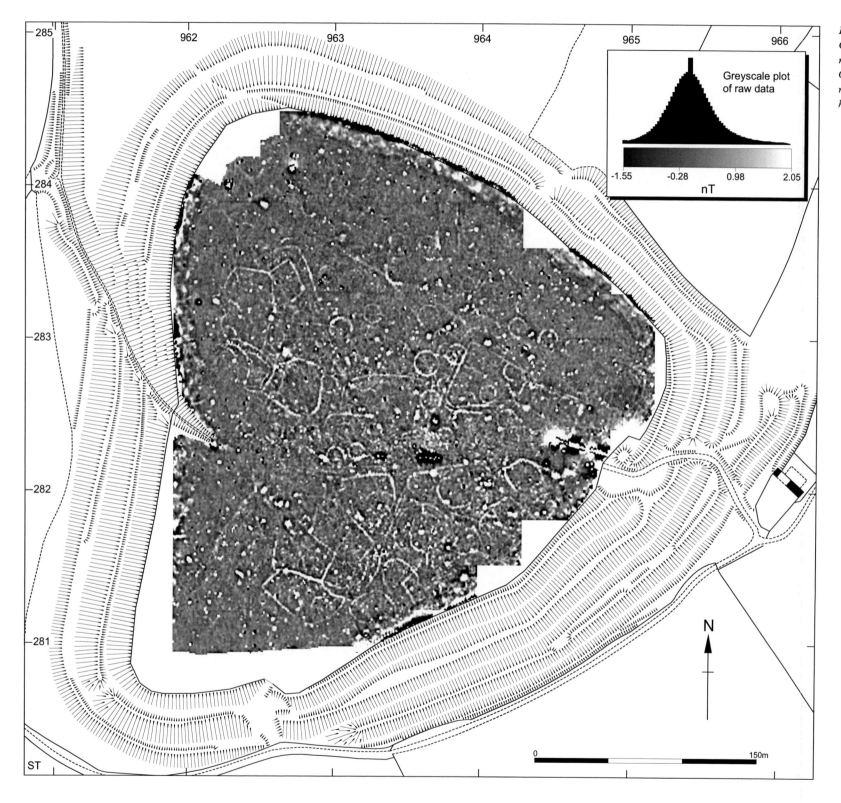

285

962   963   964   965   966

284

283

282

281

ST

Greyscale plot
of raw data

-1.55   -0.28   0.98   2.05
nT

N

0   150m

Fig 2.46
Greyscale plot of the
magnetometer data from
Castle Ditches shown in
relation to the plan of the
hillfort earthworks.

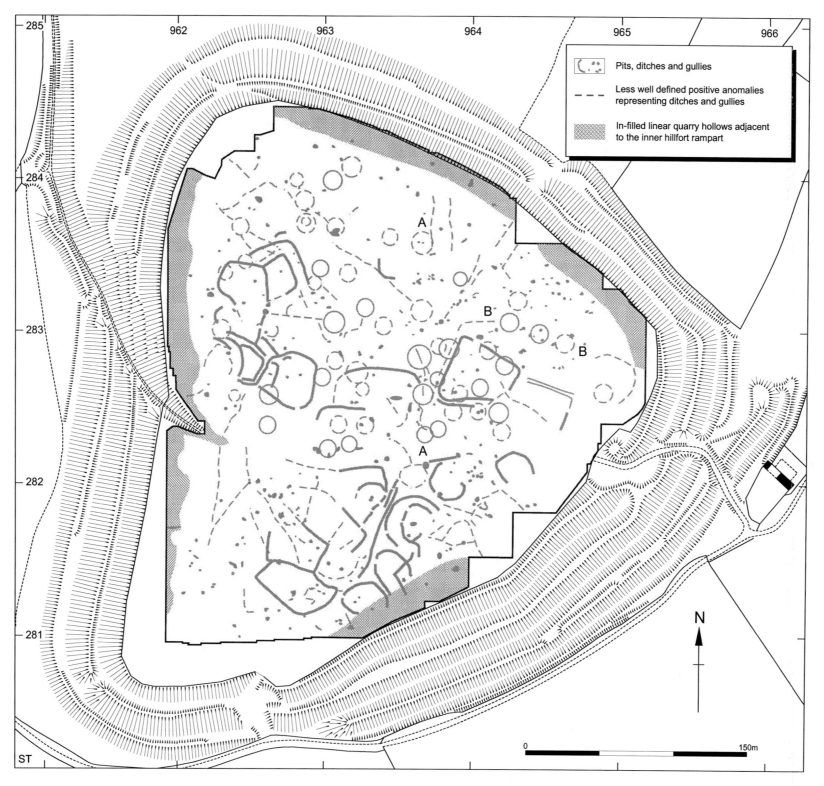

Fig 2.47
Interpretation of the
magnetometer data from
Castle Ditches.

Pits, ditches and gullies

Less well defined positive anomalies
representing ditches and gullies

In-filled linear quarry hollows adjacent
to the inner hillfort rampart

N

0   150m

ST

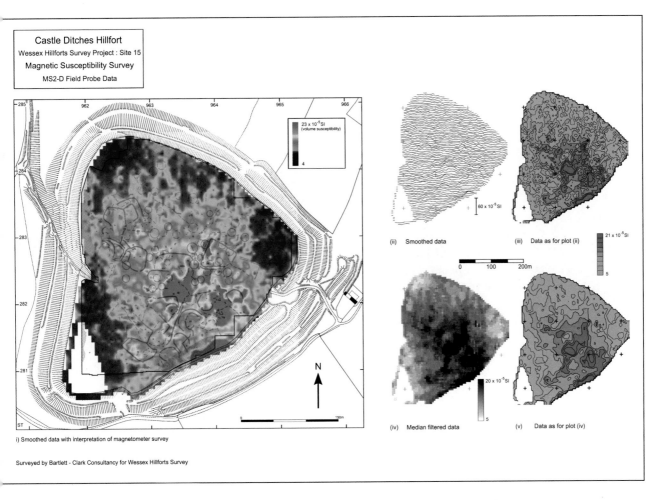

Castle Ditches Hillfort
Wessex Hillforts Survey Project : Site 15
Magnetic Susceptibility Survey
MS2-D Field Probe Data

23 x 10⁻⁵ SI
(volume susceptibility)

4

(ii) Smoothed data

(iii) Data as for plot (ii)

21 x 10⁻⁵ SI

5

0   100   200m

(iv) Median filtered data

(v) Data as for plot (iv)

20 x 10⁻⁵ SI

5

N

0   150m

i) Smoothed data with interpretation of magnetometer survey

Surveyed by Bartlett - Clark Consultancy for Wessex Hillforts Survey

oped hillforts in Wessex including Danebury, Hod Hill and Maiden Castle. The new geophysical evidence for quarry hollows, combined with the extravagant visible earthworks, all suggest that Castle Ditches underwent sustained occupation or multiple reoccupation. The quarries had not been noted previously because cultivation of the hillfort interior has caused them to become infilled with soil and obscured as surface features.

An intense east–west aligned linear magnetic magnetic anomaly (alternately positive and negative), immediately north of the point where the inner rampart is broken by the eastern entrance, is the response to a ferrous pipe leading to a covered reservoir built against the inner rampart at NGR ST 96492831.

Conclusion

The elaborate earthworks and entrances of Castle Ditches combined with the new evidence from geophysical survey for quarries, several phases of occupation, a rudimentary street-plan and numerous circular gully structures indicative of hut emplacements all reinforce the earlier view of Sumner that Castle Ditches is a hillfort of particular significance and undoubted archaeological importance.

Fosbury: Tidcombe and Fosbury; NGR SU 319 565

Summary
Date of survey:
30 September to 4 October 1996.
Landuse at time of survey:
Predominantly pasture, but the northernmost part of the interior is under woodland.
Geology:
Cretaceous Upper Chalk (soft white chalk with many flint nodules).
Soil Association:
343h – Andover 1 – shallow well drained calcareous silty soils over chalk. Striped soil patterns locally.
Approximate area enclosed:
10.5 hectares (26 acres).
Planform:
Irregular – composed of several straight lengths of rampart.

Fig 2.48
Magnetic susceptibility survey results from Castle Ditches (from Bartlett-Clark Consultancy).

107

Form of ramparts:
The defences consist of an inner bank with an equally proportioned second outer bank separated by an intervening ditch. Quarry hollows are present on the internal side of the inner rampart along the southern half of the defensive circuit.

Entrance features:
Original entrances appear to be present on the eastern and southern sides of the defensive circuit. Several possible more modern breaches through the ramparts are present in the western, north-western and northern sections of the defences.

Previous finds:
Grinsell (1957) notes that Meyrick recorded Iron Age A/B sherds from the interior.

Previous recorded excavation:
None known

Scheduled Ancient Monument:
WI 162

County SMR No.:
SU35NW200

Project Site Code:
WHSP Site 9

Morphology and setting

Fosbury hillfort (Fig 2.49) is a large bivallate enclosure of 10.5 hectares (26 acres) set just south of the crest of Haydown Hill at a height of 254m OD. The site occupies a central position in the Hampshire Downs and has extensive views in all directions, especially across eastern Wiltshire and the chalklands of western and central Hampshire. The hillforts of Walbury Camp and Chisbury lie 7km to the north-east and 10km to the north-west respectively, and the small one hectare hillfort of Godsbury is located 10km west along the same escarpment.

A rampart, ditch and a substantial second outer bank define the hillfort circuit with a well-preserved series of quarry scoops surviving within the southern arc. Of the five breaches through the defences only that on the east, with well-defined inturns, is clearly original. A possible second original entrance may exist on the south side with a staggered entrance passage formed by offset rampart terminals. Several possible more modern breaches through the ramparts are present in the western, north-western and northern sections of the defences. Of the two breaches through the western side of the fort the northernmost might be original, but has clearly been subject to modification. Although the defences appear in plan to be gently curvilinear, they are in fact constructed in a series of short, straight lengths, a feature noted on many other Wessex hillforts, including Liddington Castle (*see below* for a more detailed discussion of this phenomenon).

Within the southern half of the enclosure are extensive earthworks defining small subcircular platforms, interpreted as hut platforms and pits up to 4m in diameter and 0.5m deep. The site has never been excavated although Grinsell (1957) notes that Meyrick recorded Iron Age 'A/B' sherds from the interior. The whereabouts of this material is unknown. 250m to the north-west of the fort air photography has recorded a single ring-ditch and the Wiltshire Sites and Monuments Record (SMR) notes a find-spot of Neolithic flint in the same vicinity. Five hundred meters north-west of the western defences, on the western tip of Haydown Hill and 200m west of the ring-ditch, air photographs show a sub-square ditched enclosure of approximately 0.5ha (1.2 acres) with an east-facing entrance.

Surrounding Fosbury is a remarkably regular block of prehistoric fields that, despite recent plough damage, still present a very fine and coherent system. Best preserved on the eastern and southern slopes of the hill, the lynchets appear to be overlain by the hillfort counterscarp, thus predating it. This system can be traced over an area of at least 9 sq km and is associated with the linear ditch system that forms a major junction in the vicinity of Scot's Poor, on the extreme eastern edge of Salisbury Plain, 3.5km west of Fosbury (Massey 1998). Although Fosbury is not directly linked into a linear ditch

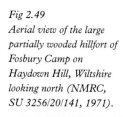

Fig 2.49
Aerial view of the large partially wooded hillfort of Fosbury Camp on Haydown Hill, Wiltshire looking north (NMRC, SU 3256/20/141, 1971).

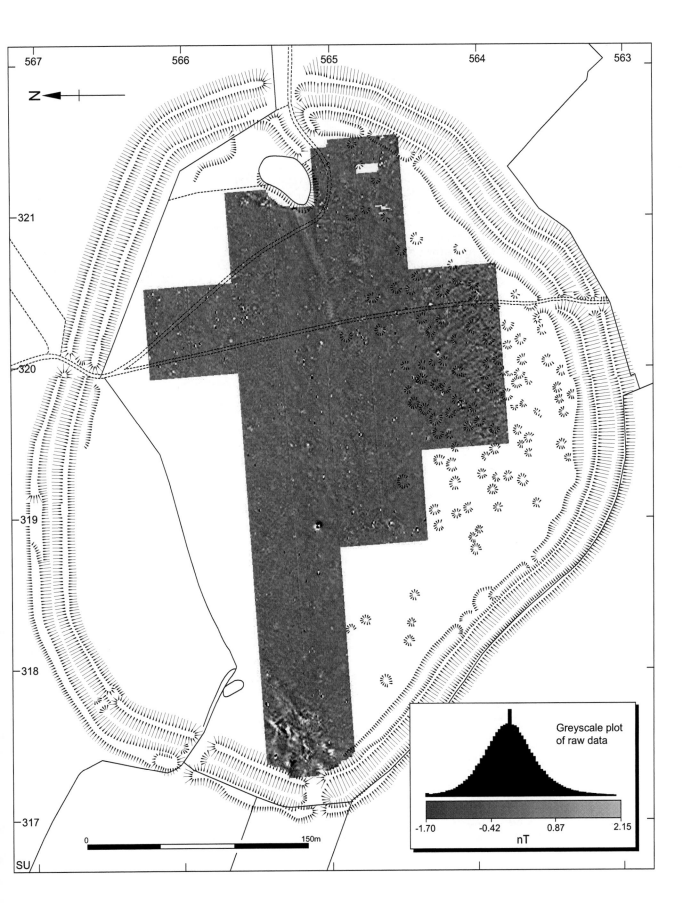

Fig 2.50 (previous page) Greyscale plot of the magnetometer data from Fosbury Camp shown in relation to the plan of the hillfort earthworks.

Haydown Hill is partially enclosed by elements of this system. A major east–west linear ditch, cutting the field system around the hillfort, passes by less than 1km from the southern rampart of Fosbury.

The small sub-square enclosure on the western end of Haydown Hill is, in terms of its general morphology and the area enclosed, very similar to settlements of Middle to Late Bronze Age date known elsewhere in Wessex (Bradley *et al* 1994; Barrett *et al* 1991). The enclosure shares the alignment of adjacent lynchets and it is tempting to see this as a settlement contemporary with the field system in the Fosbury area. If this should prove to be so then the linear ditches that cut the field system should fall within the same late Bronze Age date range proposed by Bradley *et al* (ibid) for the extensive linear ditch networks studied east of the River Avon on Salisbury Plain, only 5km from Fosbury.

Magnetometer survey (Fig 2.50)

The large-scale Ordnance Survey mapping indicates numerous recessed platforms cut out of the sloping ground in the southern half of the hillfort interior (*see* Fig 2.50). These topographical features have often been taken to indicate the presence of former hut-sites constructed on the level ground formed by the platforms. Similar features are present at hillfort sites in neighbouring Hampshire (including Beacon Hill and Old Winchester Hill) where experience has shown that they generally produce no associated magnetic signature. It is therefore not surprising that these features – even if they do indeed represent hut features – have not been detected by magnetometry at Fosbury. The magnetic signal produced by the striped soil patterns that are a feature of the underlying subsoils in this area is far more predominant in this zone of the hillfort than any response to these assumed archaeological features. More work will be required to evaluate the archaeological significance of the platforms.

Elsewhere in the sample of the hillfort covered by the magnetometer, the magnetic response is very subdued and largely lacking in significant anomalies. A few localised anomalies, sparsely distributed throughout the interior, may represent isolated pits. Other anomalies are too weakly defined to be confident of their interpretation. The response to archaeological features inside Fosbury may be weakened by the un-ploughed terrain of the interior as this has been shown elsewhere to have a adverse effect on the resolution of archaeological features in magnetometer surveys of hillforts (*see* for example Beacon Hill and Danebury, this volume). The absence of large numbers of pits would, however, be unexpected in a hillfort with plentiful evidence of hut sites.

A weakly defined, broad, positive linear magnetic anomaly extending westwards from the pond in the eastern extremity of the hillfort may represent a hollow-way leading into the interior from the eastern entrance to the hillfort. Alternatively it may represent a spring fed water course or drainage channel associated with the pond to the east. A weakly defined positive linear magnetic anomaly – which is likely to be a boundary ditch of unknown date – runs north and south of the possible hollow-way. The alignment of this feature suggests that it may be associated with an earlier underlying field-system surviving as earthworks to the south on the southern slopes of Haydown Hill (*see above*).

An area of strong magnetic disturbance adjacent to the ramparts on the far western side of the hillfort may represent some form of buried archaeological structure. Some rectilinearlity in the arrangement of the anomalies is suggestive of a possible building but without more investigation and extension of the survey coverage this interpretation can only be provisional.

Discussion

The date of the construction of Fosbury remains unresolved although the relatively large area enclosed and the relative simplicity of the defences and entrance features would suggest an earlier rather than later 1st millennium BC date.

It is intriguing to note that the earthworks within the hillfort, long thought to represent settlement remains of a density usually associated with developed hillforts in Wessex, did not produce significant magnetic anomalies indicative of human occupation. This negative evidence should not necessarily exclude the possibility of pits being present in significant numbers, however, because the survival of pits as surface indications can lead to them being less clearly resolved in a magnetometer survey compared to completely infilled pits. The magnetic evidence for internal occupation activity is suprisingly low suggesting that the survey is either giving a false impression of the true density of archaeological activity within the fort, or that occupation was of a low intensity, sporadic or short-lived.

Liddington Castle: Liddington; NGR SU 209 797

Summary

Date of survey:
[?]–6 September 1996.
Landuse at time of survey:
Pasture.
Geology:
Primarily upper chalk/partially middle chalk, found to be overlain by clay with embedded flints in excavations carried out in 1976.
Soil Association:
341 – Icknield – shallow, mostly humose, well drained calcareous soils over chalk on steep slopes and hill tops.
Approximate area enclosed:
3 hectares (7.4 acres)
Planform:
Polygonal (roughly five sided)
Form of ramparts:
Univallate defences consisting of a bank, ditch and counterscarp constructed in four main phases starting with a timber and turf rampart in the latest Bronze Age to earliest Iron Age (perhaps 7–6th century BC) culminating in a final heightening of the rampart during the later Iron Age, Roman or post-Roman period.
Entrance features:
A simple causewayed entrance is present on the east and most accessible side of the fort. A second blocked entrance is evident on the west.
Previous finds:
Finds uncovered during flint quarrying in the hillfort between 1896 and 1900 were collected by Passmore and deposited in the Ashmolean Museum. The finds included Late Bronze Age and Iron Age pottery. Additional stray finds from the hillfort documented in the Wiltshire SMR include: Neolithic stone implements including the pointed butt of a dolerite axe, and two Bronze Age barbed and tanged arrowheads.
Previous recorded excavation:
Quarrying of the north-east area of the hillfort interior for flint took place from 1896 to 1900 (Passmore 1914). Limited excavation by the University of Birmingham (School of History) in 1976 was primarily concerned with testing for occupation or re-fortification of the site in the post-Roman period linked to research into the location of the battle of Mount Badon (Hirst and Rahtz 1996).
Internal features uncovered during this excavation included: Trench A: a shallow post-hole 40–50cm in diameter, traces of an occupation feature with a slightly dished floor, and a possible ditch or palisade trench approximately a metre wide about 13m inside the inner rampart. Trench B: a deep shaft of uncertain date, 1.5m in diameter with an upper weathering cone possibly a well or flint mine excavated to a depth of 2.3m but continuing down; a shallow pit 0.4m deep cut into natural chalk and about 1.1m in diameter with pot sherds of the 5th century BC in the upper fill. The fill of the ditch terminals bounding the eastern entrance contained finds of Roman date.
Analytical earthwork survey of the site was carried out by the archaeological survey team of English Heritage in 2000 (Bowden 2000).
Scheduled Ancient Monument:
WI 127.
County SMR No.:
SU27NW209.
Project Site Code:
WHSP Site 5.

Morphology and setting

Liddington Castle (Fig 2.51) is a univallate hillfort enclosing approximately 3ha (7.4 acres), situated on the northern escarpment of the Marlborough Downs at 275m OD, overlooking the upper Thames Valley to the north and the valley of the River Og to the west. The latter is also a long established north–south route giving access to the upper Thames Valley from the chalk massif of central Wessex. Liddington Castle is one of a number of hillforts on this north-facing escarpment and is intervisible with Barbury Castle, 7km south-west, and Uffington Castle, 11km north-east.

The hillfort has one entrance on the east side. This is of simple form, being an interruption in the ditch and bank with no outworks or other substantial features. The rampart terminals at either side of the eastern entrance may have originally been faced with sarsen stones. On the western side of the circuit the earthworks display a distinct change of character at one point and it is possible to discern the position of a blocked entrance. This phenomenon is discussed in greater detail below (pp 138–9). Other sites with blocked entrances are known from within the project area and include Beacon Hill, Hampshire (Eagles 1991); Danebury (Cunliffe 1984); Uffington Castle (Miles *et al* 2003) and possibly Segsbury and Castle Ditches. The defences of Liddington also display a feature seen on a number of other Wessex hillforts; evidence of the construction methods

Fig 2.51
Aerial view of Liddington
Castle from the west,
showing several large deep
depressions in the interior,
the blocked entrance on the
west (in foreground of
photograph) and quarrying
disturbance (NMRC,
NMR 18668/09, SU
2079/49, 2000).

employed by the builders. It is clearly noticeable that the rampart is constructed in short,
straight lengths with markedly angular and
abrupt changes in alignment. This feature is
widespread and can be seen at many sites in
Wessex and beyond; notably Figsbury Rings,
Yarnbury, Fosbury (see below) and Chiselbury
– all in Wiltshire; Segsbury, Oxfordshire,
Ladle Hill in Hampshire (an unfinished hillfort) and Perborough Castle in Berkshire.
The south-western section of the inner rampart and the counterscarp bank have been
badly damaged by quarrying.

The interior of the hillfort contains several earthwork features. Some large depressions, slighter scarps and indistinct traces of
probable internal quarry scoops were
recorded by earthwork survey undertaken in
the summer of 2000 (Bowden 2000), but
because fine surface detail was obscured by
high vegetation at the time, other features
may still await discovery. Some of the earthwork features correlate with anomalies
mapped by the magnetometer survey (see
below). Erosion has been a major problem in
the past at the site and it has also suffered
considerable earlier damage from quarrying.

In the summer of 1976 the site was parally excavated to explore possible links with the battle of Mount Badon (Hirst and Rahtz 1996). The excavation found no evidence for the battle although a considerable amount of archaeological data was recovered. In particular the Late Bronze Age/Early Iron Age was well represented, suggesting a date for the inception of the hillfort as early as the 7th century BC.

The defences are an apparently simple construction of an inner rampart, ditch and counterscarp. Hirst and Rahtz (1996, 29–30, 32) identify four main phases of rampart construction. The first rampart was timber revetted at the rear and was succeeded by two phases of dump rampart beginning with a small dump rampart with a rear facing of chalk blocks and then a more massive dump rampart with a front revetment of chalk blocks. These could all date to the Late Bronze Age/Early Iron Age (7th–6th centuries BC) on the evidence of pottery, although phases 2 and 3 might be later. Phase 4 is a slight heightening of the rampart for which dating evidence was sparse and the date and context of this event is therefore uncertain. All that can be said is that it dates to later in the Iron Age or to some subsequent period. Claims for post-Roman reoccupation cannot be substantiated on the available evidence although sunken feature structures of Anglo-Saxon date and a large Roman villa are known nearby (Fowler and Walters 1981). Immediately beyond the southern rampart is a small bowl barrow of probable earlier Bronze Age date.

Liddington Castle is situated at a junction in the local linear ditch system. South of the monument a substantial linear ditch with lesser ditched components (known as the *Bican Dic*) can be traced on the ground and as cropmarks for a distance of at least 6km along the edge of the west-facing scarp overlooking the Og Valley. This feature is also associated with an extensive block of prehistoric fields and numerous finds of Bronze Age, Iron Age and Romano-British material (Wiltshire SMR). To the west another linear ditch still survives as a slight earthwork and can be seen ascending a steep west-facing scarp before apparently terminating close to the blocked western entrance. The exact relationship is obscured by later quarry activity.

Half a kilometer north of the hillfort and at the foot of the steep escarpment, recent air photographs (Fig 2.52) have revealed the plan of another large enclosure of approximately 2.5ha (6 acres). This is bivallate, but the cropmarks suggest that the ditches are very narrow and they may in fact represent trenches for a double palisade. In form it strongly resembles Boscombe Down West (Richardson 1951) and the enclosure at Suddern Farm in its later phases (Cunliffe and Poole 2000c), both dated to the Late Middle–Late Iron Age. Another morphologically similar site is known from geophysical survey at Coombe Down, Wiltshire (McOmish *et al* 2002). There have been no recorded finds from the Liddington enclosure but its proximity to the hillfort and the

Fig 2.52
Aerial photograph of the enclosed settlement of "Boscombe Down" form on the lower shelf of the escarpment below Liddington Castle (NMRC, NMR 15342/14, SU 2080/12, 1995).

Fig 2.53
The ploughed-out remains
of a large probable hillfort-
type enclosure occupying
the lower tier of the northern
escarpment of the
Marlborough Downs above
the valley of the river Og
at Chiseldon near Swindon,
Wiltshire. The site is
overlooked by Liddington
Castle 2km to the east
(NMRC, SU 1980/1/285,
1969).

character of the circuit raises intriguing questions about the character and succession of later prehistoric settlement in this region. On the edge of the north-facing lower chalk escarpment, 3km west, near Chiseldon, another large univallate enclosure is known from air photography (Fig 2.53). Enclosing at least 8ha (20 acres), this enclosure is undated but one entrance of slightly offset form is visible which may indicate a Late Bronze Age or Early Iron Age date.

Erosion has been a major problem in the past at Liddington Castle and a programme of repair and consolidation of the earthworks was carried out during 2000–2001 as part of the Countryside Agency's Ridgeway Heritage Project.

Magnetometer survey (Figs 2.54–2.56)

Magnetometer survey was conducted over the whole interior of the fort during the first season of the Wessex Hillforts Survey in 1996. The results revealed an extensive spread of occupation activity including pits,

and short lengths of curving ditches or gul lies showing a particular concentration i the northern and western areas of the for At the centre of this zone, is a large ring shaped magnetic anomaly possibly indicat ing the former position of a round timbe building of exceptional size. At 18m i diameter this is much larger than simila features found at other hillforts in the are such as Segsbury Camp, Oxfordshire an Oldbury Castle, Wilts, which generall range from 12–15m in diameter. The circu lar feature at Liddington might represent high status building of a similar size to larg round houses of Early Iron Age date previ ously excavated at sites such as Pimpern Down, (Dorset), Cow Down, Longbridg Deverill (Wiltshire) and most recently a Flint Farm (Hampshire); (Cunliffe 1991 244; Payne 2004) or possibly a buildin with a communal or specialised functio such as a shrine. Obviously the feature can not be dated at present, but it is unlikely t be a barrow because the ditch is too narro and it seems to be closely associated with the surrounding distribution of pits. The presence of a shrine or temple within Liddington Castle belonging to the Roman period, as recently cautiously suggested by Bowden (2000), is also a possibility based on the presence of small amounts of Roman pottery and other finds indicating some activity within and around the hillfort during this period.

The most notable features recorded by the earthwork survey were four large circular depressions (features **n**, **p**, **q** and **r**; *see* Bowden 2000 and Fig 2.56 this volume). Feature **n** – the largest of the four depres-sions in the southern part of the fort, 11m in diameter and 1.55m deep – coincides clearly with a positive magnetic anomaly of likely archaeological origin in the magnetometer data. Feature **r** also coincides with a possi-ble response to a pit in the magnetometer survey but also a response to ferrous mater-ial probably of relatively recent origin. Fea-ture **q** lies within an area of anomalous activity containing numerous pit-type responses but also a possible response to larger scale ground disturbance from quar-rying or geological variation. The remaining depression at **p** does not have a correspond-ing magnetic anomaly. Features **p** and **r** are

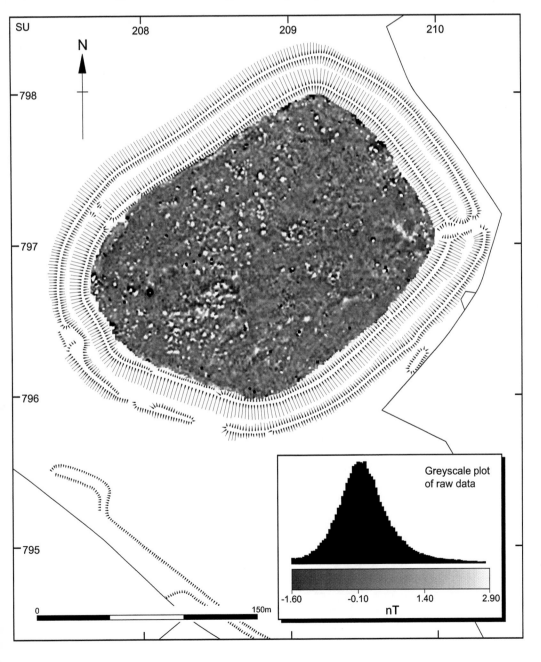

Greyscale plot of raw data

-1.60   -0.10   1.40   2.90
nT

0   150m

Fig 2.54
Greyscale plot of the magnetometer data from Liddington Castle in relation to the plan of the hillfort earthworks.

interpreted by Bowden (2000) as holes of relatively modern origin possibly linked to First World War military activity by troops stationed at nearby Chiseldon Camp. Slighter hollows just to the north-east of the centre of the fort, none more than 0.3m deep, relate to the 1896 quarrying activity noted by Passmore (1914). These and other small hollows mapped near the south and south-east edges of the enclosed area (interpreted as possible hut sites) again have no obvious magnetic anomalies associated with them. Few, if any, of the pits that produced relatively strong positive magnetic anomalies at Liddington appear to be represented by surface depressions captured by the earthwork survey, but it should be noted that the earthwork survey was carried out in the summer when much of the surface detail

within the fort was obscured by high vegetation. Because of this, other surface indications of archaeological features may still await discovery and mapping.

A suggestion of an internal quarry scoop in the form of a scarp following the inside of the rampart along the north side of the fort, and a similar feature on the south-west side of the enclosure, links in with several linear positive magnetic anomalies running parallel to the inner edge of the rampart set back a little into the fort interior. Another, wider quarry scoop, not apparent in the earthwork survey but indicated by a broad weak linear positive magnetic anomaly, seems to be present on the north-west side of the enclosure, north of the blocked western entrance. Anomalies of similar character have also been noted at

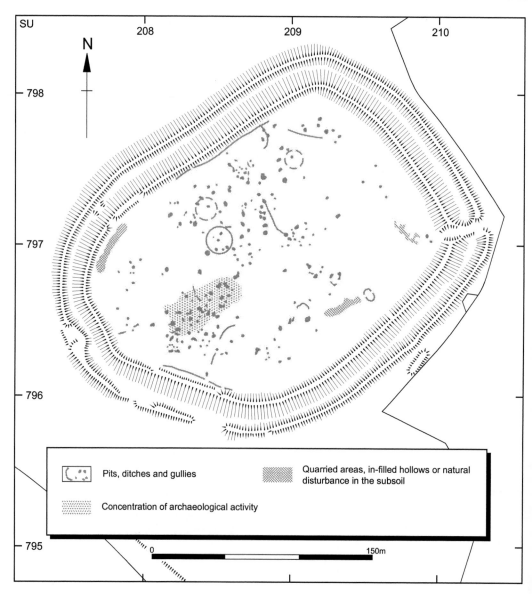

Fig 2.55
Interpretation of the magnetometer data from Liddington Castle.

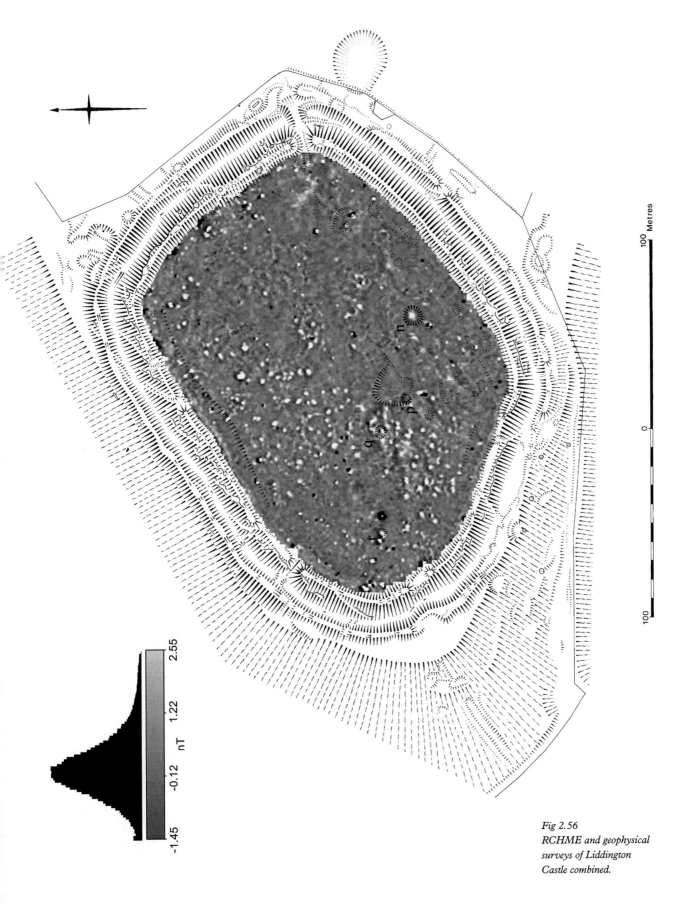

Fig 2.56
RCHME and geophysical
surveys of Liddington
Castle combined.

Alfred's Castle, Barbury Castle, Castle Ditches, Segsbury, Uffington Castle and Bury Hill following the inward facing side of the ramparts. During the 1976 excavations at Liddington Castle it was noted that the depth of topsoil over chalk increased towards the rampart tail (the area adjacent to the northern rampart of Segsbury was similar). A possible ditch or palisade trench (approximately a metre wide and about 13m inside the inner rampart) was also recorded at this time (in excavation Trench A; Hirst and Rahtz 1996). Both of these features may have some bearing on the interpretation of the magnetic anomalies subsequently mapped around the internal perimeter of the fort.

Although a possible linear ditch can be seen approaching Liddington Castle from the south-west, heading towards the blocked western entrance, there is no trace in the magnetometer data of any continuation of this feature into the hillfort interior. This is supported by the evidence of the earthwork survey which found no sign that it continued as far as the hillfort defences (Bowden 2000). It may instead turn to the south-east skirting the flank of the hill. The same lack of magnetic evidence for the presence of earlier linear ditches running through or under the hillfort applies to two slight linear hollows (interpreted as pre-hillfort land divisions) recorded by the earthwork survey emerging from under the hillfort counter-scarp on the north-east and south-east sides of the enclosure. Such negative evidence is not always reliable because some former land divisions, particularly when represented only by banks, might not neccessarily produce a sufficiently distinctive magnetic signature to be detectable.

Conclusions

The pattern of activity mapped by geophysical survey at Liddington Castle suggests that it probably never underwent prolonged or intensive occupation. This seems to be in agreement with the limited material evidence obtained to date from earthwork survey, very partial excavation in the interior and the preliminary phasing of the rampart sequence by Hirst and Rahtz (1996). A similar picture is apparent at Uffington Castle, which Liddington resembles in several aspects. In contrast the hillforts of Segsbury (east of Uffington) and Barbury Castle (west of Liddington) exhibit signs of having been more heavily occupied over longer periods of time.

The material associated with the construction of the primary ramparts (phases 1–3) at Liddington belongs to the Late Bronze Age/Early Iron Age transition. It suggests that Liddington was among the earliest hillforts in Wiltshire initially defined by a ditch and timber revetted rampart. While the timber revetted phase 1 rampart is clearly of an early date, the dump ramparts of phases 2–4 might date to the 5th–4th centuries BC (Hirst and Rahtz 1996). Liddington has produced no Iron Age pottery finds indicative of occupation after the late Early Iron Age, and by the middle of the Iron Age the site may well have been abandoned. The pottery from the site dates from at least two phases: pottery of the 7th- to 5th-centuries BC (group 1 – All Cannings Cross tradition, haematite coated, of the earliest Iron Age) and burnished and grass-marked pottery similar to ceramic phases 4–5 at Danebury dating to around the earlier 5th century BC. With the exception of Roman material, no pottery found to date at Liddington is any later than the equivalent to ceramic phases 4–5 at Danebury (that is late Early Iron Age, or the earlier 5th century BC).

Martinsell Hill Camp: Pewsey; NGR SU 177 640

Summary
Date of survey:
17–24 September 1996.
Landuse at time of survey:
Recently arable placed in set-a-side.
Geology:
Clay-with-flints deposited over upper chalk.
Soil Association:
581d – Carstens – well drained fine silty over clayey, clayey and fine silty soils, often very flinty.
Approximate area enclosed:
10 hectares (25 acres).
Planform:
Approximately rectangular.
Form of ramparts:
The defences are relatively minor in scale in comparison with many hillforts and consist of a single bank with an outer ditch, only partially preserved around some of the defensive circuit. The defences follow the curving edge of the steep escarpment on the east and south where they consist of a narrow bank, with the outer ditch only present along the north-east section. On the most easily accessible western side of the fort the defences are more substantial and better

preserved, consisting of a rampart and ditch cutting straight across the width of the promontory occupied by the fort. To the north the defences appear to have reused a straight section of an earlier east–west linear ditch. Only the rampart now survives along this section.

Entrance features:
There are two probable original entrances centrally placed on the north-east and west sides. Numerous other more modern breaches have been made through the ramparts on the western and northern sides of the enclosure.

Previous finds:
15 pottery sherds including fragments of Iron Age haematite-coated bowls, stamped, incised and finger decorated wares. 14 sherds of 1st-2nd century AD pottery (including Samian and Savernake wares) have been found on the site (Annable 1974). Previous recorded excavation : None known to have been carried out within the hillfort.

Scheduled Ancient Monument:
WI 238
County SMR No.:
SU16SE202
Project site code:
WHSP Site 7

Morphology and setting

Located on a promontory of the south-facing scarp of the Marlborough Downs, at 289m OD, the univallate hillfort of Martinsell Hill (Fig 2.57) commands extensive views of Salisbury Plain and the eastern and central zones of the Vale of Pewsey. Enclosing 10ha (25 acres), the hillfort defences follow the edge of the steep escarpment on the east and south. To the north the defences appear to re-use a section of a linear ditch that cuts off the promontory from the rest of the chalk massif and links with a large settlement complex on Huish Hill, 2km to the west. The western rampart, the most substantial component of the circuit, cuts across the plateau of the promontory. There are at least two original entrances, centrally placed on the north-east and west sides. They are both of very plain form comprising of simple gaps in the bank and ditch. The north-east entrance has been eroded by a later hollow-way which runs for about 70m to the north-east. Here the defensive ditch has an outer bank 1.0m high running for some 60m on either side of the entrance.

The site has never been excavated although a great deal of ceramic material

Fig 2.57
Aerial photograph of the large hilltop enclosure of Martinsell Hill Camp on the southern escarpment of the Marlborough Downs overlooking the Vale of Pewsey (NMRC, NMR15640/23, SU 1763/19, 1997).

Fig 2.58 (opposite)
Greyscale plot of the
magnetometer data from
Martinsell Hill Camp in
relation to the plan of the
hillfort earthworks.

has been recovered from many locations on the promontory of Martinsell Hill. From within the hillfort a small amount of pottery has been recovered, including furrowed bowls and early Roman material (Annable 1974). West of the hillfort, and spread over much of the plateau, significant concentrations of Late Bronze Age/Early Iron Age pottery, Late Iron Age pottery and early Roman material were recovered by Meyrick (Swanton G 1987). Approximately 1km to the south-west of the hillfort are two cross-ridge dykes, a plough levelled enclosure (NMR 4785/22) and a possible small promontory fort, Giant's Grave. The interior of the latter has a number of earthwork platforms representing the positions of structures. Both Giant's Grave and the ploughed-out enclosure immediately to the east have produced casual finds of Late Bronze Age and Early Iron Age pottery (Swanton G 1987). 300m beyond the north-western corner of Martinsell Hill hillfort is Withy Copse. A 'midden' excavated here by Mrs Maud Cunnington (Cunnington 1909) produced much Late Iron Age and early Roman material. Reinterpreted as a wholly early Roman feature (Swan 1975), further research has now shown that the Withy Copse feature is of Late Iron Age date and may be associated with pottery production. Evidence of possible kilns has also been recorded on the plateau west of the hillfort (Swanton G 1987). South of the hillfort, at Broomsgrove Farm, 1st- and 2nd-century AD pottery kilns have been identified (Swan 1984).

There are very few traces of prehistoric field systems on the chalk plateau in close proximity to Martinsell Hill. The drift geology of the immediate area is largely clay with flints and therefore not an area that is usually cultivated to any great extent in prehistory. The evidence for pottery production (part of the 'Savernake Ware' tradition) in the Late Iron Age and earlier Roman period suggests that much of the immediate environs of the hillfort may have been comprised of managed woodland to provide fuel for the kilns.

Below Martinsell Hill, at the eastern end of the Vale of Pewsey, our knowledge of the pre-medieval archaeological pattern is still very scant. The greensand derived soils of this area are notoriously unproductive in terms of cropmark formation and most records for the area are derived from stray finds. Ten kilometers west, at the foot of the escarpment is the important Late Bronze

Fig 2.59 (over)
Interpretation of the
magnetometer data from
Martinsell Hill Camp.

Age–Early Iron Age transition site of All Cannings Cross (Cunnington 1923). Five kilometers south another site with All Cannings Cross type ceramics has been partially investigated beneath the early Anglo-Saxon cemetery at Black Patch, Pewsey, and the 9th–8th century BC 'midden' site at East Chisenbury is 11km south-west (Brown *et al* 1994). The Vale of Pewsey and its environs is clearly an area of great importance during the early 1st millennium BC and the hillfort and associated sites on Martinsell Hill are of great regional significance.

Magnetometer survey (Figs 2.58 and 2.59)

The hill-top enclosure contains few magnetic anomalies consistent with internal settlement activity, but caution should be exercised with this interpretation because features such as small post-holes could still be present inside the fort but not detectable. Suitable recognition should be given at this juncture to Cunliffe's point (p 156) that where comparable early hill-top enclosures have been excavated, they have contained small four-posters and 'lightly built' huts. It is also possible that smaller archaeological features within the enclosed area have been gradually lost to agriculture over the course of many years. Occasional scattered positive anomalies of irregular appearance and variable magnitude do occur within the fort (particularly within the south-western zone), but their form and size suggests that they are probably of geological origin or a product of ground disturbance linked to chalk, clay or flint quarrying of unknown date. The soils on the site are very flint rich and therefore the site would be attractive for flint digging in both the prehistoric and more recent past. Weak linear and curvi-linear anomalies indicative of striped soil patterns of peri-glacial origin are also visible throughout much of the hillfort in the magnetometer data. Similar patterns are seen at Bury Hill (Hants), and Walbury (Berks). A small proportion of the magnetic anomalies at Martinsell (perhaps **A–E** on Fig 2.59) may relate to archaeological features, such as scoops or irregularly dug pits, but even so these are very sparsely distributed within the enclosed area.

The results suggest that the site functioned differently to many of the other hillforts in the region or only underwent a short episode of occupation perhaps as a temporary camp only sporadically occupied during seasonal communal gatherings. The results from Martinsell are consistent with those

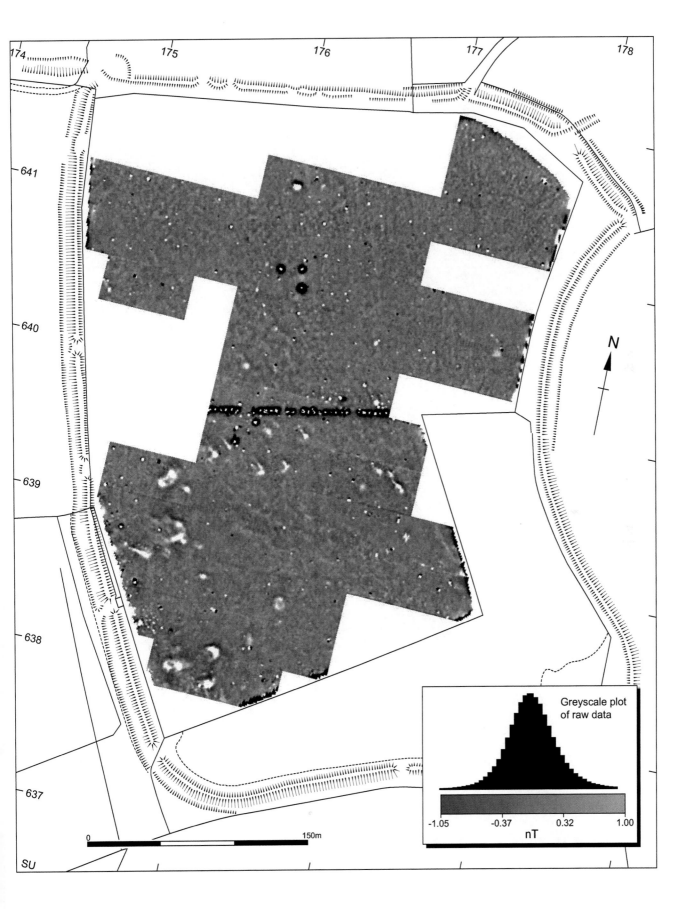

N

Greyscale plot
of raw data

-1.05   -0.37   0.32   1.00
nT

0   150m

SU

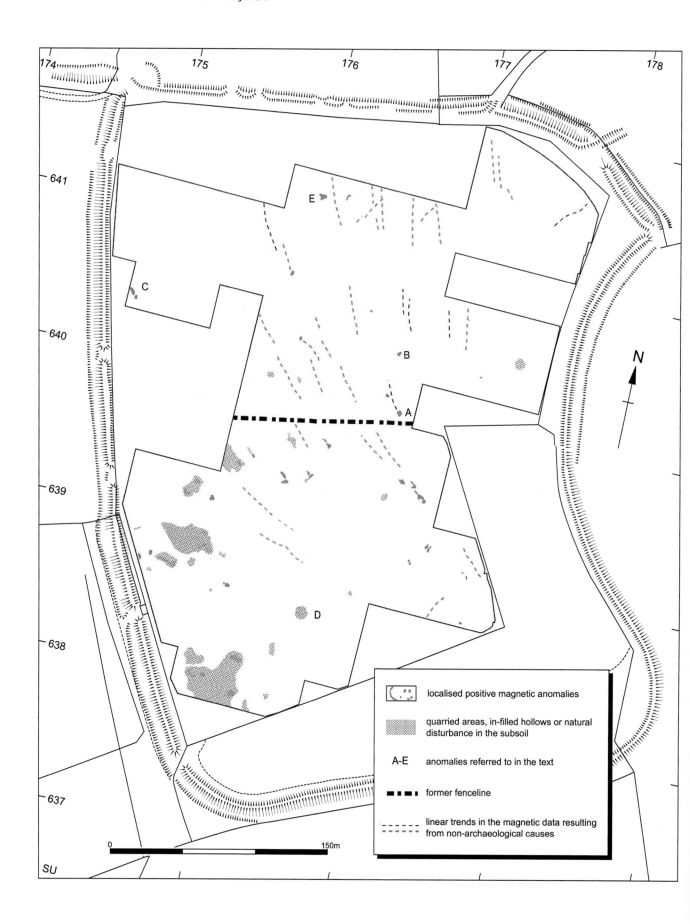

localised positive magnetic anomalies

quarried areas, in-filled hollows or natural disturbance in the subsoil

A-E anomalies referred to in the text

former fenceline

linear trends in the magnetic data resulting from non-archaeological causes

0   150m

SU

from other hillfort sites in the hill-top enclosure group such as Walbury, Balksbury and Harting Beacon, which all appear to be associated with only minor archaeological activity, suggesting a low level of internal occupation.

Oldbury: Calne; NGR SU 049 693

Summary
Date of survey:
9–17 September 1996.
Landuse at time of survey:
Permanent pasture.
Geology:
Cretaceous Upper Chalk.
Soil Association:
341 – Icknield – shallow, mostly humose, well drained calcareous soils over chalk on steep slopes and hill tops.
Approximate area enclosed:
9 hectares (22 acres).
Planform:
Irregular – bow-shaped eastern side (with central entrance) but less regular on the north, south and east where the defences follow the shape of the contours.
Form of rampats:
The defences are bivallate except on the north-west where the perimeter follows the edge of a steep escarpment and the defence consists of a nominal bank, scarp and berm. The outer ramparts show signs of being unfinished and on the south the ramparts have been damaged by flint digging. A bank and ditch running north-west – south-east divides the western part of the interior from the remainder of the fort. This cross-bank has been interpreted as an earlier phase in the construction of the hillfort defences (*see below*).
Entrance features:
An original in-turned entrance flanked by the outer rampart is present in the middle of the more regular eastern side of the hillfort. This faces the easiest gradients leading up to the site across the relatively level plateau of Cherhill Hill. There are indications of a second in-turned entrance on the far western side of the fort, partially removed by the construction of the Cherhill Monument.
Previous finds:
Early Iron Age haematite coated ware (600–500 BC) was recovered from pits excavated in the interior by Cunnington in 1875. The base of one late Iron Age vessel, Roman coins and pottery, a 5th century Saxon brooch and part of a saddle quern (undated) have also been recovered from the site.

Previous recorded excavation:
Late 19th-century excavation by Cunnington (Cunnington 1871).
Scheduled Ancient Monument:
WI 106.
County SMR No.:
SU06NW200.
Project Site Code:
WHSP Site 6.

Morphology and setting

Oldbury hillfort (Fig 2.60) is located at the western end of Cherhill Down, close to the western edge of the chalk massif of the Marlborough Downs, and has extensive views in all directions. It is the largest later prehistoric monument in the Avebury region, with Windmill Hill, Avebury henge and Silbury Hill all being visible from the eastern defences. The defences enclose an area of approximately 9ha (22 acres) and are bivallate except on the north-west where a simple ledge following the contour at the head of a steep coombe defines the boundary. The enclosing earthworks vary considerably in character, being most massive on the east and south – 'humouring the hill in its numerous sinuousities' (Colt Hoare 1812). There are two probable original entrances still visible, with that on the eastern side being the largest, with substantial inturns and a relatively complex series of outworks.

The earthwork defences display evidence of several stages of modification indicating a complex sequence of development. An earlier western limit of the monument is marked by a massive single bank and ditch that runs along the line of the 250m contour. Subsequently the defences were extended westwards along the break of slope overlooking a steep coombe that divides Cherhill Down from Calstone Down. This surface evidence, coupled with the discovery of a section of another possible smaller enclosure circuit within the north-eastern quadrant of the hillfort during the course of the magnetometer survey (*see below*), clearly indicates that Oldbury is an extremely complex site with a lengthy history of activity. Within the eastern part of the monument, slight earthwork remains indicate the presence of pits and possible structures, many of which appear to correlate with anomalies recorded by the magnetometer survey. Much of the interior of the south-western quadrant of the hillfort has been heavily disturbed by chalk and flint quarries of 18th- and 19th-century date (Colt Hoare 1812). These workings extend beyond the hillfort

Fig 2.60
Aerial photograph of
Oldbury on Cherhill
Down, near Avebury,
Wiltshire looking south.
The various phases of the
defences and the extent of
quarrying disturbance
around the periphery
of the site are clearly
visible in the photograph
(NMRC, NMR
15834/07, SU
0469/40,1997).

Fig 2.61 (opposite)
Greyscale plot of the
magnetometer data from
Oldbury in relation to
the plan of the hillfort
earthworks.

to the south and south-east and have effectively destroyed or masked any earlier remains in close proximity to the hillfort.

As a result of evidence unearthed by the flint digging, Colt Hoare (1812) states that Oldbury 'appears to have been made use of as a place of residence as well as defence, for the labourers in digging for flints within its area, throw up numerous fragments of animal bones and rude pottery, the certain marks of habitation.'

Although no detailed scientific excavation has ever been undertaken on the hillfort, informal digging has produced numerous finds that indicate activity on the hilltop over a considerable period of time (Cunnington 1871; Grinsell 1957). The ceramics include a large amount of Late Bronze Age–Early Iron Age forms and fabrics, some later Iron Age material, considerable amounts of Romano-British pottery and a penannular brooch of probable 5th–7th century AD date. The latter is of considerable interest as a very similar brooch was recently discovered 'near Calne', within 4km of Oldbury (Youngs 1995). The brooches are of British origin and of a type well-known in western Britain. The proximity of Oldbury to the western terminal of the East Wansdyke on Morgan's

Hill, only 3km south-west, may be of some importance. Eagles (1994), has argued for late 5th century AD date for the construction of the East Wansdyke. Given the presence of two 5th–7th-century brooches, one from within the hillfort, and one from nearby Calne (Youngs 1995) it is quite possible that Oldbury was re-occupied in the early post Roman period. In this context it is tempting to see the smaller enclosure within the north-eastern quadrant as a post-Roman construction. The construction of other enclosures within hillforts at this period is known in the neighbouring county of Somerset at Cadbury Congresbury (Rahtz *et al* 1992). Cherhill village, immediately north of Oldbury, is also the site of a substantial Roman villa located beneath the medieval church (Johnson and Walters 1988).

Beyond the hillfort defences there are a significant number of monuments to the east along Cherhill Down and to the south on North Down. A substantial linear ditch approaches Oldbury from the east along Cherhill Down. This can be traced for a distance of 2.5km and although partially levelled by ploughing as it approaches Oldbury, enough survives to show that the feature terminated on the edge of the escarpment just outside the northern apex

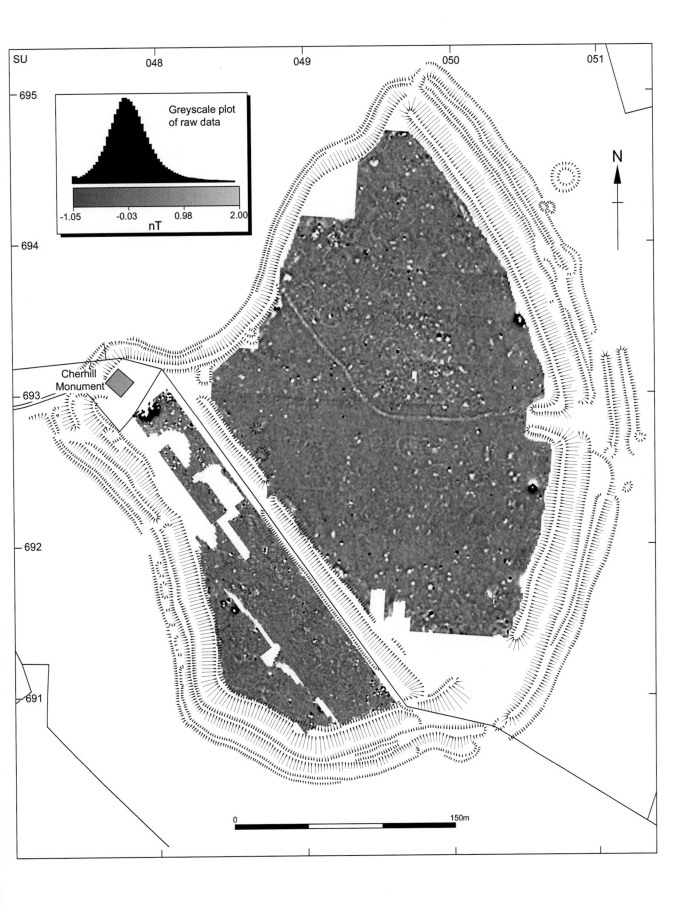

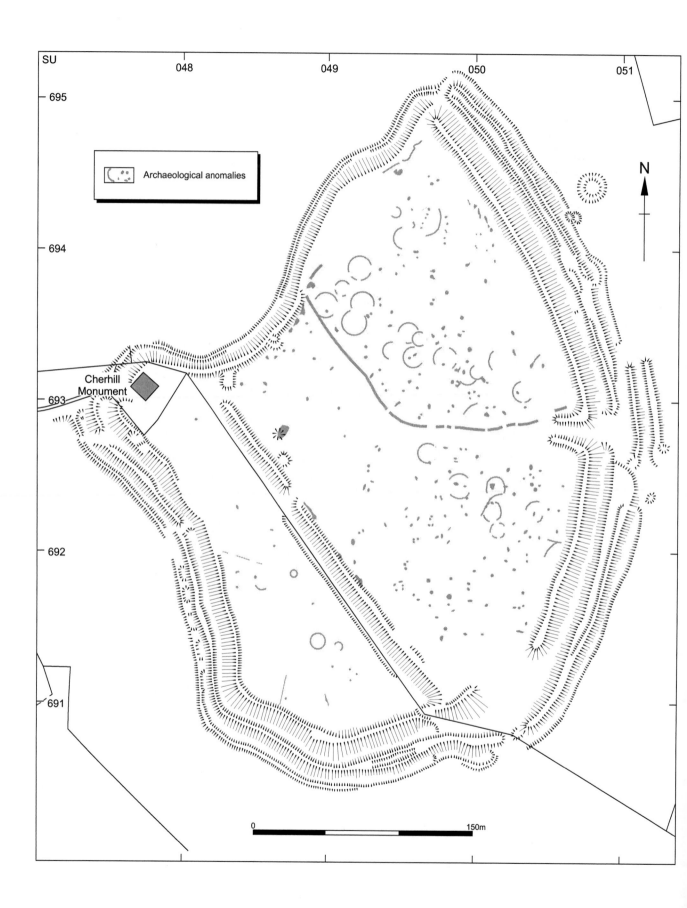

of the hillfort. Just beyond the eastern entrance of the hillfort is an extant bowl barrow, presumably of earlier Bronze Age date. Between the barrow and the linear ditch, approximately 200m beyond the hillfort defences, there is a well-defined rectangular platform that has produced finds of Romano-British pottery and pennant sandstone roof tiles. The latter suggests the presence of a structure of some status and, given the exposed and elevated location, a later Roman period temple or shrine should not be ruled out. Temples or shrines of the Romano-British period set either within or in close proximity to hillforts are relatively common occurrences in western Britain. At Uley in Gloucestershire and Cadbury Congresbury in Somerset, temples of Romano-British date are located close to hillforts (Woodward and Leach 1993; Watts and Leach 1996).

No prehistoric field systems are known in close proximity to Oldbury. To the south, however, on North Down and beyond the line of the Roman Road from London to Bath (Margary 4), there are still slight traces of an extensive field system as well as significant concentrations of earlier Bronze Age barrow cemeteries. Beyond these, on Bishop's Cannings Down, settlements and fields of later Bronze Age date have been surveyed and partially excavated (Gingell 1992) and an Early Iron Age settlement associated with early All Cannings Cross-type ceramics sampled (Swanton pers comm).

North of Oldbury, on the lower chalk plateau, evidence of later prehistoric activity has been surprisingly elusive. This may in part be a reflection of the poor response to crop mark formation on this geology. However, recent excavations in the area of Yatesbury and Compton Bassett to investigate the early medieval origins of these villages have produced some evidence of prehistoric activity.

Magnetometer survey (Figs 2.61 and 2.62)

The fluxgate magnetometer survey carried out over the majority of the hillfort interior (excluding quarried areas) in 1996 revealed the presence of a previously unrecognised internal ditch dividing the northernmost third of the hillfort from the remainder. The ditch follows a curving course from just north of the in-turned entrance on the eastern side of the hillfort to a point on the north-western perimeter of the hillfort where there is a distinct change in the form of the inner rampart. This new discovery

may indicate that the fort developed in several distinct phases and that it possibly retracted at a later date, or expanded to enclose a larger area, leaving part of the earlier defences redundant. Similar developments are known, for example, at Maiden Castle in Dorset, Torberry in West Sussex (Cunliffe 1976) and Conderton Camp in Worcestershire (Thomas forthcoming) associated with Middle Iron Age re-configuration of the defensive circuits. Another possible parallel is the hillfort on Cadbury Hill, Congresbury, Somerset where an internal rampart was constructed across the centre of the original area enclosed by the Iron Age defences associated with post-Roman reoccupation of the site (Rahtz et al 1992). If not an enclosure feature, the ditch might represent part of the course of a linear boundary ditch pre-dating the construction of the hillfort. This could be clarified by more magnetometer survey to determine if the ditch continues underneath the hillfort ramparts into the adjacent downland.

In the eastern and northern sectors of the fort, there is evidence of intensive occupation, including faint traces of up to 20 circular gullies, possibly the positions of successive phases of round timber buildings. Abundantly scattered amongst these structures, defined by localised positive magnetic anomalies, are in excess of 150 pits. The areas of occupation tend to cluster to either side of an east–west road corridor (defined by an absence of magnetic anomalies) running from the east entrance towards the Cherhill Monument (where there is the suggestion of a second in-turned entrance). Occupation activity appears to decrease in the southern and western areas, but due to the extreme weakness of the circular anomalies at Oldbury, traces of buildings could well be present elsewhere on the site which are not detectable above the threshold of instrument noise. Greater down-slope soil accumulation could also be obscuring other features in these areas. The geophysical evidence from Oldbury is not dissimilar to that obtained from Segsbury Camp (Letcombe Castle).

The new geophysical evidence from Oldbury has resulted in a major improvement to understanding of the site suggesting that it belongs in a category of hillforts typified by sites such as Danebury, Segsbury Camp and Yarnbury Castle. The site clearly has a complex history with evidence for several phases of modification of the enclosed circumference.

Fig 2.62
Interpretation of the magnetometer data from Oldbury.

127

Oliver's Castle or Camp: Bromham; NGR SU 001 647

Summary

Date of survey:
25–7 September 1996.

Landuse at time of survey:
Rough grassland/meadow.

Geology:
Cretaceous Lower Chalk.

Soil Association:
342b – Upton 2 – shallow well drained calcareous silty soils over argillaceous (clay enriched) chalk.

Approximate area enclosed:
1.6 hectares (3.9 acres).

Planform:
Approximately triangular.

Form of ramparts:
The defences consist of a modest bank and outer ditch where they cut across a natural spur on the eastern side of the fort. Around the remainder of the perimeter the defences follow and emphasise the natural contours of the steep sided promontory on which the fort is sited.

Entrance features:
A single entrance is present on the eastern side of the camp. It consists of a simple break sited centrally in the eastern rampart and on the most approachable side of the camp.

Previous finds:
The site has formerly produced finds of Bronze Age, Iron Age and Roman pottery.

Previous recorded excavation:
Partially excavated by M. Cunnington in 1907 (Cunnington, M E, 1908).

Scheduled Ancient Monument:
SAM WI 27.

County SMR No.:
SU06SW200.

Project site code:
WHSP Site 8.

Morphology and setting

Oliver's Castle (Fig 2.63) is a small univallate earthwork enclosing an area of approximately 1.6ha (3.9 acres). The fort occupies a triangular, west-facing promontory, 195m OD, at the extreme western edge of the Marlborough Downs chalk massif. The form of the natural promontory has dictated the shape of the enclosed area. Immediately south of this promontory a narrow coombe provides a natural route by which an ascent of the escarpment onto the plateau of Roundway Down can be made with ease. The clear earthwork remains of terraceways and a hollow-way demonstrate the intensity of past use of the route.

Oliver's Castle has a single entrance located on the eastern side of the monument; this is of plain form, comprising a simple

Fig 2.63
Aerial photograph of the small triangular escarpment-edge hillfort of Oliver's Camp, on Roundway Down near Devizes, Wiltshire. In the Interior two features are visible as surface relief (a circle and a rectangle). These produced intense anomalies in the magnetometer survey suggestive of ferrous material and are therefore likely to be of relatively modern origin (original photography held at Cambridge University Collection of Air Photographs, Unit for Landscape Modelling, AY 45, 1948).

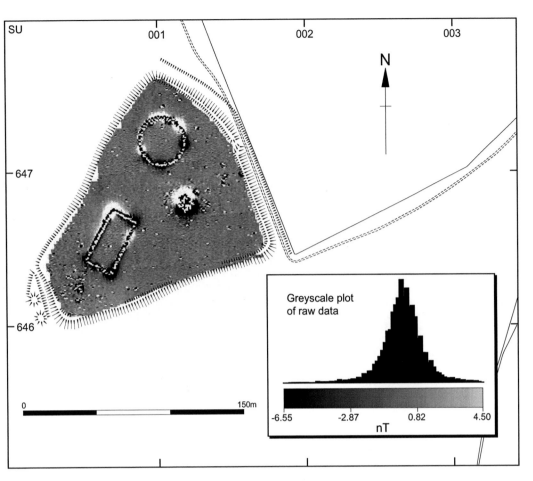

SU

001   002   003

N

647

646

0   150m

Greyscale plot
of raw data

-6.55   -2.87   0.82   4.50
nT

Fig 2.64
Greyscale plot of the
magnetometer data from
Oliver's Camp in relation
to a plan of the hillfort
earthwork.

break in the perimeter bank with a corresponding causeway across the ditch. A single rampart of relatively slight character with an external ditch defines the hillfort circuit. The greatest rampart height is seen on the east, facing the approach from Roundway Down and it rises slightly either side of the approach to the entrance. On the northern side there is a slight but well-defined counterscarp bank. At the western apex of the circuit, the hillfort ditch deviates from the line of the inner rampart to incorporate two bowl barrows of presumed earlier Bronze Age date. This deliberate inclusion of earlier features into the perimeter system is of considerable interest and is another example of a phenomenon seen in Wessex and areas beyond where earlier features were consciously incorporated into the hillfort landscape (Bowden and McOmish 1987; 1989).

Excavation of Oliver's Camp in 1907 by Maud Cunnington (Cunnington 1908) established a Late Bronze Age/Early Iron Age date for the construction of the fort, although pre-hillfort activity is attested to by the barrows (*see above*) and Bronze Age hearths sealed by the rampart (ibid). The

majority of the ceramics recovered belong to the early All Cannings Cross period and includes quantities of furrowed bowl, a form more usually associated with non-hillfort sites in Wessex. There was very little later Iron Age material although a quantity of late Roman pottery was recovered along with a substantial portion of an iron window grille. This fitting could suggest the presence of a substantial Roman building in close proximity to the hillfort, although the geophysics failed to locate any such structure within the monument. Close to the hillfort there are a number of other features that suggest the presence of a religious focus spanning the Iron Age and Romano-British periods.

Below the western apex of the hillfort, at approximately 160m OD, there is a narrow level platform following the contour. Although undoubtedly natural in origin this platform, like Oliver's Camp, also overlooks a spring known as Mother Anthony's well. This spring has, over many years, produced many casual finds of later Iron Age and Romano-British material, especially coins and metalwork (Dr P Robinson, *pers com*). Long suspected to be a temple or shrine, recent air photographs (NMR15519/25) show a pair of oval enclosures, evidence of multiple ditches (with characteristics consistent with a late Iron Age date), stone structures and a metalled road with flanking side-ditches of presumed Roman date. It is possible that the iron window grille excavated by Cunnington inside Oliver's Camp originated from this complex.

East of the hillfort is the plateau of Roundway Down. Now heavily cultivated, air photography has revealed very faint and intermittent traces of a prehistoric field system across the plateau that approaches the eastern defences of the hillfort. No obvious settlement related features are visible in close proximity to the monument.

Magnetometer survey (Fig 2.64)

Magnetometer survey carried out over the interior of Oliver's Castle in 1996 failed to identify any internal occupation features clearly contemporary with the hillfort. Two unusually conspicuous anomalies in the form of a circle 30m in diameter and a rectangle with dimensions of 37m × 19m were recorded in the north and west parts of the fort interior. These are indicative of structures incorporating ferrous material such as reinforced concrete and are therefore presumably of relatively modern origin. A possible interpretation of these unexpected features is that they represent the remains of a former military installation (possibly a WWII search light post). The position of a dew-pond, visible as a depression in the center of the site, was also detected by the magnetometer as another area of intense magnetic disturbance having been partially in-filled with magnetic detritus. The magnetic response over the rest of the site is subdued and unremarkable, suggesting that only insubstantial remains of any earlier habitation are present.

3

The Regional Pattern

by Mark Corney and Andrew Payne

The hillforts of Wessex: their morphology and environs

by Mark Corney

Introduction

The methodical study of Wessex hillforts has its origins in the late 19th century and opening two decades of the 20th century and, with the notable exception of Pitt Rivers' excavations at Winkelbury, Wiltshire (Pitt Rivers 1888), initially developed as a non-intrusive survey tradition. Given that this volume is presenting the results of non-intrusive methodologies it is worth pausing to review the development of this tradition in Wessex. Although the late 19th century marks the main starting point for investigations, any review must acknowledge the contribution of the superb surveys produced by Philip Crocker on behalf of Sir Richard Colt Hoare. These plans (Fig 3.1) are a remarkable and accurate record of many monuments, including hillforts (Colt Hoare 1812, 1819). They frequently depicted major hillforts and their environs thus presenting the first 'landscape' plans specifically executed to record the extant archaeology.

Pitt Rivers was certainly aware of the importance of recording surface features and the Cranborne Chase volumes contain many plans of his sites prior to excavation (eg Pitt Rivers 1888). In addition he also had scale models produced of many sites that depict the condition of the monument prior to excavation (Bowden 1991). Pitt Rivers' assistants, most notably Herbert Toms, were to develop this analytical survey skill further (Bradley 1989).

Earthwork depictions of most of the hillforts in the Wessex region to a common specification were first produced by the Ordnance Survey for the first edition 6-inch and 25-inch maps (Crawford 1955; Phillips 1980). In the opening years of the 20th century a small number of fieldworkers began to produce larger-scale, divorced surveys of many Wessex hillforts. In 1908 Allcroft published *Earthwork of England*, and of particular interest are the investigations of Heywood Sumner and J

P Williams Freeman. Both worked primarily in Hampshire, although Sumner also extended his survey work into neighbouring southern Wiltshire and Dorset. His pioneering survey of Cranborne Chase (Sumner 1913) resulted in the presentation of plans produced to a very high standard of draughtsmanship that had a profound influence on the graphic style of the early RCHM surveys in West Dorset. (These were largely produced during the 1930s but, owing to the outbreak of the Second World War, were not published until 1952.) Williams Freeman published surveys of many Hampshire hillforts (1915) and although his graphical style did not match that of Sumner, he provided an important record of many sites as they appeared 100 years ago (*see* for example the section on Norsebury, pp 66–71).

This auspicious start to non-intrusive investigation was to prove something of a false dawn as the emphasis began to move rapidly to hillfort excavation. In Wiltshire Maud Cunnington, assisted by her husband B H Cunnington, investigated a number of hillforts (Cunnington 1908, 1925, 1932a, 1932b, 1933; Cunnington and Cunnington 1913, 1917) as well as the important Early Iron Age settlement at All Cannings Cross (Cunnington 1923). In Hampshire it was C F C Hawkes who took the lead in hillfort excavation, investigating St Catherine's Hill (Hawkes *et al* 1930; Hawkes 1976), Buckland Rings (Hawkes 1936), Quarley Hill (Hawkes 1939) and Bury Hill (Hawkes 1940). Hawkes' excavations in Hampshire were to be central to his 'ABC' scheme for the British Iron Age (Hawkes 1931, 1956, 1959). Southwest of our study area, in Dorset, Sir Mortimer Wheeler and his team examined a number of major hillforts at Maiden Castle (Wheeler 1943), Poundbury (Richardson 1940) and Chalbury (Whitley 1943).

The growth of aerial photography in archaeology in the decades following the Second World War had a profound impact in the region. The potential of this method had already been demonstrated by Crawford and Keiller (1928) but it was not until the formation of the Cambridge University Committee for Air Photography and,

Fig 3.1
*The surveys of Oldbury
and Barbury Castle
published in 1812 by Sir
Richard Colt Hoare in his*
Ancient History of
Wiltshire, Volume 2
(from NMRC Library –
The Ancient History of
Wiltshire, Volume 2,
North Wiltshire, Plate
VIII, pages 40–41,
originally published 1812,
re-published 1975).

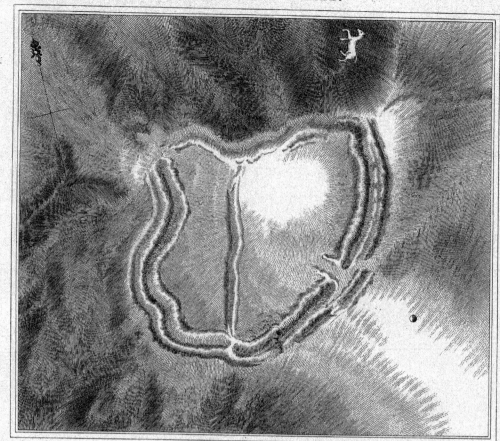

OLDBURY CAMP.

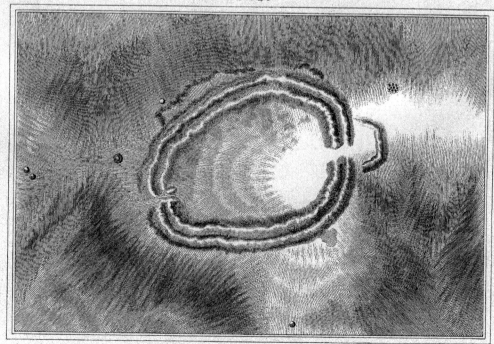

Nº. 2.

BARBURY CASTLE.

somewhat later, the Air Photography Unit of RCHME that the intensity and complexity of the later prehistoric landscape in Wessex could be fully appreciated. Collin Bowen (1975, 1978) began the elucidation of this landscape by using the results of air photography and ground survey. Building upon this came a landmark study with the publication of a major air photographic study of the Danebury environs (Palmer 1984). Using only air photographic sources, an area of 450 sq km was mapped at a scale of 1:10,000 with select windows at 1:5000 and 1:2500. This study set a new standard in air photographic analysis of extensive relict landscapes that has been repeated since over many areas of the country (eg Bowen 1990; Stoertz 1997).

In addition to pure air survey, multidisciplinary extensive projects within Wessex using air photography, earthwork survey and geophysics were undertaken by the former RCHME (now part of English Heritage). Studies of southern Wiltshire (NMR archive) and Salisbury Plain (McOmish et al 2002) demonstrate the level of detailed analysis attainable by these means and were instrumental in stimulating further projects (eg Bradley et al 1994).

The morphology of Wessex hillforts

The main morphological characteristics of the hillforts of the British Isles have been examined in detail by numerous authors in recent years (eg Cunliffe 1991, 312–70; Forde-Johnston 1976; Hogg 1975). These studies looked at the phenomenon of hillforts from both national and regional perspectives. In Wessex work has continued at a number of levels; ranging from major projects involving large scale excavation, such as at Danebury, to intensive non-intrusive survey utilising multi-disciplinary methodologies. Among the latter there have been a large number of earthwork and air photographic surveys that have added both a considerable amount of detail and important observations that, until now, have remained largely unpublished. The following section is largely based upon this work.

Location

The choice of hillfort location cannot be considered as a random decision. The correlation between hillforts and earlier monuments is well known – even though there is still considerable debate on the significance of this corre-lation. Whatever the undoubtedly complex factors behind the choice of location might have been, there were clear preferred locations within the landscape and strong regional trends can be discerned over much of the area covered by this study. There is a tendency to view Wessex hillforts as part of the classic chalkland prehistoric landscape. However, even a cursory glance at the map of Wessex hillforts immediately shows that the great majority are located on the limits of the chalk, either on the escarpment edge or overlooking the major valleys such as the Avon, Test, Kennet and Wylye. Only a relatively small number are within the main chalk massif and even here it is possible to discern preferred locations in certain regions.

It must be stressed that many of those sites grouped together below have had little if any modern excavation and the detailed chronology is far from clear. It will be seen, though, that there are certain common links in the morphology of these groupings. Obviously none of these sites will have existed in isolation; the other components of the environs of those hillforts examined by this project, and noted in the preceding section, must be borne in mind (see also pp 139–41).

Escarpment locations

There are two major groups occupying north-facing escarpments:

The Ridgeway/Marlborough Downs Group

The largest group within this category is located on the north-facing escarpment of the Berkshire Downs and Marlborough Downs – along the route of the 'Ridgeway' – comprising ten hillforts: Blewburton Hill (Harding 1976), Segsbury, Rams Hill, Uffington Castle, Hardwell Camp, Liddington Castle, Chiseldon (a ploughed out univallate site known only from air photographs (see Fig 2.53) and Barbury Castle. The latter three also overlook the junction between the Og Valley and the northern chalk escarpment, allowing easy access from the chalk massif to the upper Thames Valley. Beyond Barbury Castle there is a gap in the Avebury area and then two western fringe outliers of the group: Oldbury and Oliver's Camp.

North Hampshire Escarpment

This group comprises six hillforts and overlooks the middle reaches of the Kennet Valley with extensive views to the north. The westernmost outlier of the group, Forest Hill near Marlborough, is possibly a Late

Iron Age construct (Cunliffe 1991, 153; Corney 1997) while the remainder; Walbury, Beacon Hill, Ladle Hill, Bowry Walls and Winklebury occupy the main escarpment edge set back some distance from the Kennet Valley.

Smaller scarp edge clusters can be discerned in a number of areas. The north-western escarpment of Salisbury Plain in the Warminster area has four hillforts – Scratchbury, Battlesbury, Bratton Castle (McOmish *et al* 2002) and Cley Hill – forming a discrete cluster. At the eastern end of the Vale of Pewsey Martinsell Hill and Giant's Grave dominate the south-facing escarpment.

River Valley Foci

In Wessex a number of the major river valleys act as notable foci for hillfort locations. This applies to four principal river systems and their tributaries: the River Test in Hampshire, the River Avon in Hampshire and Wiltshire, the River Stour in Dorset and the Frome and Piddle in Dorset. Of these the Stour and the Avon have the greatest concentration of hillforts and associated landscapes.

The River Avon in Hampshire and Wiltshire

The River Avon and its tributaries, in particular the River Wylye, has the largest and most coherent group comprising 25 hillforts and the major emporium at Hengistbury Head (Cunliffe 1987) where the Stour and the Avon flow into the English Channel.

Along the lower stretches of the Avon, east of the river and on the fringe of the New Forest are four small univallate enclosures: Castle Hill, Castle Piece, Gorley and Frankenbury (Smith N 1999). Upon entering the chalk the hillforts along the Avon become more frequent and are often of larger proportions: Castle Ditches, Whitsbury (Bowen 1990; Ellison and Rahtz 1987), Clearbury, Woodbury (Bersu 1940; Brailsford 1948, 1949), Old Sarum, Ogbury (Crawford and Keiller 1928), Heale Hill, Vespasian's Camp (RCHME 1979, 20–1), Casterley Camp (McOmish *et al* 2002; Cunnington and Cunnington 1913) and Chisenbury Trendle (Cunnington 1932b). Along the River Wylye, north-west of the confluence with the Avon are Grovely Castle, Bilbury ring, Stockton (Corney 1994), Yarnbury (Cunnington 1933), Codford Circle, and then Scratchbury, Battlesbury and Cley Hill (the last three also being on scarp edge locations – *see above*). West of the Salisbury confluence, along the valley of the River Nadder are Chiselbury (Clay 1935), Wick Ball Camp, Castle Ditches (Tisbury) and Castle Rings (Donhead). North-east of the confluence with the Avon, the high ground overlooking the valley of the River Bourne has Figsbury Ring (Cunnington 1925; Guido and Smith 1982), the major complex on Boscombe Down West (Richardson 1951) and Sidbury.

The River Stour, Dorset

The Stour and its tributaries host a number of major hillforts and, by way of the Blackmoor Vale, give access through to the southern edge of the Somerset Levels and the two large and impressive Wessex fringe hillforts of South Cadbury (Barrett *et al* 2000) and Ham Hill (Dunn 1997). The main concentration of larger hillforts along the Stour Valley is between Hengistbury Head and the Blandford Forum area, effectively defining the southern and western limits of Cranborne Chase with its distinctive Iron Age Settlement pattern (Barrett *et al* 1991). This group comprises Dudsbury, Spettisbury (Gresham 1940), Badbury (Crawford and Keiller 1928), Buzbury, Hod Hill (Richmond 1968; RCHM 1970c) and Hambledon Hill (RCHM 1970b). Beyond Hambledon Hill, where the valley broadens out into the Blackmoor Vale, are smaller hillforts at Rawlsbury and Banbury Hill (RCHM 1970c). Close to the source of the Stour and also situated on the south-western extremity of the Wiltshire chalk lies White Sheet Hill, a multi-period prehistoric focus of comparable complexity to Hambledon Hill.

The Frome and Piddle, Dorset

This is the smallest of the river foci in Wessex, having five hillforts within the catchment area: Bulbury (Cunliffe 1972), Woodbury (RCHM 1970a), Weatherby Castle (RCHM 1970c), Poundbury (Richardson 1940) and Maiden Castle (Sharples 1991; Wheeler 1943). The latter is the only hillfort in Dorset to have had an intensive study of its immediate environs (Sharples ibid).

The River Test, Hampshire

The valley of the River Test is the easternmost of the major valley foci in Wessex. Beyond here the Itchen and Meon valleys have but one major fort apiece, St Catherine's Hill (Hawkes *et al* 1930; Hawkes 1976) and Old Winchester Hill (Chapter 1, this volume). The Test and its tributaries flow from the heart of the Hampshire chalk into Southampton Water and have 13 hillforts within the catchment. The largest in terms of area enclosed and complexity are north of Stockbridge: Ashley's Copse, Woolbury, Danebury, Bury Hill, Balksbury, Tidbury Ring and Norsebury. South of Stockbridge and beyond the southern limit of the chalk are other smaller and poorly understood sites: The Walls, Tatchbury, Toothill Camp, Dunwood Camp, Lockerley Camp and Holbury.

Further observations on location

One curious grouping observed in parts of the region is the occasional pairing of large hillforts in close proximity to each other. In some cases the benefit of excavation has indicated support for the model put forward by Cunliffe that sees one monument abandoned while another continues to develop and become a multivallate or developed hillfort. This is clearly the most likely case in the Dorchester area with Poundbury and Maiden Castle. In other areas the evidence is not so clear cut and the possibility of an earlier manifestation of the pairing of sites seen in parts of Wessex (Barrett et al 1991; Corney 1989) in the Late Iron Age should not be discounted. Of especial note are the close proximity of Hambledon Hill and Hod Hill in Dorset, Battlesbury and Scratchbury in Wiltshire, and Martinsell Hill and Giant's Grave also in Wiltshire. It is of passing interest to note in the cases of Hambledon Hill and Scratchbury that both hillforts enclose Neolithic causewayed enclosures, as does Maiden Castle.

Observations on the Ridgeway and Avebury Environs grouping of hillforts

The hillforts of the Ridgeway and Avebury Environs grouping were the main focus of investigation during the first season of the survey programme in 1996. The sites are arranged approximately equidistantly in a linear fashion along the escarpment edge of the Berkshire and Marlborough Downs, coincident with the route followed by the Ridgeway giving rise to the frequently used term 'Ridgeway hillforts'. Based largely on their even distribution but without the backing of reliable dating evidence, it has been contended that the Ridgeway forts represent largely contemporary centres of adjacent territorial blocks (Cotton 1962), in which case they might be expected to exhibit similar densities and character of internal occupation. One of the specific aims of the Wessex Hillforts Survey was to test this theory further by attempting, through non-destructive means, to determine if the sites do in fact contain recurring patterns of spatial organisation. Like the Danebury Environs Project before it, the Hillforts of the Ridgeway Project (Gosden and Lock 2003; Miles et al 2003; Lock et al 2005) is now beginning to provide a more detailed chronological framework for hillfort development in the Ridgeway area, which will help to resolve some of the fundamental archaeological questions concerning the group. It is encouraging to observe that all of the Ridgeway hillforts are currently under stable grassland management regimes, some formerly having been under arable cultivation. The present sympathetic management of the sites is likely to stay in place for the foreseeable future, with beneficial effects for the preservation of archaeological features contained within them (many of which have been revealed for the first time by the geophysical surveys). In some cases the increased knowledge of the hillforts derived from the geophysical programme has acted as a catalyst for improving the management of the sites. The cultural resource value of many of the sites had previously been largely ignored owing to the paucity of knowledge of their internal character. This had led to the misconception that there was little of archaeological interest surviving or worth preserving within the continuously ploughed sites.

The hillforts of the Ridgeway exhibit considerable differences in size, ranging from the largest at Segsbury Camp (Letcombe Castle) with an internal area of some 12ha, to the smallest enclosure of 1.2ha at Alfred's Castle. As well as the varying size of the areas enclosed by the Ridgeway forts, there are also obvious differences in the layout of the defensive circuits. More often than not the ground plans reflect the particular topographical position of the site, but some sites also exhibit more elaborate defensive architecture than others in the form of the entrances, the presence of additional outworks screening an entrance and multivallation of the ramparts. Univallate sites with an internal bank fronted by a ditch and an outer counterscarp are the most common defensive arrangement in the Ridgeway group (illustrated by Uffington and Liddington for example). Other sites are multivallate for part of their circuit, such as Segsbury and Oldbury (generally to reinforce sections of the defences with less of a natural terrain advantage that can be approached over level ground or to provide a more impressive symbol of strength or status visible from the main avenue of approach to the hillfort). In some cases (for example at Barbury and Segsbury) there is limited evidence for earlier pre-hillfort enclosures removed or built over by the later defences (*see* for example Bowden 1998) or remodelled and extended enclosures (for example Oldbury and Alfred's Castle). Barbury shows the greatest elaboration of the group having completely bi-vallate defences (the product of successive phases of construction) and a defensive outwork screening the approach to the eastern entrance. Segsbury has an outward projecting hornwork shielding the eastern entrance and yet another variation on entrance reinforcement is present at Oldbury, where a northerly extension of the second outer rampart screens the eastern entrance preventing a direct approach and creating an extended corridor to the entrance, which itself is deeply inturned.

The varying approaches adopted for entrance augmentation at the hillforts of the Ridgeway and the Avebury Environs have clear parallels with other hillfort sites elsewhere in Wessex. The outer rampart screening the eastern entrance at Oldbury uses exactly the same technique employed at the eastern entrance of Hod Hill in Dorset (Cunliffe 1991, fig14.13, 336). The possible out-curving of the main ramparts at the eastern entrance of Segsbury to create an extended corridor approach mirrors the construction of the eastern entrance at Danebury. The eastern outwork at Barbury Castle has some similarity with the one protecting the eastern entrance of Yarnbury Castle also in Wiltshire. A similar feature is also present at Chiselbury, Witshire. Liddington, Segsbury and Uffington all show evidence of originally having possessed two entrances – east and west – one of which was subsequently blocked. The same practice can be seen at Danebury and Beacon Hill in Hampshire and at Conderton Camp, Worcestershire (Thomas 2005). It is interesting to note that the examples of hillforts with multivallate defences in the wider Ridgeway grouping at Barbury and Oldbury retain two opposing entrances, as is also the case with other multivallate sites farther afield such as Maiden Castle (Dorset) and Castle Ditches (Tisbury, Wilts). The widespread occurrence of blocked entrances at the hillforts investigated by the project is discussed below and in Chapter 4.

Rampart Morphology

There has been a long tradition of categorising hillfort ramparts according to the nature of the circuit, construction method and the materials employed (cf Hawkes 1971; Cunliffe 1991, 313–29). This level of analysis can be based partly on surface observation, but a full elucidation of the often complex sequence of construction requires excavation. The literature on this aspect of hillfort circuits is well known and will not be repeated here. There are, however, a number of observations on the nature of hillfort ramparts that seem to have escaped attention and are especially relevant to a number of the monuments examined as part of the Wessex Hillfort project.

Detailed examination of a number of Wessex hillforts, especially although not exclusively confined to the univallate examples, reveals a geographically widespread common feature; the construction of the bank and ditch in a series of short, straight sections of relatively uniform length. Feachem (1971) noted this feature of hillfort construction in connection with unfinished hillforts but it is also visible on many complete examples. Also visible on most surviving hillforts is another characteristic feature: 'peaks' and 'troughs' along the length of the rampart tops that can be seen to correlate with similar features along the base of the ditch. Both of these traits may prove to be related to the construction of the circuits and could indicate something of the organisation of labour in the construction and maintenance of hillforts. Ralston (1996) has noted a similar trend in some of the oblong-shaped hillforts in eastern Scotland (such as Tap o'Noth, Grampian Region), where the form of the enclosure was dictated partly by the materials employed, involving the maximum use of straight lengths of timber for ease of construction.

The straight length construction form in southern Britain is most readily seen on the surviving univallate hillforts although bi-vallate and multivallate examples also display the trait. Analysis of the best surviving examples appears to indicate two main groups, each distinguished by the length of rampart unit: Group 1 with the rampart constructed in 30m to 40m lengths with the average being 32m; Group 2 featuring lengths averaging 50m.

Particularly good examples of Group 1 can be seen at Chiselbury, Wiltshire (Clay 1935), Figsbury, Wiltshire (Guido and Smith 1982), Ogbury, Wiltshire (Crawford and Keiller 1928; Hampton and Palmer 1977)

nd Uffington Castle, Oxfordshire (Miles
t al 2003). All of the cited examples are
nivallate enclosures of proven or probable
arly Iron Age date (*see* Table 2). One multi-
allate example within this group is Yarn-
ury, Wiltshire (Crawford and Keiller 1928;
Cunnington 1933) where the inner and outer
amparts display this feature with remarkable
niformity around the entire circuit.

Table 2 Group 1 hillforts

site	type	average unit length
Chiselbury	Univallate	30m
Codford Circle	Univallate	30m
Figsbury	Univallate	32m
Grovely Castle	Univallate	32m
Liddington Castle	Univallate	35m
Ogbury	Univallate	35m
Rybury	Univallate	32m
Uffington Castle	Univallate	35m
Walbury	Univallate	30m
Woolbury	Univallate	35m
Yarnbury	Multivallate	30m

That this phenomenon is so readily
apparent on the univallate examples should
not come as a surprise. When certain
hillforts develop into multivallate enclosures
the sequence of re-modelling so clearly
demonstrated by excavation can lead to a
'blurring' of the original configuration.
Even so it is still possible to see a hint of
this construction method on many multivallate or developed hillforts, such as
Danebury, Hambledon Hill, Badbury and
Maiden Castle.

Group 2 hillforts, where the unit length
averages 55m, appear to be less frequent
than Group 1, but still form a significant
number of those examined as part of this
analysis. Included in this group is the
unfinished fort on Ladle Hill, Hampshire
(*see* Fig 2.21; Piggott 1931). At Ladle
Hill this pattern is remarkably clear with
each incomplete unit still being separate
from its adjacent components. The angular-
ity of the changes in alignment is especially
clear at Segsbury and is still a striking
feature of this monument when viewed
from ground level (Fig 3.2).

Fig 3.2
*Ground view of the hillfort
defences of Segsbury Camp,
Oxfordshire illustrating the
remarkably long and straight
sections of rampart out of
which the hillfort is
constructed (James Davies).*

Table 3 Group 2 hillforts

site	type	average unit length
Alfred's Castle	Univallate	50m
Barbury Castle	Bivallate	50m
Bury Hill 2	Univallate	80m
Casterley Camp	Univallate	45m
Chisenbury Trendle	Univallate	55m
Fosbury	Univallate	60m
Ladle Hill	Univallate	45m
Martinsell Hill	Univallate	50m
Perborough Castle	Univallate	50m
Segsbury	Univallate	70m
Stockton	Univallate	50m

It was suggested above that this unit form of construction may indicate the way in which the building of the circuit was organised. Whether this indicates discrete groups from the hillforts' hinterland contributing to the communal monument or, perhaps, a reflection of seasonal construction is of some considerable interest, but beyond the scope of this discussion. However, at two of the sites where this phenomenon is especially clear, at Ogbury in Wiltshire (Crawford and Keiller 1928, plate xxiv; Hampton and Palmer 1977, fig 7) and Perborough Castle in Berkshire it is possible that the unit lengths have been influenced by the presence of an existing field system. This is especially clear at Perborough Castle (*see* Fig 2.2; Wood and Hardy 1962) where, as at Ogbury, there are indications of settlement within the field system beyond the hillfort circuit. At Ogbury air photographs and antiquarian plans also record two smaller ditched enclosures abutting the east side of the circuit (Colt Hoare 1812; Hampton and Palmer 1977). Records in the Wiltshire SMR note Middle Iron Age pottery from these and they may well postdate the construction and use of Ogbury.

Beyond Wessex this phenomenon has also been noted on Bathampton Down, Somerset. Here a large univallate hilltop enclosure was laid out over an existing field system (Crawford and Keiller 1928, plate xxiii; Wainwright 1967). This association between rampart form and earlier field systems is not common and appears to be the exception rather than the rule.

Blocked Entrances

The blocking of entrances, especially on univallate sites at the period when elaboration of the circuit commences, is a well-known feature of a number of Wessex hillforts. Within the study area blocked entrances have been examined by excavation at Danebury (Cunliffe and Poole 1991, 23–32) and Uffington Castle (Miles *et al* 2003) and other examples can be suggested on the basis of the earthwork evidence. At a number of sites there are common indications of such an event. This will usually take the form of a characteristic indentation in the rampart, marking where the rampart terminals of the former entrance have been infilled, and, occasionally, there will be the remains of outworks associated with the former entrance. The latter feature is especially pronounced at Danebury (Cunliffe and Poole 1991, 23–32). Eagles (1991), in a paper examining the surface evidence from Beacon Hill, Hampshire, has drawn attention to another probable example marked by a subtle change in the external ditch, and a marked increase in the height of the counterscarp where the former gap had been infilled. Other examples can be postulated on the basis of field observation.

One relatively common characteristic of univallate hillforts in Wessex is pairs of opposed entrances. Where only one entrance is now visible the observer will have a reasonably good idea where to seek evidence for a blocked counterpart. This very simple maxim has been used to identify blocked entrances at four Wessex hillfort sites and others doubtless exist. At Liddington Castle a single entrance survives on the east side of the monument (Figs 2.54–6). This is an unelaborate affair consisting of a simple gap through the defences with the bank displaying slightly expanded terminals. On the western side of the circuit, directly opposite the eastern entrance, the inner rampart has a slight inward kink and is slightly wider for a distance of 10m. The ditch narrows at this point and a gap through the counterscarp is still very evident on the ground. This feature has all the characteristics of a blocked entrance and is close to the probable junction between the hillfort circuit and a linear ditch that approached the site from the west (the precise relationship having been truncated by later quarrying).

At Segsbury, excavation of the eastern entrance has shown that it was protected by a projecting hornwork and that the existing southern entrance might have been a later opening, possibly Iron Age or Roman (Lock and Gosden 1998, Lock *et al* 2005). The form of the eastern entrance is clearly of earlier Iron Age type and it would be tempting to postulate that there was once a western equivalent. Study of the earthworks on the western arc of the circuit has produced two candidates. To the north-west there is an opening through the rampart and the counterscarp is noticeably narrower at this point. However, the fact that the inner rampart is broken at this point would tend to argue against this being an earlier entrance. A stronger candidate can be seen on the south-west where the inner rampart, ditch and counterscarp all make a characteristic kink over a length of 20m. This is also directly opposite the eastern entrance and the magnetometer survey shows a broad band with significantly fewer features running east–west between these points that could be interpreted as a former road. Additionally, immediately beyond this postulated blocked entrance, air photographs and magnetometer survey have located an area of possible occupation (Chapter 2).

Perborough Castle has suffered serious degradation to the earthwork circuit from modern ploughing in recent decades. However, the northern arc displays the characteristic inturned kink suggestive of a blocked entrance. Close examination of the earthwork also shows that the inner rampart at this point is slightly disjointed and may indicate an original entrance form with slightly offset terminals. The feature is clearly visible on air photographs (for example NMR 4229/17, SU 5278/9, 1988) and beyond the fort there are traces of a slight hollow-way beside one of the field lynchets that predate the monument.

In addition to these sites, at least seven more Wessex hillforts display convincing earthwork evidence for the blocking of entrances: Castle Ditches, Tisbury (*see above*); Chiselbury, Wiltshire; Eggardon Hill, Dorset; Grovely Castle, Wiltshire; St Catherine's Hill, Hampshire; Weatherby Castle, Dorset and Yarnbury, Wiltshire. In every case these are located directly opposite the principal surviving entrance.

Beyond the ramparts: hillforts in their landscape

The brief history of Wessex hillfort studies outlined above illustrates how, until recently, there had been a strong tendency to view hillforts in isolation. This myopia had created many problems with the way hillforts and indeed the Wessex Iron Age had been studied and interpreted. The growth in 'Landscape Archaeology' and

projects such as the Danebury Environs (Palmer 1984; Cunliffe 2000) and the large-scale mapping of extensive areas of the Wessex chalk (eg Bowen 1990; Bewley 2001; McOmish *et al* 2002) have begun to redress this imbalance and have graphically demonstrated the complexity of settlement forms and land division that coexisted through much of the 1st millennium BC. In this general discussion attention will focus upon the immediate environs of the hillforts and pay special attention to the growing body of evidence for enclosed and unenclosed extramural settlement. A more detailed discussion of the environs of those sites investigated by the project will be found in the gazetteer (pp 39–130).

The positioning of hillforts appears to be based on many complex factors that can include proximity to earlier monuments, significant points of junction between landscape divisions and geomorphological factors. The project under discussion in this volume has also added valuable corroboration to observations made from the study of air photography regarding potential settlements in close proximity to the hillforts. Excavation of such sites has been all too rare, although the recent examination of an extensive settlement located on a spur north of Battlesbury hillfort in Wiltshire has demonstrated a very early Iron Age date that probably precedes the first phase of the hillfort (M. Rawlings, Wessex Archaeology, pers comm).

Air photographs show potential unenclosed settlements marked by pit clusters and maculae immediately outside and south-west of Perborough Castle (*see* for example Ashmolean Museum 7093/929 held in NMRC Swindon) and Segsbury (NMR 1703/264, SU 3884/17, October 1979). In the case of Perborough Castle these features can be seen to extend right up to the outer edge of the ploughed-out ditch suggesting that they predate the construction of the hillfort defences and its associated counterscarp. At both Perborough Castle and Segsbury the cropmark evidence was confirmed by the detection of significant anomalies during the magnetometer survey (*see* Figs 2.3 and 2.40, Chapter 2). In neither case has the settlement been verified or dated.

Martinsell Hill, a large univallate hill-top enclosure overlooking the eastern end of the Vale of Pewsey, has been shown by the magnetometer survey (pp 118–23) to be largely devoid of significant archaeological features.

On the plateau to the west of the enclosure and extending as far as the small promontory fort of Giant's Grave, some 1km distant, fieldwalking by Owen Meyrick recovered spreads of Late Bronze Age and Iron Age material (Swanton 1987).

At Bury Hill air photographs indicate a mix of enclosed and unenclosed settlement over an area of at least 4ha located 150m south-east of the entrance to the hillfort. Again magnetometry has confirmed this location and added clarity to the marks observed on the air photographs (Figs 2.14–15).

There is now growing evidence that significant extramural settlement is a common feature of many hillforts in Wessex and in the case of developed or multivallate forts this often takes the form of enclosed activity in relatively close proximity to the principal entrance.

At Yarnbury in Wiltshire a large (approximately 3ha) oval enclosure is sited 400m south-east of the eastern entrance of the developed hillfort. Although unexcavated, pottery of 3rd–1st century BC date was recorded when the site was damaged by road widening in the 1970s (Wilts SMR). This material is contemporary with the ceramics recovered from the interior of the developed hillfort during the 1932 excavations (Cunnington 1933).

Still in Wiltshire, air photographs held by English Heritage at the National Monuments Record Centre (NMRC) in Swindon show oval ditched enclosures of approximately 1.5ha outside the hillforts of Battlesbury and Scratchbury. In the case of the former this is situated approximately 300m beyond the eastern entrance of the hillfort on the low spur giving access to the monument. Although undated, the form of the enclosure is typical of other later prehistoric examples in this part of the county. At Scratchbury, only 1.5km south-east of Battlesbury, another ditched enclosure occupies a similar spur-end position some 200m beyond the north-east entrance of the hillfort. Aerial reconnaissance is playing an important role in the identification of these extramural enclosures and unenclosed settlements. At Grovely Castle, another hillfort along the Wylye Valley (and in the same locational group as Yarnbury, Battlesbury and Scratchbury), an enclosure of approximately 2ha has been located in close proximity to the entrance. Farther west, along the Nadder Valley in the Vale of Wardour, another enclosure of approximately 3ha has been discovered some 500m from the western entrance of Castle Ditches, Tisbury.

At Old Sarum in Wiltshire casual finds and limited observation and excavation have recorded Iron Age material of the 4th century BC to early 1st century AD over an area of at least 10ha beyond the eastern entrance (conveniently summarised in Borthwick and Chandler 1984). Owing to the circumstances of discovery it is impossible to ascertain the exact nature and full extent of the occupation, but both enclosed and open settlement seems probable. There are similar records of extensive spreads of later Iron Age material outside the principal entrance to Badbury in Dorset. This spans the 3rd century BC to early 1st century AD and includes an area that developed into a small shrine in the Romano-British period (M Papworth pers comm).

The presence of these clusters of extramural activity appears to have been largely ignored and yet they must surely represent another potentially important component of a hillfort landscape. To date these patterns appear to have relatively discrete distributions, with a notable concentration in close proximity to the hillforts of the Wylye Valley in southern Wiltshire. Farther east, on the Hampshire chalk, this pattern has, with the exception of Bury Hill, so far failed to manifest itself convincingly. The enclosure at Houghton Down (Cunliffe and Poole, 2000e) is, at just over 2km from Danebury, too far to be considered as an example of this phenomenon. The pattern seen in Hampshire is also similar to that observed so far on the Berkshire Downs and the Marlborough Downs where, with the possible exceptions of Segsbury and Perborough Castle, evidence of potential settlements in *very* close proximity to the hillforts appears to be lacking.

There is clearly an urgent need for a carefully planned sampling strategy to obtain more information on those settlements and other features hard by hillfort entrances. Such a strategy will need to address some very fundamental questions starting with: 'are these settlements and other features contemporary with the use of the adjacent hillfort? If so, is there any discernible difference in the character of the material assemblage that may indicate a different economic/social pattern to that of the hillfort? Do these sites remain in occupation after the decline of the hillfort and if they do is there any major change in their character?' It is tempting to postulate that in the absence of any major concentrations of obvious 'high status' material from many excavated hillforts in central Wessex that such a focus, should it exist, is not within the hillfort but immediately adjacent, on the approach to the monument. In the areas where the pattern is concentrated, the recurring location, generally within 200m and 500m of an entrance, does strongly suggest a close relationship.

Hillforts of Wessex after the Iron Age

The use of hillforts in Wessex in the Late Iron Age and beyond is an aspect that has yet to be given the study it deserves. The patterns that are discernible appear again to be both regional and chronological. The Danebury excavations show that here there is very little major activity after *c* 100–50 BC (Cunliffe 1984a) and no evidence of Roman military activity in the mid-1st century AD. Unlike Dorset (Hod Hill, Maiden Castle), South Somerset (Ham Hill, South Cadbury) and East Devon (Hembury), none of the hillforts in the core area of Wessex have produced convincing evidence of Roman military intervention. Only at Forest Hill near Marlborough, probably part of a Late Iron Age regional centre (Corney 1997), and Bilbury Ring in the Wylye Valley is there a possibility of a short-lived Roman military presence. This lack of evidence can be accepted and in probability reflects the very different political and social attitudes in the region towards the Roman invasion in AD 43.

Evidence of non-military activity within hillforts throughout the Roman period in central Wessex is, however, plentiful even if, in many cases, the exact nature of this is still obscure. In some cases the activity is clearly domestic and the relationship to the hillfort may be little more than convenience in defining an area of settlement activity. This is surely the case at Balksbury, a Late Bronze Age–earliest Iron Age enclosure near Andover. Here an aisled building of later Roman date appears to be the focus of a small farming settlement (Wainwright and Davies 1995). At Yarnbury in Wiltshire excavation (Cunnington 1933) and surface collection (unpublished, National Monuments Record [NMR] archives) suggests the presence of a large settlement spanning the entire Roman period. At Stockton Earthworks, overlooking the Wylye Valley in Wiltshire, an early univallate enclosure develops into a major nucleated Late Iron Age and Romano-British settlement of 32ha (79

acres) that continues into the early 5th century AD (Corney 1989). A similar complex might also have developed adjacent to a nearby complex centred on Bilbury Ring hillfort and Hanging Langford Camp (ibid).

Two hillforts in the project area have remarkable structures within their circuits. Tidbury Ring, Bullington in Hampshire has two substantial Roman buildings, set at 90° to each other, placed centrally within the enclosure. Known only from air photographs (for example NMRC SU 4642/6, 1948) this complex appears to be a small villa complex with an aisled building and a simple corridor house. Such a siting is highly unusual and poses questions as to why this particular location was chosen. A substantial Roman building is also known within the small enclosure of Alfred's Castle. This again appears to be a domestic structure constructed in the 1st or 2nd century and demolished in the late 3rd century AD (Gosden and Lock 1999, 2001, 2003, Lock and Gosden 2000). To seek a possible parallel it is necessary to look into the Cotswold region to The Ditches at North Cerney, Gloucestershire. Excavation here has recovered details of a simple corridor house of 1st century AD date set within a plough-levelled enclosure of hillfort proportions and dated to the 1st century BC (Trow 1988; Trow and James 1989). It is possible that Tidbury Ring may be a further example of a Romano-British villa developing within a hillfort but only fieldwork can answer this question. The Roman building at Alfred's Castle was recently excavated by the Hillforts of the Ridgeway Project during 1998–2000 (Gosden and Lock 1999, 2001 and 2003; Lock and Gosden 2000) and a detailed summary of the results is included in Chapter 2. Tidbury also has other features suggesting post-Iron Age activity. South of the hillfort air photographs show a substantial linear ditch mirroring the southern arc of the hillfort and presumably of prehistoric date (Fig 3.3). Close examination of the photographs shows a series of cropmarks that may represent an inhumation cemetery. These are clustered around a small ring ditch of approximately 5–7m diameter. There are two possible contexts for this apparent cemetery. It could be very late Iron Age and compared with Mill Hill, Deal (Parfitt 1995) or, and perhaps more plausibly, be an early pagan Anglo-Saxon cemetery. Tidbury Ring is a site that requires a great deal of further investigation and it is to be very much regretted that

Possible cemetery
adjacent to linear feature

Roman building

Fig 3.3
Aerial photograph of
Tidbury Ring, Bullington,
Hampshire showing linear
earthwork south of the fort
with possible adjacent
inhumation cemetery
(NMRC, SU 4642/19/16,
1976).

access for geophysical survey as part of the Wessex Hillfort Project was denied.

In the Vale of Wardour in south-west Wiltshire both surface finds and geophysical survey suggest an extensive Roman period settlement within Castle Ditches, Tisbury (pp 103–7). None of the features located by the geophysical survey resembles a temple of Romano-Celtic form and the settlement may be a largely secular one. The area is intriguing as it is one where there is good survival of pre-English place names indicating possible continuity from the Roman to post-Roman period (Eagles 1994).

In western Britain the most common occurrence of substantial Roman buildings on or in close proximity to hillforts is usually associated with a religious focus. There are numerous examples ranging from 'intramural' cases such as Maiden Castle (Wheeler 1943), and Lydney (Wheeler and Wheeler 1932) to those in close proximity to the hillfort such as Uley (Woodward and Leach 1993) and Henley Wood (Watts and

Leach 1996). Within our study area Romano-British religious activity has been postulated at a number of examples including Uffington Castle (Lock and Gosden 1997a), Old Sarum (Corney 2001), Liddington Castle (this volume) and Oldbury (pp 123–7). Others, such as Ashley's Copse on the Wiltshire-Hampshire border, are also likely candidates.

The phenomenon of post-Roman reoccupation and refortification of hillforts is, like reuse as a religious focus, best known in western Britain. Here, hillforts such as Cadbury Congresbury (Rahtz *et al* 1992), South Cadbury (Alcock 1995, Barrett *et al* 2000) and Ham Hill (Burrow 1981) have all produced good evidence of reoccupation. The nature and character of this activity is still far from understood but clearly involved long distance contacts with the Byzantine world as evidenced by ceramic imports. This focus on Somerset is probably more a reflection of the work of individual archaeologists such as Philip Rahtz, rather than a true geographical pattern. In Dorset there is good evidence for post-Roman activity at Maiden Castle in proximity to the Romano-British temple (Woodward 1992) and Hod Hill has produced some items of late Roman style metalwork, weapons and two 5th century AD Germanic brooches, the latter coming from the site of a Roman building just below the hillfort defences (Eagles and Mortimer 1994).

At Oldbury, Wiltshire, close to the western terminal of the East Wansdyke, a penannular brooch of probable 5th-century date is known with another example from nearby Calne (Youngs 1995). In this context the proximity of the hillfort to a major Roman villa below Cherhill village church, only 1km to the north-west (Johnson and Walters 1988) and the possibility of an extramural Romano-British temple (p 127) makes the geophysical evidence for a possible reduction of the hillfort circuit especially interesting. The proximity of major Roman structures to hillforts with evidence for post-Roman reoccupation is impressive and includes Cadbury Congresbury, South Cadbury, Ham Hill, Crickley Hill and Old Sarum.

In Hampshire, small-scale excavations by Philip Rahtz recovered post-Roman ceramics and evidence for refurbishment of the defences at Castle Ditches, Whitsbury (Ellison and Rahtz 1987). This site is in some ways comparable to Oldbury in that it is close to another probable 5th century AD boundary, Bokerley Dyke (Bowen 1990).

Such hints do suggest that reoccupation of hillforts in southern Britain may be far more widespread than hitherto thought, and to this author it would appear that it may be related to the area once covered by the former late Roman province of Britannia Prima. The region has a growing body of evidence for very late Roman activity in both coins and other artefacts (ibid) and it is here that we may expect to see evidence of a social evolution develop before the final assertion of Anglo-Saxon hegemony.

An overview of the geophysical survey results

by Andrew Payne

The results of the programme of geophysical surveys span a wide range and do not divide simply into clear groups. The classification of sites based on the geophysical results is to a degree a matter of personal interpretation and a range of quite different classifications are clearly possible based upon using a range of different attributes for grouping the sites. The system adopted below is based on similarities in the density, form and pattern of magnetic anomalies within the hillforts and the presence of recurrent features such as circular gully structures.

At one end of the spectrum, there are a number of hillforts that exhibit a low level of internal activity. These could be termed 'empty hillforts'. In the case of Ladle Hill this is entirely compatible with the unfinished status of the hillfort, suggested by the irregular form of the earthwork. In other cases, such results could reflect early abandonment of the site (as happened at many hillforts in the early Iron Age) or sporadic, perhaps seasonal, usage. The small hillfort of Oliver's Camp appears to represent another example of this type of site.

A second category of sites that appear to show features in common are the group known as hill-top enclosures – vast enclosures following the contours of a plateau area defined by relatively slight earthwork defences and datable to the very beginning of the Iron Age. The examples of these sites that were surveyed at Walbury and Martinsell appear to contain mainly geological disturbances or areas of quarrying with little evidence for a settlement function. Total coverage of these sites was thought to be unnecessary after this disappointing response. The internal areas were nevertheless extensively sampled.

The third category consists of sites with evidence for scatters of pit-type anomalies such as St Catherine's Hill (only sampled because of tree cover), Woolbury, Perborough Castle and Uffington Castle. In many cases distinct clustering of pits can be observed in specific areas of the hillfort – either around the perimeter of the enclosure or at the centre, often on the highest ground – but the overall quantity and density of pits is low.

In the fourth category are sites such as Bury Hill II and Barbury Castle that contain very dense and even pit distributions. This response is consistent with the stronger, more developed, multivallate earthworks defending these forts, usually indicative of continued and prolonged occupation into the Middle Iron Age and beyond or re-occupation at a late period in the Iron Age.

The fifth category includes a range of hillforts that all contain similar patterns of occupation, although the density of the anomalous activity varies. It is quite clear that all these sites functioned as settlements or at least foci of activity at one time or another because they contain zones of pits associated with small numbers of round structures defined by ring-gullies. This group makes up about a third of all the sites surveyed and therefore seems to be the most representative of hillforts in general in our sample region. It includes Segsbury Camp, Beacon Hill Camp, Liddington Castle and Oldbury Castle.

Finally we are left with two very distinctive sites that exhibit rather more elaborate patterns of internal layout suggesting an element of settlement planning and division of the internal area into functional zones for different activities. One site is more coherent as a single phased layout; the other is more suggestive of two separate distinct phases of internal arrangements.

The first site – Norsebury – contains linear sub-divisions and there is a particular concentration of occupation features adjacent to the ramparts along the western side of the hillfort, while the central area appears to have been reserved for a large circular enclosure of unknown date and purpose but possibly a shrine. Complex entrance features are indicated by the magnetometer in the ploughed-out section of the hillfort defences now clearly defined by the survey.

At Castle Ditches the site is occupied by large numbers of circular structures defined by ring-gullies, with enclosures and roadways aligned on the four entrances into the fort.

The enclosures are clearly of a different phase to the ring-gullies which they appear to intersect in several places. The round structures appear to be aligned in rows suggesting an element of planning in their layout. Pits appear to be less plentiful at Castle Ditches than the round structures and enclosure features.

Small hillforts

More work needs to be done on understanding the function of smaller hillforts as the results from those included in the study were uninformative (Oliver's Camp) or complicated by later occupation (Roman in the case of Alfred's Castle and relatively recent activity at Oliver's Camp). One question that is frequently asked of such sites is, 'do they represent a different level of social organisation to the larger hillfort enclosures?' The ranking of such sites in a settlement hierarchy depends on them being permanent settlements. The evidence from Oliver's Camp suggests it was never intensively occupied, implying that there may be some functional distinction between some small hillforts and larger hillforts. In contrast, the magnetometer data from Alfred's Castle shows signs of considerable activity within the enclosure indicated by a high density of pits. Some of these have now been excavated producing a rich assemblage of Early Iron Age material suggestive of a high status site (Gosden and Lock 1999, 2001, 2003; Lock and Gosden 2000).

Other aspects of the results

The results from ploughed or previously cultivated sites (such as Norsebury Ring and Castle Ditches) were generally much clearer than those from uncultivated sites under permanent grassland. Surveying sites that have been ploughed for many years is therefore a clear advantage for magnetometer survey despite the likelihood of loss or truncation of archaeological deposits from agricultural erosion.

The grassland sites often preserve earthwork evidence for archaeological features in their interiors that can more easily be interpreted from analytical earthwork surveys of the type carried out by the former Royal Commission on the Historical Monuments of England (RCHME; now part of English Heritage). At Beacon Hill the earthwork evidence (Eagles 1991) and the evidence from magnetometer survey tie in with one another remarkably well, but there is less of a clear match at Barbury Castle where sub-surface features are much more prolific. It is likely that the two forms of survey at Barbury are picking up separate phases of occupation and therefore providing a more complete picture of the sequence of activity in the enclosure than would be gained by using the techniques in isolation. The sub-surface features detected by the magnetometry are most likely earlier than the features visible as surface indications. The land-use history of the site and variation in past land-use across the site again plays a part in the visibility of both surface and sub-surface features – one set of features often being detectable at the expense of the other.

Notable discoveries at specific sites

Important information on specific aspects of a number of sites has also been recorded. At Oldbury a previously unknown boundary ditch partitioning the hillfort (no longer clearly visible on the ground) suggests two distinct phases of hillfort development, involving expansion or retraction of the enclosed/defended area. This may reflect several stages of fortification of the site during the Iron Age involving phased expansion of the hillfort across high ground, as is already known, for example, at Maiden Castle and Torberry (West Sussex) (Sharples 1991, Cunliffe 1976). Alternatively, it might represent a second line of defence added as a later partition of the enclosed area to provide greater protection to the core area of settlement. Such a feature has been recognised through excavation at Conderton Camp (Worcestershire), where a secondary rampart was inserted across an earlier hillfort enclosure, and the smaller area so formed occupied by a settlement, leaving an outer annex that was unoccupied (Thomas 2005). Cadbury Hill, Congresbury, in Somerset provides another example of later partition of a pre-existing hillfort (Rahtz *et al* 1992). The internal ditch at Oldbury might have functioned simply to keep out animals or to divide agricultural or other activities from habitation areas. Yet another alternative explanation for the ditch is that it represents an earlier prehistoric linear boundary running through the area later occupied by the hillfort, although it does not appear to line up with any of the known 'linears' in the area. Further magnetometer survey could be used to determine if the ditch does continue outside the hillfort.

The magnetometer data from Liddington Castle raises interesting questions about the nature of the activity within this hillfort. The singular nature and impressive diameter of the large round structure revealed by the geophysics inside the fort is suggestive of a specialised function, such as a shrine or temple. The large oval enclosure set apart from the rest of the activity in the hillfort of Norsebury may represent a similar sacred enclosure, shrine or temple site. An enclosure mapped by magnetometry within the defences of Maiden Castle in 1985 (Baalam *et al* 1991) may represent another example of this type of feature.

A group of unusual features revealed inside Oliver's Camp are thought to relate to relatively modern (possibly Second World War) activity.

Parallels with Danebury and other excavated Wessex hillforts

Based on the magnetometer survey evidence, the hillforts of St Catherine's Hill (with a central zone of pits), Segsbury, Liddington (containing discrete zones of pits with round structures), Oldbury (a moderately high pit density, but more evenly scattered, plus round structures) and at the lower end of the scale Beacon Hill (a thin scatter of pits plus round structures) all show elements of the early Danebury layout in the 6th–5th century BC.

St Catherine's Hill also shares other features in common with Danebury in the early period, such as entrance/gate structures known as a result of excavation in the 1930s. In Period 2 of the St Catherine's Hill sequence there is evidence of major reconstruction and heightening of the original dump rampart in parallel with narrowing and lengthening of the entrance passageway. At St Catherine's Hill these modifications are linked to a major change of pottery style to saucepan pots of the St Catherine's Hill group. Similar developments took place at Danebury about 270 BC (Danebury Period 4) when the original box rampart built in the middle of the 6th century BC was replaced by a more substantial dump rampart fronted by a large V-shaped ditch and the entrance passage was also narrowed and lengthened. The first hillfort entrance at St Catherine's Hill also closely resembles Danebury Gate 2a-b (a wide dual carriageway entrance closed by double gates) in the early period of Danebury. St Catherine's Hill shows evidence of destruction not long after the new rampart build. Elsewhere in the region now covered by Hampshire the hillforts at Quarley Hill and Woolbury also seem to have declined after the end of the 4th century in common with St Catherine's Hill. Only Danebury continued as a major centre in the region after this decline (Cunliffe 2000, Cunliffe 1995).

Zones of dense pitting and occasional small round/oval structures also occur at Norsebury although these concentrate towards the edges of the enclosure in areas bordering the ramparts rather than the central area which seems to have been reserved for a large, circular ditched feature. The deeply in-turned, slanted entrance on the south side of Norsebury is a possible parallel with remodeled strengthened approaches through hillfort defences dating to the Middle Iron Age at sites such as Torberry, Danebury and St Catherine's Hill (Cunliffe 1991, 330–4). The eastern entrance at Norsebury also shows signs of elaboration in the form of additional projecting outworks similar in design to the south-east entrance at Beacon Hill and the blocked west entrance at Danebury.

The majority of the other sites do not seem to compare well with Danebury in its earlier phases. Barbury could correspond with Danebury nearer the end of its occupation history – along with Maiden Castle the product of cumulative phases and a long sequence of activity. The resemblance between the magnetic results from Barbury and Maiden Castle (which is well understood from excavation) is quite striking. Sites such as Perborough and Ladle Hill have most in common with emptier sites such as Bury Hill I and Woolbury (plus Figsbury and Quarley) examined during the Danebury Environs Project (Cunliffe 2000) and the smaller promontory-type fort of Oliver's Camp would fit in here too. Martinsell and Walbury probably belong in the earliest, sparsely occupied, class of hillfort in their region similar to Balksbury in the Danebury Environs – but this is difficult to state conclusively because of geological complications – and there is a question mark over whether archaeological features are really absent. Features of an ephemeral nature such as post-holes may not be adequately resolved by the fluxgate type magnetometers and 'standard' recording intervals employed by the project.

There are other anomalous hillforts that do not easily fit in with our current understanding. These include Fosbury,

Alfred's Castle and Castle Ditches. On the basis of the paucity of evidence for activity inside it, Fosbury is similar to Woolbury or Bury Hill I – but it has elaborate defensive architecture and a suggestion of internal quarry ditches more in keeping with a developed hillfort. This may indicate that the enclosure circuit was redefined at regular intervals involving heightening of the ramparts but never actually brought into use as a fortified static community. Alfred's Castle is complicated by Romano-British occupation but appears to be a densely used, primarily early, small hillfort akin to the previously excavated site of Lidbury Camp in the east of Salisbury Plain that produced eleven storage pits in a limited area of excavation (Cunnington and Cunnington 1917; Cunliffe 1991, 348). Castle Ditches stands out on its own as an untypical hillfort in the sample of sites included in the Wessex Hillforts Survey, but is peripheral to the main area sampled and possibly belongs to a geographically distinct group with more in common with hillforts in Dorset and Somerset. If Castle Ditches does belong in this group it might have been occupied until a much later date than the hillforts farther east in what became the territory of the Atrebates in the Late Iron Age. Although defensively a hillfort Castle Ditches has, in one phase, the internal characteristics of an oppida-type settlement or 'valley-fort' such as Salmonsbury in Gloucestershire or Dyke Hills in Oxfordshire. Non-hillfort Iron Age settlement in the Danebury Environs shows considerable variety to the extent that it is difficult to discern any regular pattern. There is no reason why this variety should not extend to hillfort settlement.

Some overall conclusions

The project has revealed a wealth of new evidence for the nature of the internal utilisation of Wessex hillforts. While supporting some of the existing models of hillfort development, the surveys also show that the pattern is considerably more complex and varied than previously realised (*see* Chapter 4). Some hillforts exhibit a very low density of archaeological features, while others contain evidence for prolonged and intensive usage (indicated by a very high density of magnetic anomalies mapped). In some cases several discrete phases of settlement activity are suggested by the magnetic results.

The character of internal activity revealed by the magnetometer surveys can not always be correctly anticipated from the layout and sophistication of the hillfort defences, showing the value of magnetometer survey for rapidly revealing the character of occupation within a hillfort. This in turn can shed light on the likely duration of occupation and the character and intensity of past activity on the site. The case of Norsebury is a good example where the design of the earthworks at first sight would suggest a relatively simple form of hillfort, belying the complex internal activity now revealed by the magnetometer. The reverse seems to be the case at Fosbury.

Many sites that are superficially similar in terms of size, siting and rampart construction contain very different and sometimes unusual or unexpected patterns of activity. Two sites that appear very similar on the ground based on the size of the areas enclosed and the form and layout of the enclosing earthworks are Perborough Castle and Norsebury Ring but they exhibit very different patterns of occupation. Differential preservation may also have some part to play in these results but this is difficult to quantify without excavation.

The size of a site and the complexity of the defences visible on the surface are not, therefore, necessarily related to function or socio-economic complexity. The large enclosed area of Segsbury (12ha) contains a similar pattern of occupation to that observed inside the 3ha enclosed at Liddington Castle. Norsebury, enclosed by a simple bank ditch and counterscarp, displays a density of internal occupation on a par with larger sites with massive multivallate defences such as Yarnbury, Oldbury, Bury Hill II and Castle Ditches. Univallate sites can contain a similar density and complexity of internal activity as multivallate sites, but multivallate sites generally, but with the notable exception of Fosbury, contain dense internal activity.

The overall impression given by the results is that far from all hillforts were inhabited or functioned primarily as settlements. Although in some cases forts may have been constructed to house settlements perhaps when the need arose or for socio-political reasons, in many cases the sites may not have been inhabited for very long or served other purposes, leaving few detectable traces in the archaeological record. Fosbury is one possible example of this. Some hillforts were obviously centres

Fig 3.4
Aerial photograph of
Conderton (or Dane's)
Camp, Worcestershire, a
small 1.5 hectare hillfort
located on a narrow ridge
between two dry valleys
on the side of the upland
massif of Bredon Hill
(NMRC; NMR
18035/11, SO 9738/18,
1998, Crown Copyright).

of large permanent settled communities (as illustrated by the houses, streets and enclosures mapped at Castle Ditches). Others were probably only temporarily or sporadically occupied while some may have had more specialised functions possibly as religious or ceremonial centres or seasonal gathering places. The overall results of the survey allow for a considerable range of functional variability between hillforts.

The internal planning and layout of structures in hillfort interiors is highly varied. Some sites appear more organised than others. At some sites the pattern of features appears to be quite random and disorganised although nearly all sites display some clustering of activity. In other cases there is more evidence of zoned activities. One example is Norsebury, where there are zones containing a very high concentration of archaeological features in two discrete areas of the hillfort including pits, quarries and circular structures, while the remaining third of the hillfort appears much emptier. Segsbury and St Catherine's Hill both have concentrations of occupation near the centre of the site, on the highest ground, dominating the whole of the enclosed area. At Oldbury occupation is concentrated in the northernmost third of the hillfort on a steep natural promontory separated at some time by a cross boundary ditch from the remainder of the area enclosed by the hillfort.

Some sites contain large numbers of pits apparently with few house sites (Liddington, Barbury and Segsbury). At others, house sites are fairly plentiful, but have few pits (Beacon Hill, Castle Ditches). Sites such as Perborough Castle appear to have only ever been sparsely occupied leaving evidence only of limited scatters of pits. Barbury Castle appears to have been the most intensively used or longest occupied of all the sites surveyed. The sheer profusion of anomalies at this site suggests numbers of pits running into the thousands.

A significant sample of the hillforts in central-southern England has now been surveyed, considerably broadening our knowledge and understanding of the sites. The more detailed information that has emerged from the project is already beginning to show the diversity of patterns of activity within Iron Age hillforts. The evidence suggests that hillforts were constructed for a number of purposes and that these purposes will have changed over time.

The results prove that it is not possible easily to predict the character of hillforts from surface evidence alone and therefore there is clearly justification for the continued and expanded use of geophysical methods for hillfort investigation. Preliminary results of magnetic survey from a limited number of hillforts in the neighbouring Severn-Cotswold Region (Figs 3.4 and 3.5;

Fig 3.5 (page 148)
Magnetometer and
earthwork surveys of
Conderton Camp showing
the bi-lateral division of the
hillfort into storage and
occupation areas represented
by distinct zones of densely
packed pits and round
structures. The remains of
a field system survive as a
series of lynchets to the east
of the fort and were partially
subsumed by it (Mark
Corney and Andrew
Payne).

Fig 3.6 (page 149)
The results of the magne-
tometer survey carried out
inside the hillfort of Castle
Hill, Little Wittenham,
Oxfordshire. The newly
identified inner enclosure
circuit revealed by the
survey is clearly visible in
the plot.

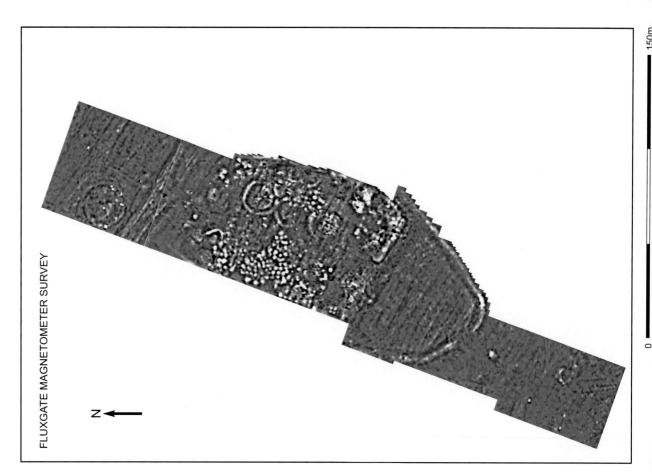

FLUXGATE MAGNETOMETER SURVEY

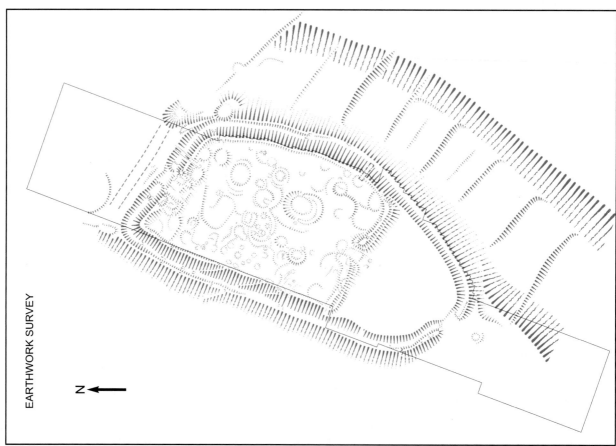

EARTHWORK SURVEY

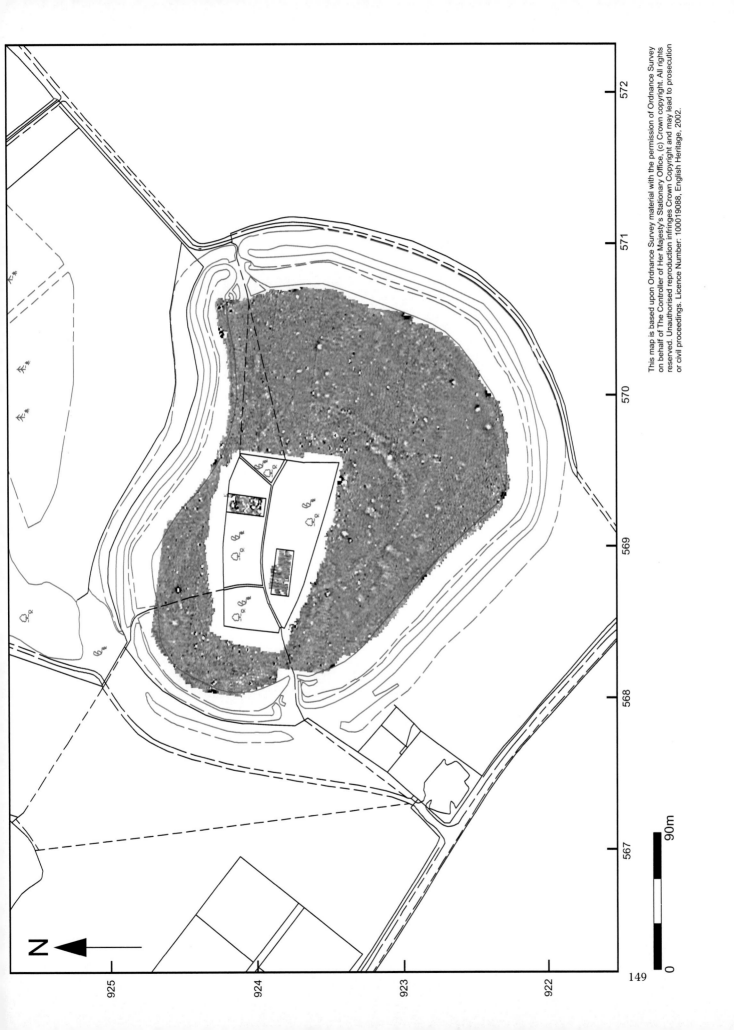

N

90m

0

This map is based upon Ordnance Survey material with the permission of Ordnance Survey on behalf of The Controller of Her Majesty's Stationary Office, (c) Crown copyright. All rights reserved. Unauthorised reproduction infringes Crown Copyright and may lead to prosecution or civil proceedings. Licence Number: 100019088, English Heritage, 2002.

149

925

924

923

922

567   568   569   570   571   572

Conderton Camp, Worcestershire) suggests that here there is considerable future promise for further expansion of our knowledge of hillforts. Recent survey within the hillfort at Castle Hill, Little Wittenham, Oxfordshire – a site overlooking the Thames Valley – has continued to demonstrate the potential, revealing the presence of a previously unknown inner enclosure circuit provisionally dated to the late Bronze Age (Fig 3.6; Payne 2002). The work of the Wessex Hillforts project has also demonstrated the complementary academic and practical value of thematic geophysical survey aimed at a single type of archaeological site, for which there is a recognised range of management challenges and a clear research agenda.

To end with a final note of caution – we need to ask the question: does magnetometry really represent the reality beneath the ground in a hillfort? The answer, it has to be acknowledged, is probably 'no – not totally' based on the retrospective survey of Danebury, but if the results are interpreted with care they can still tell us much.

4

Understanding hillforts: have we progressed?

by Barry Cunliffe

By their very nature hillforts have been a source of fascination for antiquarians and archaeologists alike over many centuries. Prominently sited and redolent of power, these sites have challenged the imagination. When were they built, in what circumstances, who lived there and what were their lives like? – the questions have remained much the same for generations and still demand answers. The explanations of early antiquarians were imaginative, inevitably involving mythical beings, historical figures or races of invaders – the giant Bevis, Caesar or Alfred, the Danes and the Saxons: folk tales and pseudo histories merged. The 19th century saw the beginnings of serious intrusive investigation. Sometimes excavations were carried out on a large scale. At Worlebury in Somerset the Reverend Francis Warre excavated nearly a hundred Iron Age pits within the protection of the fort's defences and later C W Dymond sectioned the ramparts and gates, publishing the results in a creditable monograph (Dymond 1886). This was antiquarianism of a serious kind, but the beginning of systematic archaeological research into hillforts can be fairly said to lie with General Pitt Rivers. In 1867 Colonel Augustus Henry Lane Fox (as Pitt Rivers was then known) conducted a survey of the hillforts of the Sussex Downs, carefully observing them all and offering a soldier's-eye perspective of their significance (Lane Fox 1869). Ten years later, between 1877 and 1878, he turned to excavation in an attempt to answer some of the questions he had raised earlier, sampling Cissbury, Highdown, Mount Caburn and Caesar's Camp, Folkestone (Lane Fox 1881; Pitt Rivers 1883).

In the 20th century hillforts have featured large in the research designs of archaeologists. In the first four decades of the century about 80 forts were sampled by excavation (Cunliffe 1991, 1–20). Many of them were concentrated in central-southern Britain. In Wiltshire Maud Cunnington examined eight forts between 1907 and 1932, in Sussex E C Curwen tackled five

between 1926 and 1932, Christopher Hawkes sampled a similar number in Hampshire between 1925 and 1939, while in Dorset Mortimer Wheeler and his team excavated three, one of them, Maiden Castle, on an heroic scale showing, for the first time, the great potential of area excavation within the interior (Wheeler 1943).

The excavations of the period 1900–60 were carried out within the invasionist paradigm. The forts were believed to be the result of turbulent times when Britain was subject to waves of invasion and internal strife. In consequence excavation tended to focus on defences and gates where, it was believed, signs of the history of these invasions, and responses to them, could be read. Although Wheeler's area excavation at Maiden Castle was an exception in providing details of the occupation within, 'invasions' featured large in the site's interpretation. At an early stage in the development of hillfort studies Christopher Hawkes had outlined the invasionist hypothesis in his famous paper 'Hillforts' published in *Antiquity* in 1931. He was to restate his views in a much elaborated form in an equally famous paper 'The ABC of the British Iron Age' published in *Antiquity* in 1959. In many ways this was the valedictory appearance, for the 1960s were to see the wholesale rejection of invasionist explanations and with that came a refocusing of interest on the hillfort phenomenon.

Questions now began to centre on hillfort functions, redirecting attention away from the defences and on to the interiors. Between 1960 and 1970 in the Welsh borderland three hillforts – Croft Ambrey, Credenhill and Midsummer Hill Camp – were examined by Stan Stanford who devoted considerable attention to their interiors (Stanford 1971, 1974, 1981). Meanwhile, at South Cadbury in Somerset extensive sampling of the interior was undertaken by Leslie Alcock from 1966–70 as part of an ambitious project of investigation (Barrett *et al* 2000). This decade of activity amply demonstrated the value of large-scale excavation. It was now possible to begin to glimpse something of the ordered arrangement of the structures within and, from the comparatively large quantities of material recovered, to gain a clearer idea of the activities that went on within the enclosure.

In 1969 the excavation of Danebury began. It was planned from the outset to be a long-term programme designed to examine the hillfort thoroughly and to explore its regional context. In the event the excavation of the fort extended over 20 seasons (1969–88) (Cunliffe 1984a, 1995; Cunliffe and Poole 1991) and excavations on broadly contemporary sites in the surrounding landscape, including the forts of Bury Hill and Woolbury, lasted another eight (1989–97) (Cunliffe 2000; Cunliffe and Poole 2000a, 2000b).

In parallel with the Danebury programme other hillforts became the focus of extensive area excavation, the most notable being Maiden Castle in Dorset (Sharples 1991), and Winklebury (Smith K 1977) and Balksbury (Wainwright 1969; Wainwright and Davies 1995; Ellis and Rawlings 2001) in Hampshire. Thus, in the last 40 years of the 20th century, the sample of hillfort interiors examined on a suitably large scale had greatly increased and something of the variation among them was beginning to become apparent, allowing a number of possible development scenarios to be offered. The more relevant of these have been summarised above in Chapter 1.

Area excavation had shown the great potential of the patterns, inherent in the mass of features found inside the forts, to modelling socio-economic systems, and a number of geophysical surveys had amply demonstrated the power of these techniques in realising these patterns inexpensively and without recourse to destructive excavation. Thus it seemed logical that a profitable next step in hillfort studies would be to undertake thorough surveys of a sample of forts to enhance the anecdotal database that had accrued through excavation and one-off surveys. In this way the Wessex Hillforts Project was conceived. The results of that work have been fully presented in this volume and the project evaluated, and it remains now to offer some brief assessment of what has been learned in the broader context of Iron Age studies.

Some parameters

It is as well to begin by reminding ourselves of two basic truths: first, the main period of hillfort building and use spans the Late Bronze Age and Iron Age – a period of about a thousand years; and second, magnetometry reflects, but does not necessarily fully represent, what is beneath the ground, irrespective of age. As an illustration of the first point the survey of Castle Ditches (*see* Figs 2.46, 2.47) is instructive. The complex of features revealed within the fortifications is evidently of more than one period but without excavation they are impossible to phase or date. One might hypothesise that the ditched enclosures, and many of the hut circles, should belong to the Late Iron Age or even to the Roman period, and might therefore be of much later date than the initial construction of the fortifications, but magnetometry alone will not tell us. Similarly at Oldbury (*see* Figs 2.61, 2.62) the internal ditch that divides off one part of the fort could represent an earlier, smaller, fortification but it could equally have been constructed much later after the main fortifications had reached their fully-evolved form. Again, without excavation the question must remain open.

The second reservation – the difficulties of relating the magnetometry to the archaeology – is nicely displayed by the survey of Danebury (pp 58–62). The survey gives the impression only of a very 'noisy' response without allowing the true density of the discrete features, demonstrated by excavation, to be fully appreciated. The survey is a fair reflection of what is known to be there without actually representing it in fine detail.

Magnetometry, therefore, provides a valuable way of seeing, even though our vision is often blurred and lacking depth of focus. So long as this is realised it can be used, along with other classes of evidence, to excellent effect in the exercises of pattern recognition that enable some structure and direction to be given to our precepts of 1st millennium BC society.

Before proceeding further it is as well to attempt a general definition of 'hillfort'. For the purposes of the present discussion it is characterised as an enclosed place constructed in a highly-visible location to serve as a focus (if sporadic) for communal activity. Even in so bland a definition there are implications that some might find unacceptable but further restriction would be overcautious, so let us accept

- enclosure,
- visibility, and
- communal functions

as the most common denominators of 'hillfort'.

Once built the *boundary* and the *visibility* remain consistent features, although their meaning might change. The functions performed, if indeed there are any following the act of construction, are likely to vary from site to site, and at any one site they would also vary through time. The functions might also affect the boundary, which could be enlarged, enhanced or redefined in some other way, depending on its meaning in the social context of the time.

To attempt to understand the complexity of meaning embedded in hillforts, using the physical evidence that remains, a reasonable approach would be to seek to discern patterning in the data. The most easily accessible categories to examine are:

- size
- location
- boundary form/complexity
- activity
- chronology

Size, location and boundary form are generally accessible through topographical survey, but understanding of the boundary can usually be enhanced considerably through excavation.

The range of activities that went on within the enclosure is more difficult to discern. Surface survey may, in circumstances where preservation is good, allow coherent plans of earthworks to be produced, as in the case of Beacon Hill (Eagles 1991), but interiors are seldom undamaged and such features as there are may not represent all phases of activity. Aerial photography may enable more details to be added, but since many interiors are now unploughed opportunities for observing crop marks or soil marks are few. The value of geophysical survey is that it overcomes this difficulty and can provide a total plan of the large features present, but such surveys are usually without much chronological refinement. Only by recourse to excavation can questions of activity and chronology be adequately addressed, and excavation on a large scale is required if detailed diachronic models are to be constructed. These reservations need to be spelled out if only as a firm reminder of the limitations that restrain hillfort studies.

That said, 100 years of survey and excavation among the hillforts of Wessex, 80 years of aerial photography and 20 years of geophysical survey have created a database

unparalleled in Europe. It is not unreasonable therefore to expect some patterns to emerge, the explanations of which may contribute to our understanding of society in the 1st millennium BC.

Different ways of seeing

Since the publication of Hawkes' famous paper 'Hillforts' (Hawkes 1931) archaeologists have attempted to categorise hillforts using what little evidence was to hand. For the most part the divisions made were usually based on size, location, rampart structure and date. In a comparatively recent attempt the present writer offered a scheme for Wessex (Cunliffe 1984b), which recognised certain broad categories of fort:

- *early hilltop enclosures*, usually in excess of 10ha in area
- *small, strongly-defended settlements* in prominent positions, usually 1–3ha in area
- *early hillforts*, univallate contour works of usually 3–7ha
- *developed hillforts*, also usually in 3–7ha range but often multivallate and with complex entrance features

Dating evidence was consistent enough to suggest that the early hilltop enclosures belonged to the Late Bronze Age or earliest Iron Age (*c* 800–600 BC). The small, strongly-defended settlements seemed to date towards the end of this period. The early hillforts belonged to the Early Iron Age (600–400 BC) while the developed hillforts seemed to be more a feature of the Middle Iron Age (*c* 400–100 BC). This simple scheme, which takes with it no particular implications of social status or function, still holds good in broad terms but many refinements can be made.

In this volume Mark Corney has drawn attention to subtle differences in rampart morphology, noting that in many forts the enclosing earthworks seem to have been built in a series of roughly straight lengths. He has identified two distinct groups, one with the length averaging 32m and another with length of about 50m. What this means is difficult to say, but if each straight length was built by a social group then it could reflect different social structures.

A second observation concerns the blocking of entrances. Most *early hillforts* had two entrances, usually at opposite sides of the enclosure, while many of the *developed hillforts* had only one. Excavations at Danebury showed that at this fort one of the entrances of the early hillfort was blocked when the fort's defences were elaborated and strengthened (Cunliffe and Poole 1991, 23–32). This phenomenon now appears to be quite widespread in Wessex, as Corney has demonstrated in this volume (pp 138–9). It is now possible to list five certain examples, with another seven as possibilities. This reflects a pattern of behaviour evident throughout Wessex, and if the entrance blocking took place at broadly the same time, then it must represent a significant socio-political horizon. The evidence at Danebury indicates a date in the late 4th to early 3rd century BC for this event.

Another pattern to be recognised is a certain regionalism in the type of entrance earthworks preferred. Two distinct groups can be defined, one in Dorset characterised by the entrance of Hambledon Hill, the other in Hampshire where entrances like those of Beacon Hill are preferred (Cunliffe 1991, 339). It would no doubt be possible to refine this approach still further with more detailed work.

Sufficient will have been said to show that, using a restricted range of typological observations enhanced with some knowledge of chronology where available, it is possible to discover significant variation among the earthworks grouped together as hillforts.

Assessing function

To take the study of hillforts further, beyond generalising comments based on their typologies, it is necessary to generate new portfolios of evidence, principally from excavation and from geophysical surveys. Within the area of Wessex covered by this study six hillforts have been sampled by excavation on a comparatively large scale: Balksbury; Danebury; Winklebury; Maiden Castle; Bury Hill; and Woolbury, while a significant number (most of them described in this volume) have been subjected to large-scale geophysical surveys. The excavated hillforts of the Danebury region (Danebury, Balksbury, Woolbury and Bury Hill) have been discussed as a group quite recently in the report on the Danebury Environs Programme (Cunliffe 2000, 135–203) and a summary of the main conclusions has been given above (pp 10–14). Andrew Payne has also, in this volume, provided an overview of the results of the geophysical survey programme (pp 143–150) in which he emphasises the varied patterns of activities

reflected in the survey plots indicating everything from 'empty hillforts' to forts densely packed with settlement evidence. While the Danebury Environs Programme showed that the development of hillforts was far more complicated than previously thought, the Wessex Hillfort Project has added another level of complexity, although it is without the chronological control necessary to enable the two types of evidence to be directly compared. This should not, however, prevent us from attempting to offer a general model consistent with our much enhanced database.

Before proceeding to create a narrative it is necessary to explore the potential range of functions to which hillforts may have been put. Some of the more likely possibilities include:

- the act of building as a demonstration of group cohesion
- enclosure used for communal pastoral activities
- defined space for social/religious interactions
- storage for communal surplus
- settlement for a community on a cyclic basis
- settlement for a community on a permanent basis
- settlement for elite and entourage
- focus for redistribution and production
- defence in time of unrest
- territorial marker

Several points need to be emphasised. The list does not claim to be definitive. Each of the functions listed could be divided into subsets and there is also a degree of overlap between them. The act of listing does, however, provide a way of focusing the question of how hillforts functioned in the social system of which they are so dramatically a part. The starting point for any discussion must be the acceptance of the fact that the defined place, which we characterise by the portmanteau term 'hillfort', may well have been used for a variety of functions and that these functions may have changed over time, new uses being introduced and old discontinued. So many are the possibilities of combination that each fort may have its own distinctive 'history' of use. Put more starkly: there may be no such thing as a typical hillfort.

There is also the question of time span to be addressed. A few examples will be instructive. At Balksbury it is evident from the more recent excavations (Wainwright 1969; Wainwright and Davies 1995; Ellis and Rawlings 2001) that the early hilltop enclosure of the 9th to 7th centuries BC was most likely abandoned for some while before being reused again in the Middle Iron Age as a convenient place to establish a farming settlement, typical of many others in the region. The excavated evidence would support (but does not prove) the interpretation that this farm continued in use into the Roman period when a masonry-built hall was erected. Occupation lasted into the 4th century AD. In this particular case it is best to regard Balksbury as two totally different sites, the early hilltop enclosure and the later farmstead, the later use being unrelated to the earlier. That said there is the question of legitimacy. Could it be that the community founding the farm was claiming an ancestral link with builders of the enclosure? If so then it could be argued that there is a real thread of continuity.

There is a comparable situation at Alfred's Castle. Here magnetometry supported by excavation has shown a densely-used 'hillfort' of the Early Iron Age to have been reused by a Roman farmstead. Similarly at Tidbury aerial photography has shown there to be a substantial Roman villa within the hillfort defences. Alfred's Castle and Tidbury are small fortifications, which *could* have housed the permanent settlements of elites from the Early Iron Age, in which case it might reasonably be argued that the Roman phase was, functionally, a continuation of the Early Iron Age use. In other words, although Balksbury, Alfred's Castle and Tidbury could all be described as 'hillforts' with Roman villas in them, their histories might have been very different, Balksbury showing a discontinuity in social function while Alfred's Castle and Tidbury might have retained their elite status over many centuries.

Continuity, discontinuity and the strengths of the thread of legitimacy are difficult issues to deal with even when there is excavated data to bring to bear. Can the building of the medieval chapel in St Catherine's hillfort be argued as continuity of legitimacy? And to take it still further, what significance, if any, should we attach to the burial of Lord Carnarvon in Beacon Hill? An elite burial found within the confines of a hillfort may have many explanations! Perhaps the simplest way to view all this is to accept that once a prominent boundary has been set up to define a place the enclosure thus formed is likely to have been used in many different ways by subsequent communities. Their uses

will reflect local and regional needs. It is the task of archaeology to examine the disparate and highly incomplete data that may survive, and be potentially discoverable, in an attempt to establish what patterns may be discernible and to offer explanations for them.

Towards a narrative

Writing a narrative requires a chronology. The time frame adopted here can be summarised as follows:

- Late Bronze Age–earliest Iron Age (900–600 BC)
- Early Iron Age (600–350 BC)
- Middle Iron Age (350–100 BC)
- Late Iron Age (100 BC–AD 43)

The dates can be regarded only as approximate but the scheme provides a general structure that is compatible with the available evidence (Cunliffe 1995, 13–18; Cunliffe 2000, 149–96).

Late Bronze Age–earliest Iron Age (900–600 bc)

Two quite different types of 'hillfort' belong with this period: large *hilltop enclosures* and small *strongly defended forts*.

The hilltop enclosures form a cohesive type. They are usually more than 10 ha in area, their 'defences' are comparatively slight, the emphasis being on the ditch rather than on the banks of spoil thrown out from it, and the enclosures are often sited at high and rather exposed locations. Examples in the study region include Balksbury, Danebury (outer enclosure), Walbury and Martinsell. Beyond the study area Harting Beacon, West Sussex (Bedwin 1978, 1979), Bathampton Down, Avon (Wainwright 1967) and Norbury Camp, Glos (Saville 1983) belong to the same category.

Balksbury is the most informative. It has been subject to a number of campaigns of excavation during the last 60 years or so as the result of which much of the interior has been excavated (Hawkes 1940; Thompson 1958; Wainwright 1969; Wainwright and Davies 1995; Ellis and Rawlings 2001). The work has shown that the enclosure bank and ditch was built in the 9th–8th centuries BC and the enclosure continued in use for about two centuries during which time the bank and ditch was refurbished on at least two occasions. Internally the only significant features of this phase to be identified were a number of small four-post 'granaries' and a few lightly-built circular 'huts'. The most interesting aspect of the recent work has been the examination of the build-up of colluvium, containing midden material, against the inside of the enclosing bank. Analysis suggested that the high organic component of the deposit probably derived from animal waste and other organic material brought in for fodder and litter (Ellis and Rawlings 2001, 87–8).

Excavations at the other sites of this type, Danebury, Norbury and Harting Beacon, have emphasised the lack of internal features, other than small four-post structures, but add little more to the discussion. The two early hilltop enclosures chosen for geophysical survey in this project, Martinsell and Walbury, confirmed that the interiors of these sites were without significant features such as pits and ditches and showed very little evidence of any type of human activity.

Taken together the evidence suggests that the primary function of these enclosures was pastoral, to provide corral space for livestock at certain times during the year. In this context the four-post structures could be interpreted as fodder ricks, while the light circular buildings could have provided shelter for those tending the beasts. The size of the enclosures might suggest that they served large communities and this takes with it the possibility that they were places where the community could gather at certain times during the year for ceremonies and feasting when the more practical tasks of culling, castration and the redistribution of stock were being undertaken. Some supporting evidence for this comes from Balksbury, where it was found that the colluvium contained midden material possibly derived from feasting. As to the size of the territory to which the enclosure belonged, it may be relevant to note that some of the pottery found in these deposits came from as far away as 10–15km.

If we are correct in accepting that the early hilltop enclosures served as meeting places associated with livestock management, then they may be seen to reflect a level of socio-political organization representing a community spread over a considerable landscape. The demise of the majority of these sites by the Early Iron Age implies a significant shift in organisation. It

is at this time that many of the more conventional hillforts came into existence.

There is another, rather ill-defined, category of enclosure that should be mentioned at this stage, since most appear to have been built in the earliest Iron Age though some continued in use into the Early Iron Age. These are difficult to define precisely but might be characterised as small, strongly defended, early hillforts and would include such sites as Budbury, Avon (Wainwright 1970), Lidbury, Wiltshire (Cunnington and Cunnington 1917), Oliver's Camp, Wiltshire (Cunnington 1908 and this volume, pp 128–30), Highdown Camp, West Sussex (Wilson 1940, 1950) and Alfred's Castle, Oxfordshire (this volume, pp 81–9). The sites are of less than 3ha in extent, they favour ridge-end locations (although some are found in less defensible and more open central downland settings) and often have more than one line of defence. All seem to have been intensively occupied with the exception of Oliver's Camp, which produced comparatively little material and no major internal structures. The recent excavation at Alfred's Castle by Gary Lock and Chris Gosden will, when published, provide a much-needed insight into sites of this kind. At present all that can be said – and it is no more than a suggestion – is that they might have been elite settlements of some kind, the prominent location and impressive defences being the symbols of elite status distinguishing them from contemporary farmsteads. On present evidence they are broadly contemporary with the large hilltop enclosures and seem not to have continued in use much after the beginning of the Early Iron Age. At Alfred's Castle, however, as we have seen, the enclosure was later used for a Roman villa establishment.

It is tempting to suggest that the early hilltop enclosures and small, strongly defended early hillforts characterise a particular type of social system operating throughout much of Wessex, and adjacent regions, at the end of the Bronze Age and beginning of the Iron Age, c 900–600 BC. The enclosures are only part of the picture and there is much new evidence now available from other categories of contemporary sites. This is not the place for a more extended discussion but the overall impression is that this was a period of transition in the course of which the economic, social and belief systems changed rapidly. The great majority of our hillforts belong to the subsequent period.

The Early–Middle Iron Age (c 600–100 bc)

In a general scheme for the development of hillforts in Wessex, put forward nearly 20 years ago (Cunliffe 1984b), the writer suggested that it was possible to define two broad phases. In the first, dating to the Early Iron Age, many hillforts were built. They were usually contour works averaging about 5ha in extent and defined by a single rampart and ditch with two entrances on opposite sides of the enclosure. The ramparts, where they had been sectioned, were found to have been faced externally with timber or stone to create a vertical wall. Forts of this sort were called *early hillforts*. By the Middle Iron Age many of the forts built in the early period had gone out of use. The few that remained were more strongly redefended, often with one or more lines of defence and complex entrance earthworks. Some were extended in area. In all cases ramparts built in this second period were unrevetted, giving rise to a continuous slope, or *glacis*, from the top of the rampart to the bottom of the ditch. Forts with these characteristics were referred to as *developed hillforts*.

At a basic level of characterisation this simple model remains valid but other excavations, at Maiden Castle, Uffington, Segsbury, Danebury, Bury Hill and Woolbury, together with the results of the geophysical surveys published in this volume, make it possible to add new levels of complexity. Perhaps the most striking thing to emerge is that while a broad sequence of development can be offered based on plan and defensive form and complexity, evidence for internal activity shows that there need be no direct correlation between the form of the fort and what went on within. The situation is complex, though not entirely without pattern. It will be convenient to discuss the forts in a broad chronological sequence based on the form of their defensive circuits before considering the variations apparent in the intensity of their use.

Reviewing all the evidence at present available for the development of hillfort enclosures in Wessex it is possible to distinguish five distinct categories. These can be placed in a chronological sequence to which broad dates can be assigned (Table 4).

Not all phases may be represented at every site, and without excavation it is often impossible to be sure if a particular phase is present or absent, but that said, the scheme does comfortably contain the array of data presently available. A brief survey of some of the key evidence from excavations will help to demonstrate the validity of the scheme.

Early 1 hillforts by definition have ramparts faced with timber or stone walling. Many could have had two opposed entrances but in the absence of excavation this cannot always be demonstrated. The key examples from the wider study area include Chalbury (Whitley 1943) and Maiden Castle in Dorset, Danebury, Winklebury and Bury Hill 1 in Hampshire and Torberry I in West Sussex (Cunliffe 1976). All have produced pottery dating to the 6th or 5th century BC.

Their relationship to the early hilltop enclosures of the preceding period is not immediately clear but the early hillfort at Danebury was built within the early hilltop enclosure, suggesting a degree of continuity. It could also be argued that Bury Hill 1 'replaced' Balksbury and Torberry I 'replaced' Harting Beacon by virtue of their proximities. What is known of their chronologies would support this interpretation.

Early 2 hillforts are similar in plan and size to Early 1 hillforts and have opposed entrances but are characterised by the *glacis* style of rampart. Examples include Woolbury and Quarley Hill in Hampshire and Figsbury in Wiltshire. All three were constructed on sites not previously enclosed and all have evidence that their ramparts were enhanced on more than one occasion. The associated pottery suggests a date in the 5th to 4th centuries BC. It is probable that some, at least, of the Early 1

Table 4 Summary of the five distinct hillfort categories

enclosure type	characteristics	ceramic phase	date	example
Early 1	vertical faced rampart	cp 2 3	6th–5th BC	Bury Hill 1
Early 2	*glacis* rampart	cp 3	5th–4th BC	Quarley Hill
Developed 1	entrances modified	cp 4/5 6	4th–3rd BC	Beacon Hill
Developed 2	only one gate;	cp 7	3rd–2nd BC	Danebury 5
	ramparts and gate enhanced			
Late	circular and multivallate	cp 7	late 2nd BC early 1st AD	Bury Hill 2

hillforts continued in use during this period: at Bury Hill 1 which began as an Early 1 hillfort the rampart was enhanced at this time.

Developed 1 hillforts. To divide Developed 1 and Developed 2 hillforts is somewhat arbitrary but the reality of this was demonstrated by the Danebury sequence. Developed 1 hillforts can be defined as earlier forts with enhanced entrances, sometimes with external hornworks added to create a more impressive approach. Danebury 3 and 4 is of this type. Beacon Hill would also appear to be a good example in one of its phases. Fosbury and Oldbury are other possibilities, but without excavation it is impossible to be sure. At Danebury the dating evidence suggests a 4th to 3rd century BC date.

Developed 2 hillforts. Hillforts of this type usually have only one entrance and there may be evidence that one or more earlier entrances have been deliberately blocked. In the cases where only the one gate remains it is usually elaborate with a long passage approach created by outer hornworks, inturns or a combination of the two. The ramparts have usually been considerably enhanced in size with material quarried from immediately inside. Examples include Danebury 5 and 6, Winklebury, Beacon Hill, St Catherine's Hill, Segsbury, Uffington, Barbury Castle, Castle Ditches, Oldbury Castle, Yarnbury and Maiden Castle. Where dating evidence is available it suggests a date in the 3rd or 2nd century BC.

Late hillforts is a category designed to accommodate double banked enclosures of the type represented by Bury Hill 2, Chisbury and Suddern Farm, all of which seem to have taken this form some time in the early 1st century BC.

Without far more excavation it will be impossible to give a definitive account of all the possible sequences embedded within the earthworks of hillforts, but of the sites beginning as *Early 1 hillforts* some were abandoned (eg Chalbury), some develop as Early 2 hillforts (eg Bury Hill 1) and some continue to be modified to the stage of Developed 2 hillforts (eg Danebury, Maiden Castle and Winklebury). *Early 2 hillforts* are known which were built *de novo* and did not develop further (eg Figsbury, Quarley Hill and Woolbury). Ladle Hill may well be an example of a fort of this type, begun but never completed. No examples are known of

sites that began as Early 2 hillforts continuing to develop, but this does not imply that there were none.

The *developed hillforts* present a different problem. All the examples from which there is excavated data (Danebury, Maiden Castle, Winklebury, Yarnbury, Torberry, Uffington, Segsbury, and others) began as early hillforts. None can be shown to have been built in the developed style on virgin sites. In contrast the few *late hillforts* known were all built on new or abandoned sites.

Always remembering that arguments based on absence of evidence are inherently weak, a few generalisations may be offered by way of summary:

- most of the hillforts built in the 6th to 5th centuries BC continued to be developed to the 2nd century BC, although this need not imply continuous use
- many of the hillforts built in the 5th–4th century BC were short-lived
- there appears to have been a period in the early 3rd century BC when forts with two gates had one blocked
- the few distinctive *late hillforts*, of the early 1st century BC, did not develop from earlier forts (although in the case of Bury Hill 2 it occupied part of the site of a long-abandoned early fort)

The discussion so far has been based largely on the evidence of excavation, augmented in part by topographical considerations. We must now extend the debate to examine what was going on inside the hillforts using the data from excavations, now greatly enhanced by the results of the recent geophysical surveys of 18 hillforts published in this volume.

In his summary of the results of the geophysical surveys (Chapter 3) Andrew Payne has stressed the variety of activity patterns represented. Five broadly defined arrangements can be identified:

- no recognisable activity
- limited pit scatters usually clustered in discrete areas
- dense, even pit scatters
- zones of pits interspersed with circular structures
- complexes of enclosures associated with circular structures and pits

What is particularly striking is that there is no direct correlation of activity pattern and hillfort type. Norsebury, a comparatively small site with simple earthworks, was densely packed with features while Fosbury, a large seemingly developed hillfort, appears to be largely empty in contrast to others of the same type (eg Barbury Castle and Danebury) the interiors of which were packed with features.

This apparent lack of correlation also gains support from several excavations. Danebury, Winklebury and Uffington all began as typical early forts with timber-faced ramparts and were later developed. In all three cases one gate was blocked and the rampart heightened when the defences were turned into a *glacis*. The further elaboration of the Danebury entrance and the massive final heightening of the rampart may belong to a later stage not represented at Winklebury and Uffington. Even so the settlement pattern in the three hillforts is very different in all comparable periods. While Danebury was densely packed with pits and other structures throughout, Winklebury appears to have been far less intensively occupied, and the excavators of Uffington, basing their reasoning on magnetometry supported by trial trenching, believe that the fort was used only slightly and sporadically (Miles *et al* 2003). The early hillfort of Bury Hill 1 adds further contrast in that the part of it not obscured by the later fort was totally empty of features – a fact supported by a comparatively large excavation.

Sufficient will have been said to show that the evidence, both from excavation and geophysics, argues strongly for the need to separate hillfort type from internal activity when attempting to understand the functions of hillforts. How, then, can we approach the problem if indeed it is at all possible to take the debate further?

One way would be to suppose that the actual enclosure was the all-important feature to the community who built it. It was, at the very least, a symbol of social cohesion and the dominant positions chosen visibly proclaimed the community's power over a wide area. The excavations at Danebury produced an array of evidence suggestive of the regular renewal of the enclosure boundary. It was possible to show that the ditch had been cleared out on a frequent cycle and the debris piled up to form a gradually growing outer bank (often called by the military term 'counterscarp'), while the rampart was added to several times, but far less frequently than the ditch renewal. We have suggested that these different cycles of renewal were symbolic rather than practical (Cunliffe 1995). At several sites, including Bury Hill 1, Quarley Hill, Figsbury and

Woolbury, where there is little or no evidence of internal occupation, the ramparts were enhanced often on more than one occasion. This would support the idea that renewal is likely to have been a symbolic act – perhaps the reaffirmation of the boundary enacted at a moment of significance in the life of the community.

The entrances are also worth considering in this context. The opposed entrances, so common among the early forts, are more appropriate to a society structuring its comings and goings and perhaps indulging in formal processions than one wishing to defend itself against aggression. It may not be entirely irrelevant to point out that the henge monuments of the 3rd millennium BC were similarly arranged with opposed entrances. The gates themselves – the liminal spaces that linked the inner and outer worlds – must have been endowed with special significance. When, during the Middle Iron Age, the enclosures were reconfigured to have only a single gate, that structure was usually greatly elaborated to make the liminal space much more extensive by creating a long passage formed by hornworks and inturns. It is conventional to explain these complex entrances in terms of their military capabilities or as symbols of elite power. Both explanations are possible and reasonable, but there need be no conflict between these aspects and the ritual significance of entrance passages.

If we extend this line of reasoning to suggest that each hillfort was the result of a community creating its own social place, then the appearance of a fort could symbolise the crystallising out of a socially cohesive group who, through the act of construction, proclaimed their identity while also making a claim to territory. If this, admittedly tenuous, line of reasoning is allowed, it could be further argued that in the hillforts we see a direct reflection of regional history, and that from them a socio-political narrative can be constructed.

A tentative narrative

In the 9th century BC or thereabouts Late Bronze Age communities occupying the chalklands of Wessex created large enclosures (*early hilltop enclosures*) in upland areas where communities could come together at certain times during the agro-pastoral year when livestock needed to be closely managed. At other times they dispersed to their farms, the elites occupying prominent settlements defined by banks and ditches.

The 7th century BC saw a marked change with the abandonment of the old enclosures and the creation of new communal enclosures (Early 1 hillforts) some of which might have directly succeeded the earlier enclosures while others were constructed without precedents. New forts continued to be created (Early 2 hillforts) in the 6th and 5th centuries BC, gradually filling up the landscape. As focal points for their communities they are likely to have been used in a variety of ways quite possibly governed by a strict annual calendar. One can imagine assemblies associated with religious rituals and feasting at which the 'business' of the community was enacted – gift exchanges, marriage settlements, law giving, the forming of allegiances and the host of social interactions necessary for society to sustain and reproduce itself.

The archaeological evidence gained from excavation shows that some sites were intensively used while others produce very little sign of activity. A convincing explanation for this disparity is not immediately apparent. Why, for example, was Danebury (in period 2) packed with storage pits, 'granaries' and circular houses arranged in zones and separated by streets when the neighbouring contemporary sites of Quarley, Figsbury, Bury Hill 1 and Woolbury appear to have been largely empty of structures? The simplest explanation would be that at this early stage Danebury began to perform a range of functions that the other forts did not. This does not necessarily mean that the other forts fell out of use – indeed there is evidence of continued, if sporadic, activity in each. They could have been maintained for assembly, while Danebury began to acquire the trappings of a more permanent settlement with a very considerable capacity for the storage of commodities in underground silos ('storage pits') and above ground 'granaries'. If we are correct in assuming that the underground silos were used predominantly for storing seed corn, then the community using Danebury had the capacity to store the seed for a considerable area of planting. The presence of what appears to be small rectangular shrines indicates another activity.

It is not, perhaps, too fanciful to suggest that the differences that appear at this time reflect two different aspects of the economy: enclosures for predominantly pastoral-related functions and enclosures reflecting agrarian production, the two being the components of a single system. Another way of viewing the pattern is to see Danebury as a focal site articulating all communal activities, while Quarley, Figsbury, Woolbury and Bury Hill 1 were peripheral locations for a more limited range of interactions. The enclosures were broadly similar in form. What went on in them was not.

For all its limitations the Danebury region provides an incomparable set of data but it need not be typical of the whole of Wessex. Each region should be considered on its own merit. At Winklebury the early phase was quite different from Danebury. A number of scattered circular houses were identified, together with many four-post 'granaries', but pits were rare. In the comparatively large area stripped only 3 of the 79 pits excavated belonged to the early period (Smith K 1977). Clearly the grain storage function, so evident at Danebury, was insignificant at Winklebury. Winklebury then, like Danebury, might have assumed 'settlement' as one of its functions but without the large-scale storage capacity. Another site that may be comparable with Winklebury is Chalbury, Dorset (Whitley 1943) where a number of houses have been identified but few pits. Few other early forts in Wessex have been excavated on a scale suitable for assessing internal arrangements.

To summarise, in the early forts we have tentatively identified three functions:

- assembly
- settlement
- storage

Assembly is assumed to have been a function of all early forts. Of these, fewer developed settlements within their defences and far fewer a large storage capacity in underground silos. This divergence can begin to be recognised at least as early as the 6th century BC.

The excavation at Danebury suggested a phase of disruption at the end of period 2 (coincident with ceramic phase 5) at the end of the 4th century BC when there is evidence of a widespread fire followed by a period of diminished use (Cunliffe 1995, 13–18). It is tempting to ascribe this to social unrest. How widespread this might have been remains to be defined, but that it coincides with a major change in pottery style recognisable over a considerable area may indicate that we are observing here a social dislocation of more than regional significance. After this distinctive horizon many of the early hillforts show no sign of any further use, while others continued to be utilised, their enclosing earthworks being refurbished.

The horizon of dislocation is of very considerable interest and deserves more attention than can be given here. The simplest explanation of the phenomenon is that there was a widespread social crisis brought about perhaps by the emergence of competing polities. Once it was resolved some of the old polities, who had maintained their integrity and dominance, continued while others were disbanded or absorbed. This could explain the abandonment of some of the hillforts and the development of others.

In this scenario the developed hillforts of the 3rd to 1st centuries BC represent the successful polities. At Danebury it is possible to show how the fort was re-established in period 3 with heightened rampart, an elaborated south-west entrance and an annex. Occupation continued (period 4) and further modifications were made when the rampart was refurbished once more. At this time the south-west entrance was blocked and the east entrance greatly elaborated (period 6). Excavation within the fort shows a continuation of the processes already apparent in the earlier period. Roads were maintained and the 'shrines' rebuilt, zones were set aside for rows of large six-post storage buildings, storage pits were dug in large number and circular houses, rebuilt on up to six occasions, clustered in the lee of the rampart. Altogether the structural evidence suggests heavy and continuous activity (although it is impossible to say that it was entirely without interruption). Added to this, the material remains point to a wide range of activities being undertaken, including manufacturing and redistribution.

The evidence is sufficient to suggest that Danebury, in its developed phase, had acquired central place functions (Cunliffe 1995, 91–5). Danebury, therefore, can be characterised as an intensively used developed hillfort.

A number of other hillforts belong to the same category. Maiden Castle is a well-known example and needs no further comment. The recent excavation at Segsbury suggests that it, too, might be considered in the same class (Lock and Gosden 1997b, 1998; Lock et al 2005). The geophysical survey (this volume, pp 92–3) seems to imply rather less activity when compared to Danebury but this is belied by the excavation, which demonstrated densely packed features including a large number of pits. The rampart was greatly increased in size in the later period and there is a strong probability that one of the earlier gates was blocked.

On the basis of the geophysical surveys Norsebury Ring, Barbury Castle and Castle Ditches all give the appearance of having been densely occupied. Barbury Castle and Castle Ditches have the massive ramparts and complex gates typical of the Developed 2 hillforts. The latter has a complex pattern of enclosure within, but it remains a distinct possibility that this is Late Iron Age or Roman in date, in part obscuring a plan dominated by pits. Norsebury Ring remains something of an anomaly because of its small size and comparatively slight defences. Lack of excavation means that little more can be said. It seems, then, that a number of the developed forts like Danebury continued to be densely occupied and were provided with extensive storage facilities in underground silos.

Other forts that continued in use into the Middle Iron Age display much less evidence of activity. Uffington, Liddington, Beacon Hill, Winklebury and probably St Catherine's Hill all had one of their earlier entrances blocked and except for Beacon Hill, which is unexcavated, all had their early ramparts refurbished. Thus they conform to our Developed 2 hillfort type. In all five cases the magnetometry shows that internal occupation was restricted in extent and not apparently very intense. Excavation at Uffington (Miles et al 2003) and limited trial trenching at Liddington (Hirst and Rahtz 1996) confirmed this.

From what has been said it will be clear that sufficient evidence, both from excavation and from geophysical survey, is now available to allow certain generalizations to be made. After the phase of social dislocation in the 4th century BC a number of forts continued to be maintained. Some were intensively used and were provided with a large grain storage capacity while others were used to a very much lesser extent and some may have been abandoned altogether. Those that were intensively used were refurbished on a number of occasions and by the late 2nd century BC their ramparts were substantial and their gates massively elaborated. It would be tempting to equate the Developed 2 hillforts with intensive occupation but Fosbury proves to be the exception. The nature of its earthworks puts it squarely within the Developed 2 hillfort category but the geophysical survey shows it to have been largely devoid of internal features. Except for this example, one might have argued that all Developed 2 hillforts were likely to have been intensively occupied!

The first half of the 1st century BC seems to have been a time of massive social and economic change and for the first time we can begin to glimpse a difference between two regions of Wessex. The area which, by the second half of the century, had become the territory of the Atrebates (approximately Hampshire, Wiltshire, West Sussex and Berkshire) developed in one way while the territory of the Durotriges (broadly Dorset and southern Somerset) developed in another.

In the territory of the Atrebates the earliest sign of a change is the construction, within the long-abandoned hillfort of Bury Hill, of a new defended enclosure consisting of a ditch almost circular in plan with a substantial bank both inside and out. The magnetometer survey showed that the inside was quite densely packed with storage pits, a fact confirmed by excavation which suggested that the pits and associated buildings dated to a late phase in the Middle Iron Age (ceramic phase 7) and that occupation was comparatively short-lived (Cunliffe and Poole 2000b).

One possibility that suggests itself is that Bury Hill 2 was constructed by a polity that was in some way challenging the authority of the nearby, long-established, Danebury. It may be relevant that it was about this time that Danebury was abandoned and its entrance destroyed by fire. Whether or not Bury Hill outlived this phase is impossible to say on the basis of the ceramic evidence at present available. Other sites broadly similar in form to Bury Hill 2 developed elsewhere in Atrebatic territory in the 1st century BC and into the 1st century AD. Examples include Suddern Farm (Cunliffe and Poole 2000c), Boscombe Down West (Richardson 1951) and possibly Chisbury (Cunnington 1932a). There is no evidence that the old hillforts continued in regular use after the beginning of the 1st century BC.

In what can be regarded as Durotrigian territory there is evidence to suggest that some of the forts were maintained or at least reused. Excavation shows this to have been so at Maiden Castle (Wheeler 1943; Sharples 1991), Hod Hill (Richmond 1968) and South Cadbury (Barrett et al 2000) and it could well be that the ditched enclosures, defined by geophysical sources, within Castle Ditches (p 106) belong to this phase of use, but without excavation this must remain speculative.

Standing back from the great mass of detail summarised so briefly above it is possible to discern a distinct patterning. On one level there is an increase in the number of hillforts during the period from the 6th to 4th centuries BC. This is followed by a phase of social disruption after which some of the hillforts continue in use into the 3rd century BC but only a few are maintained in strengthened form to the end of the 2nd century BC. The early 1st century BC was a period of rapid social and economic change that saw the demise of forts across much of the region, except in the territory of the Durotriges where some continue into the 1st century AD. Overall, after a peak in the number of forts in use in the 5th century BC, there is a gradual decline in the number maintained.

Among the early hillforts, irrespective of form, a variety of uses can be defined. All were probably used for some kind of assembly, some for settlement as well and among this group a few were intensively occupied and provided with a substantial storage capacity. From the 4th century BC onwards, the developed hillforts that continued in use divide into the same three functional types.

There seems to have been a direct continuity between early and developed forts in that no developed fort is known, in Wessex, to have been built *de novo*: where there is direct archaeological evidence each developed fort can be shown to have begun in the early period. The late hillfort of Bury Hill 2 was, however, without direct precedent, although it occupied a site fortified in the early period.

The thread of continuity that runs through all this is particularly interesting. A hillfort such as Danebury was first built within an early hilltop enclosure in the 6th century BC and continued in use into the early 1st century BC performing a wide, and probably increasing, range of functions. As such it was a *preferred location* throughout the Early and Middle Iron Age. There were others of the same kind. Maiden Castle and South Cadbury are well known, and recent excavation suggests that Segsbury probably conforms to the type. Other strong contenders are Badbury Rings, Yarnbury and Sidbury. It may be that with the development of these preferred locations and the focusing on them of more and more communal functions, hillforts occupying the more peripheral locations gradually fell out of use.

If this sketch approximates to reality then it might imply an increasing centralisation, the population focusing on fewer and fewer centres. These are issues wide open to debate. So long as that debate is firmly rooted in the reality of the data it cannot fail to be profitable.

Bibliography

Ainsworth, S, Oswald, A and Pearson, T 2001 'Discovering Our Hillfort Heritage', *PAST* (*The Newsletter of the Prehistoric Society*), **39**, November 2001, 3-4

Aitken, M J 1974 *Physics and Archaeology*, 2 edn. Oxford: Clarendon Press

Aitken. M J and Tite, M S 1962 'Proton magnetometer surveying on some British hill-forts', *Archaeometry*, **5**, 126-34

Alcock, L 1968a 'Cadbury Castle', 1967, *Antiquity*, **42**, 47-51

— 1968b 'Excavations at South Cadbury Castle, 1967, a summary report', *Antiq J*, **48**, 6-17

— 1969 'Excavations at South Cadbury Castle, 1968, a summary report', *Antiq J*, **49**, 30-40

— 1970 'South Cadbury Excavations, 1969', *Antiquity*, **44**, 46-9

— 1971 'Excavations at South Cadbury Castle, 1970, summary report', *Antiq J*, **51**, 1-7

— 1972 *'By South Cadbury is that Camelot…' Excavations at Cadbury Castle 1966-1970*. London

— 1980 'The Cadbury Castle sequence in the first millennium BC', *Bull Board Celtic Stud*, **28**, 656-718

— 1995 *Cadbury Castle, Somerset: the Early Medieval Archaeology*. Cardiff

Allcroft, H 1908 *Earthwork of England*. London

Annable, F K 1974 'A Bronze Military Apron Mount from Cunetio' in 'Notes', *Wiltshire Archaeol Natur Hist Mag*, **69**, 176-9

Anderton, M 1998 'Barbury Castle and the Second World War', *in* Bowden, M *Barbury Castle – An Archaeological Survey by the Royal Commission on the Historical Monuments of England*, AI/3/1998, Appendix 1

Avery, M 1976 'Hillforts of the British Isles: a Student's Introduction', *in* Harding, D W (ed) *Hillforts: Later Prehistoric Earthworks in Britain and Ireland*. London: Academic Press, 1-58

Balaam, N D, Corney, M, Dunn, C and Porter, H 1991 'The surveys', *in* Sharples, N M *Maiden Castle, Excavations and Field Survey 1985-6*. London, 37-42

Bartlett, A D H 1999 *Castle Ditches, Wiltshire and Norsebury Ring, Hampshire. Magnetic Susceptibility Surveys for the Wessex Hillforts Project 1998-9*. Unpublished report

Barrett, J, Bradley, R and Green, M (eds) 1991 *Landscape, Monuments and Society: the Prehistory of Cranborne Chase*. Cambridge

Barrett, J C, Freeman, P W M and Woodward, A 2000 *Cadbury Castle, Somerset: the later prehistoric and early historic archaeology*. English Heritage Archaeol Rep, **20**. London

Bayley, J (ed) 1998 *Science in Archaeology: an agenda for the future*. London: English Heritage

Bedwin, O 1978 'Excavations inside Harting Beacon Hill-fort 1976', *Sussex Archaeol Coll*, **116**, 225-40

— 1979 'Excavations at Harting Beacon, West Sussex: second season', *Sussex Archaeol. Coll*, **117**, 21-36

— 1980. Excavations at Chanctonbury Ring, Wiston, West Sussex 1977', *Britannia*, **11**, 173-222

Bersu, G 1940 'Excavations at Little Woodbury, Wiltshire, part I', *Proc Prehist Soc*, **6**, 30-111

Bewley, R H 2000 'Aerial Survey in the Danebury Environs area, 1981-1997', *in* Cunliffe, B *The Danebury Environs Programme – the Prehistory of a Wessex Landscape, Volume 1 – Introduction*. Oxford, 20-28

— 2001 'Understanding England's Historic Landscapes: an Aerial Perspective', *Landscapes*, **2** (1). Windgather Press

— 2003 *Prehistoric Settlements*. Stroud, Gloucestershire: Tempus Publishing

Bonney, D J 1966 'Pagan Saxon Burials and Boundaries in Wiltshire', *Wiltshire Archaeol Natur Hist Mag*, **61**, 25-30

Borthwick, A and Chandler, J 1984 *Our Chequered Past: the archaeology of Salisbury*. Trowbridge

Bowden, M 1991 *Pitt Rivers. The life and archaeological work of Lieutenant-General Augustus Henry Lane Fox Pitt Rivers, DCL, FRS, FSA*. Cambridge

— 1998 Barbury 'Castle: an Archaeological Survey by the Royal Commission on the Historical Monuments of England'. *RCHME Survey Report*, AI/3/1998

— (ed) 1999 *Unravelling the Landscape, an Inquisitive Approach to Archaeology*. Stroud: Tempus

— 2000 *Liddington Castle Archaeological Earthwork Survey*. English Heritage survey report, AI/4/2001

Bowden, M 2005 'The Middle Iron Age on the Marlborough Downs', *in* Brown, G, Field, D and McOmish, D (eds) *The Avebury Landscape – Aspects of the Field Archaeology of the Marlborough Downs*. Oxbow Books, Oxford, 156-63

Bowden, M, Ford, S and Gaffney, V 1993 'The excavation of a Late Bronze Age artefact scatter on Weathercock Hill', *Berkshire Archaeol J*, **74**, 69-83

Bowden, M and McOmish, D 1987 'The Required Barrier', *Scottish Archaeol Rev*, **4**, 76-84

— 1989 'Little Boxes: more about hillforts', *Scottish Archaeol Rev*, **6**, 12-16

Bowen, H C 1975 'Air photography and the Development of the Landscape in Central Parts of Southern England', *in* Wilson, D (ed) *Aerial Reconnaissance for Archaeology*, CBA Res Rep, **12**. London, 103-18

— 1978 ' "Celtic" fields and "ranch" boundaries in Wessex', *in* Limbrey, S and Evans, J (eds) *The Effect of Man on the Landscape: the lowland zone*, CBA Res Rep, **21**. London, 115-23

— 1979 'Gussage in its Setting', *in* Wainwright, G J *Gussage All Saints: An Iron Age Settlement in Dorset*. London, 179-83

— 1990 *The Archaeology of Bokerley Dyke*. London

Bradley, R 1989 'Herbert Toms – A Pioneer of Analytical Field Survey', *in* Bowden, M, Mackay, D and Topping, P (eds.) *From Cornwall to Caithness: Some Aspects of British Field Archaeology*, Brit Archaeol Rep, Brit Ser, **209**. Oxford, 29-48

Bradley, R and Ellison, A 1975 *Rams Hill*, Brit Archaeol Rep, Brit Ser, **19**. Oxford

Bradley, R, Entwhistle, R and Raymond, F 1994 *Prehistoric Land Divisions on Salisbury Plain. The Work of the Wessex Linear Ditches Project*, English Heritage Archaeol Rep, **2**. London

Bradley, R and Richards, J 1978 'Prehistoric Fields and Boundaries on the Berkshire Downs', *in* Bowen, H C and Fowler, P J (eds) *Early Land Allotment*, Brit Archaeol Rep, Brit Ser, **48**. Oxford, 53-60

Brailsford, J 1948 'Excavations at Little Woodbury, part II', *Proc Prehist Soc*, **14**, 1-23

— 1949 'Excavations at Little Woodbury, parts IV and V'. *Proc Prehist Soc*, **15**, 156-68

Brown, G, Field, D and McOmish, D 1994 'East Chisenbury Midden Complex, Wiltshire', *in* Fitzpatrick, A and Morris, E (eds) 1994 *The Iron Age in Wessex: Recent Work*. Salisbury, 46-8

Burrow, I 1981 'Hillfort and Hill-top Settlement in Somerset in the First to Eighth Centuries AD, Brit Archaeol Rep, Brit Ser, **91**. Oxford

Chapman, H P and Van de Noort, R 2001 'High-Resolution Wetland Prospection, using GPS and GIS: Landscape Studies at Sutton Common (South Yorkshire), and Meare Village East (Somerset)', *J Archaeol Sci*, **28**, 365-75

Champion, T C and Collis, J R (eds) 1997 *The Iron Age in Britain and Ireland: recent trends*. J R Collis/University of Sheffield

Childe, V G 1935 *The Prehistory of Scotland*. Edinburgh

— 1946 *Scotland before the Scots*. Edinburgh

Clark, A J 1996 *Seeing Beneath the Soil – Prospecting Methods in Archaeology*, 2 ed. London: B T Batsford

Clay, R C C 1935 'Chiselbury Camp', *Wiltshire Archaeol Natur Hist Mag*, **47**, 20-24

Coles, J M, Leach, P, Minnitt, S C, Tabor, R and Wilson, A S 1999 'A Later Bronze Age shield from South Cadbury, Somerset, England', *Antiquity*, **73**, 33-48

Collins, A E P 1947 'Excavations on Blewburton Hill, 1947', *Berks Archaeol J*, **50**, 4–29

Collins, A E P and F J 1959 'Excavations on Blewburton Hill, Berks, 1953', *Berks Archaeol J*, **57**, 52–73

Collis, J 1981 'A theoretical study of hill-forts', *in* Guilbert, G (ed) *Hill-fort Studies. Essays for A H A Hogg.* Leicester University Press, 66–77

Collis, J R 1994 'Foreword', *in* Fitzpatrick, A and Morris, E (eds) *The Iron Age in Wessex: Recent Work.* Salisbury, ix

Colt Hoare, Sir R 1812 *Ancient Wiltshire*, Vol 1. London

— 1819 *Ancient Wiltshire*, Vol 2. London

Corney, M C 1989 'Multiple Ditch Systems and Iron Age Settlement in Central Wessex', *in* Bowden,M, Mackay, D and Topping, P (eds.), *From Cornwall to Caithness: Some Aspects of British Field Archaeology,* Brit Archaeol Rep, Brit Ser, **209**. Oxford, 111–28

— 1994 'Recording the Prehistoric Landscape of Wessex', *in* Fitzpatrick, A and Morris, E (eds) *The Iron Age in Wessex: Recent Work.* Salisbury, 35–7

— 1997 'The Origins and Development of the 'Small Town' of *Cunetio*, Wiltshire', *Britannia*, **xxviii**, 337–50

— 2001 'The Romano-British Nucleated Settlements of Wiltshire', *in* Ellis, P (ed) *Roman Wiltshire and After.* Devizes, 5–38

Cotton, M A 1960 'Alfred's Castle', *Berkshire Archaeol J*, **58**, 44–8

— 1962 'Berkshire Hillforts', *Berkshire Archaeo J*, **60**, 30–52

Crawford, O G S 1955 *Said and Done.* London

Crawford, O G S and Keiller, A 1928 *Wessex from the Air.* Oxford

Cunliffe, B 1972 'The Late Iron Age metalwork from Bulbury, Dorset', *Antiquaries Journal*, **52**, 293-308

Cunliffe, B 1976 *Iron Age sites in central southern England*, CBA Res Rep, **16**. London

— 1984a *Danebury: An Iron Age Hillfort in Hampshire. The excavations 1969–1978. Volumes 1 and 2.* CBA Res Rep, **52**. London

— 1984b 'Iron Age Wessex: continuity and change', *in* Cunliffe, B and Miles, D (eds) *Aspects of the Iron Age in Central Southern Britain.* Oxford, 12–45

— 1987 *Hengistbury Head, Dorset. Volume I: prehistoric and Roman settlement, 3500 BC–AD 500.* Oxford

— 1990 'Before Hillforts', *Oxford J Archaeol*, **9**, 323–36

— 1991 *Iron Age Communities in Britain: an account of England, Scotland and Wales from the Seventh Century BC until the Roman Conquest*, 3 edn. London

— 1995 *Danebury: an Iron Age Hillfort in Hampshire. Volume 6 A hillfort community in perspective*, CBA Res Rep, **102**. York: Council for British Archaeology

— 1996 'The Celtic Chariot: a footnote', *in* Rafferty, B (ed) *Sites and Sights of the Iron Age.* Oxford, 31–9

— 2000 *The Danebury Environs Programme: the prehistory of a Wessex landscape, Volume 1, Introduction*, English Heritage/Oxford U Committee Archaeol Monogr **48**. Oxford

Cunliffe, B 2003 *The Danebury Environs Roman Project, 7. Rowbury Farm Excavation 2003, Interim Report.* Danebury Trust, Institute of Archaeology, Oxford.

Cunliffe, B W and Poole, C 1991 *Danebury: an Iron Age Hillfort in Hampshire. The excavations 1979–1988. Volumes 4 and 5*, CBA Res Rep, **73**. London: Council for British Archaeology

— 2000a *The Danebury Environs Programme – the Prehistory of a Wessex Landscape, Volume 2, Part 1 – Woolbury, Stockbridge, Hants, 1989.* English Heritage/Oxford U Committee Archaeol Monogr **49** (Part 1). Oxford

— 2000b *The Danebury Environs Programme – the Prehistory of a Wessex Landscape, Volume 2, Part 2 – Bury Hill, Upper Clatford, Hants, 1990.* English Heritage/Oxford U Committee Archaeol Monograph **49** (Part 2). Oxford

— 2000c *The Danebury Environs Programme – the Prehistory of a Wessex Landscape. Volume 2, Part 3 – Suddern Farm, Middle Wallop, Hants, 1991 and 1996.* English Heritage/Oxford U Committee Archaeol Monogr **49** (Part 3). Oxford

— 2000d *The Danebury Environs Programme – the Prehistory of a Wessex Landscape, Volume 2, Part 5 – Nettlebank Copse, Wherwell, Hants, 1993.* English Heritage/Oxford U Committee Archaeol Monogr **49** (Part 5). Oxford

— 2000e *The Danebury Environs Programme – the Prehistory of a Wessex Landscape, Volume 2, Part 6 – Houghton Down, Stockbridge, Hants, 1994.* English Heritage/Oxford U Committee Archaeol Monogr **49** (Part 6). Oxford

Cunnington, B H and Cunnington, M 1913 'Casterley Camp Excavations', *Wiltshire Archaeol Natur Hist Mag*, **38**, 53–105

Cunnington, H 1871 'Oldbury Camp, Wilts', *Wiltshire Archaeol Natur Hist Mag*, **28**, 277

Cunnington, M 1908 'Oliver's Camp, Devizes', *Wiltshire Archaeol Natur Hist Mag*, **35**, 408–44

— 1909 'Notes on a Late Celtic rubbish heap near Oare', *Wiltshire Archaeol Natur Hist Mag*, **36**, 125–39

— 1923 *The Early Iron Age Inhabited Site at All Cannings Cross.* Devizes

— 1925 'Figsbury Rings: an account of the excavations in 1924'. *Wiltshire Archaeol Natur Hist Mag*, **43**, 48–58

— 1932a 'Chisbury Camp', *Wiltshire Archaeol Natur Hist Mag*, **46**, 4–7

— 1932b 'The Demolition of Chisenbury Trendle', *Wiltshire Archaeol Natur Hist Mag*, **46**, 1–3

— 1933 'Excavations in Yarnbury Castle Camp 1932', *Wiltshire Archaeol Natur Hist Mag*, **46**, 198–213

Cunnington, M E and Cunnington, B H 1917 'Lidbury Camp', *Wiltshire Archaeol Natur Hist Mag*, **40**, 12–36

Cunnington, M E 1934 'Wiltshire in Pagan Saxon Times', *Wiltshire Archaeol Natur Hist Mag*, **46**, 147-175

David, A and Payne, A 1997 'Geophysical Surveys within the Stonehenge Landscape: A Review of Past Endeavour and Future Potential' *in* Cunliffe B and Renfrew C (eds) *Science and Stonehenge*, Proc Brit Acad, **92**. Oxford. Oxford University Press

Dixon, P 1976 'Crickley Hill, 1969–1972', *in* Harding, D W (ed) *Hillforts: Later Prehistoric Earthworks in Britain and Ireland.* London: Academic Press, 162–75

Dixon, P 1994 *Crickley Hill: the hillfort defences.* Crickley Hill Trust/University of Nottingham

Donachie, J D and Field, D J 1994 'A survey of Cissbury Ring, Worthing, West Sussex', Royal Commission on the Historical Monuments of England. Unpublished report

Dunn, C J 1997 *Ham Hill, Somerset.* RCHME

Dymond, C W 1886 *Worlebury an ancient stronghold in the county of Somerset.* Bristol

Eagles, B N 1989 'Woolbury Fields, Stockbridge Down, Hampshire', *in* Bowden, M, Mackay, D and Topping, P (eds) *From Cornwall to Caithness,: Some Aspects of British Field Archaeology,* Brit Archaeol Rep, Brit Ser, **209**. Oxford, 93–8

— 1991 'A new survey of the hillfort on Beacon Hill, Burghclere, Hampshire', *Archaeol J*, **148**, 98–103

— 1994 'The Archaeological Evidence for Settlement in the Fifth to Seventh Centuries AD', *in* Aston, M and Lewis, C (eds) *The Medieval Landscape of Wessex.* Oxford, 13–32

Eagles, B N and Mortimer, C 1994 'Early Anglo-Saxon Artefacts from Hod Hill, Dorset', *Antiq J*, **73** (for 1993), 132–40

Ellis, C J and Rawlings, M 2001 'Excavations at Balksbury Camp, Andover 1995–97', *Proc Hampshire Fld Club Archaeol Soc*, **56**, 21–94

Ellison, A and Rahtz, P A R 1987 'Excavations at Whitsbury Castle Ditches, Hampshire, 1960'. *Proc Hampshire Fld Club Archaeol Soc*, **43**, 63–81

English Heritage 1995 *Geophysical Survey in Archaeological Field Evaluation.* Research and Professional Services Guideline, **1**

English Heritage 1998 *Corporate Plan 1998–2002*

Fasham, P 1987 *A Banjo enclosure in Micheldever Wood, Hampshire.* Winchester

Feacham, R W 1971 'Unfinished Hillforts', *in* Jesson, M and Hill, D (eds) *The Iron Age and its Hillforts: papers presented to Sir Mortimer Wheeler.* Southampton, 19–40

Fell, C I 1937 'The Hunsbury hill-fort, Northants: a new survey of the material', *Archaeol J*, **93**, 57–100

Fielden, K (ed) 1991 'Excavation and Fieldwork in Wiltshire 1989', *Wiltshire Archaeol Natur Hist Mag*, **84**, 144

Ford, S 1982 'Fieldwork and Excavation on the Berkshire Grim's Ditch', *Oxoniensia*, **47**, 13–36

Forde-Johnston, J 1976 *Hillforts of the Iron Age in England and Wales*. Liverpool

Fowler, P J 1983 *The Farming of Prehistoric Britain*. Cambridge

— 2000 *Landscape Plotted and Pieced: Landscape History and Local Archaeology in Fyfield and Overton Down, Wiltshire*. London

Fowler, P J and Walters, B 1981 'Archaeology and the M4 Motorway, 1969–71, Tormarton, County of Avon to Ermin Street, Berkshire', *Wiltshire Archaeol Natur Hist Mag*, **74/75** (for 1979/1980), 69–132

Frodsham, P (ed) 2004 *Archaeology in Northumberland National Park* CBA Res Rep, **136**. York: Council for British Archaeology

Gaffney, V L, Gaffney, C F and Corney, M 1998 'Changing the Roman landscape: the role of geophysics and remote sensing', *in* Bayley, J (ed) *Science in Archaeology: an agenda for the future*. London: English Heritage, 145–56

Geological Survey of Great Britain 1959 *One inch geology map – Sheet 283 (drift)*. Andover

Gingell, C 1992 *The Marlborough Downs: a Later Bronze Age Landscape and its Origins*. Devizes

Gosden, C and Lock, G 1999 'The Hillforts of the Ridgeway Project: Excavations at Alfred's Castle 1998', *South Midlands Archaeol*, **29**, 44–53

— 2001 'Hillforts of the Ridgeway Project: excavations at Alfred's Castle 2000', *South Midlands Archaeol*, **31**, 80–9

— 2003 'Becoming Roman on the Berkshire Downs: the evidence from Alfred's Castle', *Britannia*, Vol. XXXIV (2003), 65-80

Gresham, C A 1940 'Spettisbury Rings, Dorset', *Archaeol J*, **96** (for 1939), 114–31

Grinsell, L V 1957 'Archaeological Gazetteer', *in Victoria County History of Wiltshire, Volume 1, part 1*, 21–79

Guido, C M and Smith, I, 1982 'Figsbury Rings: a Reconsideration of the Inner Enclosure', *Wiltshire Archaeol Natur Hist Mag*, **76**, 21–6

Gwilt, A and Haselgrove, C (eds) 1997 *Reconstructing Iron Age Societies: new approaches to the British Iron Age*, Oxbow Monogr, **71**. Oxford

Hamilton, S and Manley, J 1997 'Points of View – Prominent Enclosures in 1st Millennium BC Sussex', *Sussex Archaeol Coll*, **135**, 93–112

Hampton, J and Palmer, R 1977 'Implications of aerial photography for archaeology', *Archaeol*, **134**, 157–93

Harding, D W 1976 'Blewburton Hill, Berkshire: Re-excavation and reappraisal', *in* Harding, D W (ed) *Hillforts: Later Prehistoric Earthworks in Britain and Ireland*. London, 133–46

Haselgrove, C 1994 'Social organisation in Iron Age Wessex', *in* Morris, E and Fitzpatrick, A (eds) *The Iron Age in Wessex: recent work*. Salisbury, 1–3

— 1999 'The Iron Age', *in* Hunter, J and Ralston, I (eds) *The Archaeology of Britain – An introduction from the Upper Paleolithic to the Industrial Revolution*. London and New York: Routledge, 113–34

Hawkes, C F C 1931 'Hillforts', *Antiquity*, **5**, 60–97

— 1936 'The excavations at Buckland Rings, Lymington, 1935', *Proc Hampshire Fld Club Archaeol Soc*, **13**, 124–64

— 1939 'The excavations at Quarley Hill, 1938', *Proc Hampshire Fld Club Archaeol Soc*, **14**, 136–94

— 1940 'The Excavations at Bury Hill, 1939', *Proc Hampshire Fld Club Archaeol Soc*, **14**, 291–337

— 1956 'The British Iron Age: cultures, chronology and peoples', *Cong In. Sciences pre- et Protohistoriques, Actes de la IV Session*. Madrid 1954, 729–37

— 1959 'The ABC of the British Iron Age', *Antiquity* **33**, 170–82

— 1971 'Fence, Wall, Dump, from Troy to Hod', *in* Jesson, M and Hill, D (eds) *The Iron Age and its Hillforts: papers presented to Sir Mortimer Wheeler*. Southampton, 5–18

— 1976 'St Catharine's Hill, Winchester: the Report of 1930 Re-assessed', *in* Harding, D W (ed) *Hillforts – Later Prehistoric Earthworks in Britain and Ireland*. London: Academic Press

Hawkes, C F C, Myres, J N L and Stevens, C G 1930 'St Catharine's Hill, Winchester', *Proc Hampshire Fld Club Archaeol Soc*, **11**

Hawkes, J 1940 'The excavations at Balksbury, 1939', *Proc Hampshire. Fld Club Archaeol Soc*, **14**, 338–45

Hewett, H 1844 *History and Antiquities of the Hundred of Compton, Berks*. Reading

Hill, J D 1995 'How should we understand Iron Age societies and hillforts? A contextual study from southern Britain', *in* Hill, J D and and Cumberpatch, C (eds) *Different Iron Ages: studies on the Iron Age in temperate Europe*, Brit Archaeol Rep, Internat Ser, **602**. Oxford, 45–66

Hill, J D 1996 Hillforts and the Iron Age of Wessex in Champion and Collis 1996, 95–116.

Hill, J D and Cumberpatch, C (eds) 1995 *Different Iron Ages: studies on the Iron Age in temperate Europe*, Brit Archaeol Rep, Internat Ser, **602**. Oxford

Hingley, R 1990 'Boundaries surrounding Iron Age and Romano-British settlements', *Scottish Archaeol Rev*, **7**, 96–103

Hirst, S and Rahtz, P 1996 'Liddington Castle and the Battle of Badon: excavation and research 1976', *Archaeol J*, **153**, 1–59

Hogg, A H A 1975 *Hillforts of Britain*. London

Johnson, P and Walters, B 1988 'Exploratory Excavations of Roman Buildings at Cherhill and Manningford Bruce', *Wiltshire Archaeol Natur Hist Mag*, **82**, 77–91

Lane Fox, A H 1869 'An examination into the character and probable origin of the Hill Forts of Sussex', *Archaeologia*, **42**, 27–52

— 1881 'Excavation at Mount Caburn Camp, near Lewes', *Archaeologia*, **46**, 1–73

Leach, P and Tabor, R 1997 *The South Cadbury Environs Project. Fieldwork Report 1997*, Birmingham, Birmingham University Field Archaeology Unit, Report 457.01

Liddell, D M 1933 'Excavations at Meon Hill', *Proc Hampshire Fld Club Archaeol Soc*, **12**, 127–62.

Linford, N T 1995 'Caesar's Camp, Windsor Forest, Berkshire. Report on geophysical survey, October 1995', *Ancient Monuments Laboratory Reports*, **46/95**

Lock, G and Gosden, C 1997a 'The Hillforts of the Ridgeway Project: excavations on White Horse Hill, 1995', *South Midlands Archaeol*, **27**, 64–9

— 1997b 'The Hillforts of the Ridgeway Project: excavations at Segsbury Camp 1996', *South Midlands Archaeol*, **27**, 69–77

— 1998 'The Hillforts of the Ridgeway Project: excavations at Segsbury Camp 1997', *South Midlands Archaeol*, **28**, 53–63

— 1999 'Hillforts of the Ridgeway Project: excavations at Alfred's Castle 1998', *South Midlands Archaeol*, **29**, 44–53

— 2000 'The Hillforts of the Ridgeway Project: excavations at Alfred's Castle 1999', *South Midlands Archaeol*, **30**, 82–90

Lock, G, Gosden, C and Daly, P 2005 *Segsbury Camp – Excavations in 1996 and 1997 at an Iron Age hillfort on the Oxfordshire Ridgeway*. Oxford University School of Archaeology, Monograph 61. Oxford University School of Archaeology, Oxford

MacGregor, M and Simpson, D D A 1963 'A group of iron objects from Barbury Castle, Wilts', *Wiltshire Archaeol Natur Hist Mag*, **58**, 394–402

Massey, R 1998 *Walbury, Fosbury and Tidcombe Down: a Prehistoric Wessex Landscape*. Unpublished MA assignment, U Bristol

McOmish, D, Brown, G and Field, D 2002 *The Field Archaeology of Salisbury Plain*. London: English Heritage

Meany, A 1964 *A Gazetteer of Early Anglo-Saxon Burial Sites* volume 1. London: George Allen and Unwin

Meyrick O, 1947 'Notes on some early Iron Age sites in the Marlborough District', *Wiltshire Archaeol Natur Hist* Mag, **51** (1945–7), 256–63

Miles, D and Palmer, S 1995 'White Horse Hill', *Current Archaeol*, **142**, XII, 10, 372–8

Miles, D, Palmer, S, Lock, G, Gosden, C and Cromarty, A M 2003 *Uffington White Horse Hill and its Landscape: investigations at White Horse Hill, Uffington, 1989–95 and Tower Hill, Ashbury, 1993–4*. Thames Valley Landscapes Monograph, **18**, Oxford Archaeology, Oxford

Musson, C R 1968 'A geophysical survey at South Cadbury Castle, Somerset', *Prospezioni Archaeologiche*, **3**, 115–21

Neal, D S 1980 'Bronze Age, Iron Age and Roman settlement sites at Little Somborne and Ashley, Hampshire', *Proc Hampshire Fid Club Archaeol Soc*, **36**, 91–143

Newman, C 1997 *Tara – An Archaeological Survey*, Discovery Programme Monographs, **2**, Royal Irish Academy, Dublin

Officers' Reports 1971 'Accessions to the Museum, 1970', *Wiltshire Archaeol Natur Hist Mag*, **66**, 196–200

Ordnance Survey 1962 *Map of Southern Britain in the Iron Age.* Chessington, Surrey

Oswald, A, Barber, M and Dyer, C 2001 *The Creation of Monuments: Neolithic causewayed enclosures in the British Isles.* London: English Heritage

Oxford Archaeology 2004 *A Interim Summary Report on Excavations at Castle Hill, Wittenham Clumps, Summer Season 13th July to 5th September 2003.* Unpublished report, Oxford

Palmer, R 1984 *Danebury. An Iron Age Hillfort in Hampshire. An aerial photographic interpretation of its environs*, Royal Commission on Historical Monuments (England), Supplementary Series, **6**. London

Parfitt, K 1995 *Iron Age Burials from Mill Hill, Deal.* London

Passmore, A D 1914 'Liddington Castle (Camp)', *Wiltshire Archaeol Natur Hist Mag*, **38**, 576–84

Payne, A 1993a 'Buckland Rings, Lymington, Hampshire: report on geophysical survey, April 1993', *Ancient Monuments Laboratory Reports*, **80/93**

— 1993b 'Segsbury Camp or Letcombe Castle, Letcombe Regis, Oxfordshire: interim report on geophysical survey, November 1993', *Ancient Monuments Laboratory Reports*, **119/93**

— 1996 'The use of magnetic prospection in the exploration of Iron Age hillfort interiors in Southern England', *Archaeol Prospection*, **3**, 163–84

— 2000a 'Enhancement of the site record by magnetometry', in Cunliffe, B 2000 *The Danebury Environs Programme: the Prehistory of a Wessex Landscape, Volume 1, Introduction*, English Heritage/Oxford U Committee Archaeol Monogr 48. Oxford, 29–34

— 2000b 'Commentary on the geophysical survey (Chapter 7 Appendix)' in Cunliffe, B and Poole, C 2000 *The Danebury Environs Programme – The Prehistory of a Wessex Landscape, Volume 2, Part 1 – Woolbury, Stockbridge, Hants, 1989*, English Heritage/Oxford U Committee Archaeol Monogr 49 (Part 1). Oxford, 81

— 2000c 'Commentary on the geophysical survey (Chapter 7 Appendix)' in Cunliffe, B and Poole, C 2000 *The Danebury Environs Programme – The Prehistory of a Wessex Landscape, Volume 2, Part 2 – Bury Hill, Upper Clatford, Hants, 1990*, English Heritage/Oxford U Committee Archaeol Monogr 49 (Part 2). Oxford, 83–4

— 2000d 'Commentary on the geophysical survey (Chapter 7 Appendix)' in Cunliffe, B and Poole, C 2000 *The Danebury Environs Programme – The Prehistory of a Wessex Landscape, Volume 2, Part 6 – Houghton Down, Stockbridge, Hants, 1994*, English Heritage/Oxford U Committee Archaeol Monogr 49 (Part 6). Oxford, 161–7

— 2001 'Cissbury Ring, Worthing, West Sussex, Report on Geophysical Surveys, April 2000', *Centre for Archaeology Reports Series*. **91/2001**. Portsmouth: English Heritage

— 2002a 'Perborough Castle, Cow Down, Compton', in Greenaway, D and Ward, D (eds) 2002 *In the Valley of the Pang*. Reading: The Friends of the Pang and Kennet Valleys

— 2002b 'Castle Hill or Sinodun Hill Camp, Little Wittenham, Oxfordshire: Report on Geophysical Survey, June 2002', *Centre for Archaeology Reports Series*. **70/2002**. Portsmouth: English Heritage

— 2002c 'A Hillfort within a Hillfort. The Wittenham Clumps Heritage Landscape Project', *CfA News*, **4** (The Newsletter of the Centre for Archaeology), Winter 2002-3, 5.

— 2003a 'Uffington Castle Geophysical Survey', in Miles, D, Palmer, S, Lock, G, Gosden, C and Cromarty, A M 2003

Uffington White Horse and its Landscape – Investigations at White Horse Hill, Uffington, 1989–95 and Tower Hill, Ashbury, 1993–4, Thames Valley Landscapes Monograph, **18**. Oxford Archaeology, Oxford, 98–102

— 2003b 'Rowbury Farm Enclosure, Fullerton Down, Hampshire: Report on Geophysical Survey, February 2003', *Centre for Archaeology Reports Series*. **69/2003**. Portsmouth: English Heritage

— 2004 'Flint Farm Enclosure, Fullerton, Hampshire: Report on Geophysical Survey, February 2004', *Centre for Archaeology Reports Series*. **70/2004**. Portsmouth: English Heritage

— forthcoming 'The geophysical surveys', in Thomas, N forthcoming *Excavations at Conderton Camp, Worcestershire*

Peake, H J E 1931 *The Archaeology of Berkshire.* London

Perry, B 1970 'Iron Age enclosures and settlements on the Hampshire chalklands', *Archaeol J*, **126** (1969), 29–43

— 1986 'Excavations at Bramdean, Hampshire, 1983 and 1984, with some further discussion of the 'Banjo' syndrome', *Proc Hampshire Fid Club Archaeol Soc*, **42**, 35–42

Phillips, C W 1980 *Archaeology in the Ordnance Survey 1791–1965.* London: Council for British Archaeology

Piggott, C M 1950 'The excavations at Hownam Rings, Roxburghshire, 1948', *Proc. Soc. Antiq. Scotl.*, **82**, (1947–1948), 193–224

Piggott, S 1931 'Ladle Hill – an unfinished hillfort', *Antiquity* **5**, 474–85

— 1966 'A Scheme for the Scottish Iron Age', in Rivet, A L F (ed) *The Iron Age in northern Britain*. Edinburgh, 1–16

Piggott, S and Piggott, C M 1940 'Excavations at Ram's Hill, Uffington, Berkshire', *Antiq J*, **20**, 465–80

Pitt Rivers, A H L F 1883 'Excavation at Caesar's Camp near Folkestone, conducted in June and July, 1878', *Archaeologia*, **47**, 429–65

— 1887 *Excavations in Cranborne Chase Volume I.* London

— 1888 *Excavations in Cranborne Chase Volume II.* London

— 1892 *Excavations in Cranborne Chase Volume III.* London

— 1898 *Excavations in Cranborne Chase Volume IV.* London

Rahtz, P A, Woodward, A, Burrow, I, Everton, A, Watts, L, Leach, P., Hirst S, Fowler, P and Gardner, K 1992 *Cadbury Congresbury 1968–73. a late/post-Roman hilltop settlement in Somerset*, Brit Archaeol Rep, Brit Ser, **223**. Oxford

Ralston, I 1996 'Fortifications and defence', in Green, M J (ed) 1996 *The Celtic World*. London and New York: Routledge, 59–84

Richards, J 1978 *The Archaeology of the Berkshire Downs.* Reading

Richardson, K M 1940 'Excavations at Poundbury, Dorchester, Dorset', *Antiq J*, **20**, 429–48

— 1951 'The excavation of Iron Age villages on Boscombe Down West', *Wiltshire Archaeol Natur Mag*, **54**, 123–68

Richmond, I A 1968 *Hod Hill Vol. 2: Excavations carried out between 1951 and 1958.* London

Riley, H and Dunn, C J 2000 'The earthworks', in Barrett, J C, Freeman, P W M and

Woodward, A 2000 *Cadbury Castle, Somerset: The later prehistoric and early historic archaeology*, English Heritage Archaeol Rep **20**. London, 10–13

Riley, H and Wilson-North R 2001 *The Field Archaeology of Exmoor.* Swindon: English Heritage

Robertson Mackay, R 1977 'The defences of the Iron Age Hill-fort at Winklebury, Basingstoke, Hampshire', *Proc Prehist Soc*, **43**, 131–54

Royal Comission for the Historical Monuments of England 1952 *An Inventory of Historical Monuments in the County of Dorset. Volume One. West Dorset.* London

— 1970a *An Inventory of Historical Monuments in the County of Dorset. Volume Two. South-East Dorset. Part 3.* London

— 1970b *An Inventory of Historical Monuments in the County of Dorset. Volume Three. Central Dorset. Part 1. London.* London: Her Majesty's Stationery Office

— 1970c *An Inventory of Historical Monuments in the County of Dorset. Volume Three. Central Dorset. Part 2.* London: Her Majesty's Stationery Office

— 1979 *Stonehenge and its Environs.* Edinburgh University Press

— 1987 *St Catherine's Hill and Twyford Down near Winchester,*

Hants – A plan of Archaeological features recorded by aerial photography, RCHME manuscript report, NMR Collection No. AF0997213

Saville, A 1983 *Uley Bury and Norbury Hillforts*. Bristol

Scollar, I, Tabbagh, A, Hesse, A and Herzog, I 1990 *Topics in Remote Sensing 2: Archaeological Prospecting and Remote Sensing*. Cambridge

Sharples, N M 1991 *Maiden Castle. Excavations and field survey 1985–6*, English Heritage Archaeol Rep, **19**. London

— 1994 'Maiden Castle, Dorset', *in* Fitzpatrick, A P and Morris, E L (eds) *The Iron Age in Wessex: Recent Work*, Association Francaise D'Etude de L'Age du Fer and Trust for Wessex Archaeology, 91–93

Small, F 2002 *The Lambourn Downs, Report for the National Mapping Programme*. English Heritage, AER/13/2002

Smith, K 1977 'The excavation of Winklebury Camp, Basingstoke, Hampshire', *Proc Prehist Soc*, **43**, 31–129

— 1979 'Winklebury Camp, Basingstoke – a note', *Proc Prehist Soc*, **45**, 321–2

Smith, N 1999 'The earthwork remains of enclosure in the New Forest', *Hampshire Stud*, **54**, 1–56

Stanford, S C 1967 'Croft Ambrey hillfort', *Trans Woolhope Natur Fld Club*, **39**, 31–9

— 1971 'Credenhill Camp, Herefordshire: an Iron Age hill-fort capital', *Archaeol J*, **127** (1970), 82–129

— 1972 'Welsh Border Hill-forts', *in* Thomas, C (ed) *The Iron Age in the Irish Sea Province*, CBA Res Rep, **9**. London, 25–35

— 1974 *Croft Ambrey*. Hereford

— 1981 *Midsummer Hill; an Iron Age hillfort on the Malverns*. Leominster

Stoertz, C 1997 *Ancient Landscapes of the Yorkshire Wolds*. London

Stone, J F S 1948 'A Beaker interment on Stockbridge Down, Hampshire, and its Cultural Connexions', *Antiq J*, **28**, 149–56

Stone, J F S and Hill, N G 1940 'A Round Barrow on Stockbridge Down, Hampshire', *Antiq J*, **20**, 39–51

Stuart, J D M and Birkbeck, J M 1936 'A Celtic Village on Twyford Down, Winchester, Excavated 1933–34', *Proc Hampshire Fld Club Archaeol Soc*, **XIII**, Pt 2, 188–207

Sumner, H 1913 *Ancient Earthworks of Cranborne Chase*. London

Sumner, H 1988 *The Ancient Earthworks of Cranborne Chase*. Stroud: Alan Sutton

Swan, V 1975 'Oare reconsidered and the origins of Savernake Ware in Wiltshire', *Britannia* **vi**, 36–61

— 1984 *The Pottery Kilns of Roman Britain*. London

Swanton, G 1987 'The Owen Meyrick Collection', *Wiltshire Archaeol Natur Hist Mag*, **81**, 7–18

Swanton, M J 1973 *The Spearheads of the Anglo-Saxon Settlements*. London

Tabor, R and Johnson, P 2000 'Sigwells, Somerset, England: regional application and interpretation of geophysical survey', *Antiquity*, **74**, 319–25

Thomas, G 2005 *Conderton Camp, Worcestershire: a small middle Iron Age hillfort on Bredon Hill*, CBA Research Report **143**. Council for British Archaeology, York

Thompson, M W 1958 'Recent building at Balksbury Camp, Andover'. *Proc Hampshire Fld Club Archaeol Soc*, **21**, 53

Tite, M S 1972 *Methods of Physical Examination Archaeology*. London

Tite, M S and Mullins, C 1971 'Enhancement of the magnetic susceptibility of soils on archaeological sites', *Archaeometry*, **13**, 209–19

Trow, S 1988 'Excavations at Ditches Hillfort, North Cerney, Gloucestershire, 1982–3, *Trans Bristol Gloucestershire Archaeol Soc*, **106**, 19–85

Trow, S and James, S 1989 'Ditches Villa, North Cerney: an Example of Locational Conservatism in the Early Roman Cotswolds', *in* Branigan, K and Miles, D (eds) *The Economies of Romano-British Villas*, 83–7. Sheffield

Trow, S, Payne, A, David, A, Batchelor, D, Cunliffe, B and Lock, G 1996 *Non-destructive assessment of the interiors of selected Wessex hillforts*. London: English Heritage unpubl project design

Wainwright, G J 1967 'The excavation of an Iron Age hillfort on Bathampton Down, Somerset', *Trans Bristol Gloucestershire Archaeol Soc*, **86**, 42–59

— 1969 'The excavation of Balksbury Camp, Andover, Hants', *Proc Hampshire Fld Club Archaeol Soc*, **26**, 21–55

— 1970 'An Iron Age promontory fort at Budbury, Bradford-on-Avon, Wiltshire', *Wiltshire Archaeol Natur Hist Mag*, **65**, 108–66

— 1979 *Gussage All Saints: an Iron Age Settlement in Dorset*. London: English Heritage

Wainwright, G J and Davies, S M 1995 *Balksbury Camp, Hampshire, Excavations 1973 and 1981*, English Heritage Archaeol Rep, **4**. London

Watts, L and Leach, P 1996 *Henley Wood, Temples and Cemetery Excavations 1962–69 by the late Ernest Greenfield and others*, CBA Res Rep, **99**. York

Wheeler, R E M 1943 *Maiden Castle, Dorset*, Soc Antiq Res Rep, **12**. London

Wheeler, R E M and Wheeler, T V 1932 *Report on the Excavation of Prehistoric, Roman and post-Roman site in Lydney Park, Gloucestershire*. London

Whinney, R 1994 'Oram's Arbour: the Middle Iron Age Enclosure at Winchester, Hampshire', *in* Fitzpatrick, A and Morris, E (eds) *The Iron Age in Wessex: recent work*. Salisbury, 86–90

Whitley, M 1943 'Excavations at Chalbury Camp, Dorset, 1939', *Antiq J*, **23**, 98–121

Williams-Freeman, J P 1915 *Field Archaeology as illustrated by Hampshire*. London

Wilson, A C 1940 'Report on the excavation at Highdown Hill, Sussex, August 1939', *Sussex Archaeol Coll*, **81**, 173–204

— 1950 'Excavations on Highdown Hill 1947', *Sussex Archaeol Coll*, **89**, 163–78

Wood, P and Hardy, J R 1962 'Perborough Castle and its field system', *Berkshire Archaeol J*, **60**, 53–60

Woodward, A 1992 *Shrines and Sacrifice*. London: English Heritage/Batsford

Woodward, A and Leach, P 1993 *The Uley Shrines. Excavations of a ritual complex on West Hill, Uley, Gloucestershire: 1977–9*, English Heritage Archaeol Rep, **17**. London

Woolley, C L 1913 'Excavations on Beacon Hill in Hampshire, August 1912', *Man*, **13**, 8–10

Youngs, S 1995 'A Penannular Brooch from near Calne, Wiltshire'. *Wiltshire Archaeol Natur Hist Mag*, **88**, 127–31

Index